ROYAL MUGHAL LADIES
And Their Contributions

ROYAL MUGHAL LADIES
And Their Contributions

By
Soma Mukherjee

GYAN

Published by

Gyan Publishing House
5, Ansari Road
Daryaganj, New Delhi-110002
Phone: 011-47034999, 9811692060
E-mail: books@gyanbooks.com

Distribution Network
gyanbooks.com
India, USA, Canada, UK, Australia, France

ISBN: 978-81-212-0760-7 (HB)

Reprint in India, 2024
First Published, 2011

Printed at: Gyan Press, Delhi.

Royal Mughal Ladies: And Their Contribution
Author: Soma Mukherjee

Offered with Prayer and Love
At
The Lotus Feet of
Bhagawan Sri Sathya Sai Baba

Contents

Preface 9

1. The Ladies of the Mughal Harem 15

2. Adornment of the Mughal Harem: Education and Beauty 69

3. Amusements and Festivities 93

4. Mughal Ladies in Contemporary Politics 113

5. Literary Contributions 163

6. Artistic Contributions 193

7. Contributions of Royal Mughal Ladies in Economic Life 235

8. Travels of the Mughal Harem 249

9. Conclusion 257

Bibliography 263

Index 283

Preface

Since ancient times Indian women have always played an important role in the development of social, cultural and philosophical values and trends. The position of women have changed from age to age. During the ancient times women held a respectable position in the society. Education of women was encouraged and the presence of women seers was found in the society. The women could even choose a husband of their choice. This high position that women occupied in the society deteriorated gradually. Society became more complex and so did the social norms and manners.

The position of women in the Indian society changed considerably with the coming of Islam. The Indian women now came to occupy an even lower status. Muslim inroads made strict enforcement of *purdah* and seclusion of women. Women's education was not encouraged. The birth of a girl was not regarded as a happy event. The women of the noble and royal families, even though kept in seclusion, enjoyed a better position in comparison to the middle and lower classes. They received good education and had ample opportunities for the cultivation of their talents. Sometimes they even took an active part in politics. During the Delhi Sultanate, Razia Sultan, an intelligent, courageous and capable daughter of Iltutmish became the only woman ruler in the history of Ilbari Sultans. Though her reign was short but eventful, yet the unparalleled courage and sagacity displayed by her makes her name memorable in history. The Sultanate period also witnessed some other politically ambitious ladies who played a conspicuous role in the contemporary harem politics like Shah Turkan, a wife of Iltutmish and mother of Ruknuddin Firoz; Malika-i-Jahan, queen of Jalaluddin Khalji; Khudavandzada, the sister of

Muhammad Tughlaq; Shams Khatun, the chief queen of Bahlol Lodi; and Bibi Ambha, the Hindu wife of Bahlol Lodi and the mother of Sikander Lodi.

Sixteenth century India witnessed the arrival of the Mughals from Central Asia, who became the rulers of Hindustan for the next two and half centuries. With the coming of the Mughals many new elements were introduced to the Indian society which mingled with the existing culture in course of time. They not only influenced the country in the political sphere, but in almost all spheres of social, cultural and artistic life of Hindustan. Their influences in these spheres were so great that even after hundreds of years the Mughal influence is still felt in their existing monuments, the Mughlai cuisine, the embroideries in gold and silver wire, the Zardozi and Chikankari embroideries, the famous Kim-Khwab silk brocade weaving of Banaras, the leather shoes and sandals of Kashmir, Delhi, Lucknow and Amritsar, leather water vessels of Bikaner, the Kashmiri shawls and carpets, or the Mughal influence in Indian music and musical instruments like *tabla, sitar, sarod, sarangi, shennai* and *santoor*. The Mughal past in India does not merely linger, it overwhelms us. The Mughals had contributed much in various fields and have left behind them their monuments which even today make us feel the essence of these Persian words written in the walls of the Red Fort Delhi:

Agar Firdaus Bar Rue Zameen Ast
Hameen Ast, Hameen Ast wa Hameen Ast.

The Mughal Age not only witnessed the glorious achievements of its emperors and princes, but also that of the princesses, queens and other ladies of the royal Mughal harem. The ladies of the Mughal dynasty were almost as remarkable as their men and in certain cases even more cultivated. These beautiful, educated and extremely talented women not only contributed towards the social, cultural, literary, artistic and economic fields, but also yielded great power and played a dominant role in contemporary politics. It is indeed praiseworthy that hidden behind veils and confined within the four walls of the Mahal, these ladies could achieve so much that some of their contributions even today form a part of our rich cultural heritage.

There are hundreds of books written on Mughal history. But

whenever we read about the Mughals, it is most of the times, the illustrious men of the Mughal royal family who happen to get the attention and appreciation. Rarely we come across a book which deals with the royal Mughal ladies in detail and is concerned with their life, activities and achievements. Commencing from the Mughal times, the contemporary Persian accounts were mostly court histories concerned with the various eventful happenings in the life of the reigning emperor. These accounts mention the royal Mughal ladies in certain places as a part of the narrative, but separate and detailed accounts of their lives are missing considerably. The memoirs of Babar and Jehangir also speak of the royal ladies connected to them but here too elaborate details are not found regarding the various aspects of the lives of these ladies. Gulbadan Begam's *Humayun Nama* is the best contemporary work where the life and activities of the royal ladies during Babar's and Humayun's time are concerned. The accounts of the contemporary foreign travellers also speak of the Mughal ladies though not usually in details.

In the historical writings of the modern times also we find mention of these royal Mughal ladies, but the information given is very limited and concise. There are writings on prominent Mughal ladies like Nur Jahan, or dealing with the Mughal harem system, or the *purdah* system prevalent in those days. Other works deal with certain aspects of the life of Mughal women as a part of the study of the condition of women during the medieval times, or as a part of the study of social and cultural life of the Mughal Age. Rekha Misra's Women in Mughal India certainly speaks of the life and contributions of royal Mughal ladies, but her work does not elaborately deal with these women alone. The position of middle and lower class women is also discussed in this book. Zinat Kausar's *Muslim Women in Medieval India* emphasizes on the social aspects of the life of Mughal ladies but here too not the Mughal ladies alone, but the Muslim women of the Medieval times are spoken about on the whole. K.S. Lal's *The Mughal Harem* gives a vivid picture of the Mughal harem system, the ladies who resided in it and their activities. He also emphasizes on the life and contributions of very prominent Mughal ladies like Nur Jahan, Mumtaz Mahal, Jahanara, Roshanara and Zeb-un-Nisa. But the

Mughal dynasty certainly witnessed the contributions and achievements of other royal ladies too who ought to be mentioned side by side with the very prominent ones if we attempt at presenting a comprehensive account of the life and contributions of the royal Mughal ladies. It is very difficult to find any work dealing exclusively and elaborately with the life and achievements of the royal Mughal ladies alone. Scattered or scanty information available in different works do not help in giving the reader a clear picture of these women, their life and achievements, and therefore fail to do justice to these extraordinarily talented and intelligent women.

The present study is therefore an attempt to present collectively and in details a comprehensive account of the life and contributions of the royal Mughal ladies from the times of Babar to Aurangzeb, with special emphasis on the most prominent of them like Aisan Daulat Begam and Qutluq Nigar Khanum, respectively the maternal grandmother and mother of Babar; Babar's sister Khanzada Begam; Babar's daughter Gulbadan Begam; Humayun's wife and Akbar's mother Hamida Banu Begam; Akbar's nurse Maham Anaga; Akbar's wives Ruqaiya Begam, Salima Sultan Begam and Jodha Bai; Nur Jahan, Man Bai and Jagat Gosain, the important wives of Jahangir; Shahjahan's beloved wife Mumtaz Mahal; Dara Shukoh's wife Nadira Begam; Jahanara and Roshanara, the daughters of Shahjahan; Zeb-un-Nisa and Zinat-un-Nisa, the daughters of Aurangzeb and a few others.

A feeling of awe and mystery even today fills one's mind when one thinks of the life of the Mughal ladies who resided inside the emperor's harem. The manner in which the Mughal ladies spent their lives in their palaces, their outdoor and indoor activities, dress and jewellery, *purdah* and religion, learning and education and even their loves and resentments side by side with their ambitions, achievements and contributions have always remained matters of interest to many. It does no harm to present their story of joy and sorrow, pain and pleasure, longing and disappointment and love and hatred to all those who would like to know about them. The story of women in Indian history is long and detailed. History of Indian women in every age has different features and aspects which should be dealt separately and in much details. Therefore, I have chosen in all humility, to deal with elaborately the life and contributions of the royal Mughal ladies from the time of Babar to Aurangzeb, and highlight the various aspects of their much colourful and eventful lives.

I am extremely grateful to my parents, Mr. Gopal Mukherjee and Mrs. Sabita Mukherjee for their help, encouragement and for being always by my side throughout the work. My husband, Dr. Sandipan Chatterjee has been very supportive to my efforts. His wise counsel and constructive criticism gave shape to my work. I thank him for being so special to me. I acknowledge with gratitude my teachers for all their help and guidance: Dr. J. Chaube, Late Dr. Shefali Banerjee and Dr. Md. Arif - all of them of Banaras Hindu University. I wish to express my sincere gratitude to Dr. B.N. Naidu, Professor of History, Bangalore University for his useful suggestions. I am thankful to my Persian teacher Dr. Shamim Akhtar for her kind assistance in consulting certain Persian manuscripts. I am also thankful to the Librarians and staff of National Library, Calcutta, Asiatic Society of Bengal, Calcutta, National Museum, New Delhi and the National Archives, New Delhi, for the kind help they extended to me. A special thanks to the staff of High Commission of the Islamic Republic of Pakistan, New Delhi and Iran Culture House, New Delhi for their assistance and co-operation.

Soma Mukherjee

Place: Bangalore
Date: July, 2001

One

The Ladies of the Mughal Harem

The Mughal ladies spent their entire lives inside the emperor's harem. A feeling of awe and mystery even today fills one's mind when one hears of the Mughal harem. Many things have been written and many things have been guessed about the life of Mughal ladies. The manner in which the Mughal women spent their lives, their places of residence, their food and clothes, *purdah* and religion, pleasures and pastimes, learning and education and even their love and resentments, have always remained matters of interest to many. The Mughal women were no ordinary women. They were royal women. And therefore, their social life was certainly very much different from that of the ordinary women of the medieval times.

Inmates of the Harem, their Everyday Life and their Relationship with the Emperor

The harems of the Mughal emperors consisted of a large number of women and in it lived women of different races, provinces and communities. Manucci stated that there were "within the palace two thousand women of different races."[1] Apart from Muslim women, there were Hindu women including Rajput ladies, and even Christian women in the harem of the Mughal emperors. The harems of Babar and Humayun were modest in size. But from Akbar's time onwards the Mughal harem became an elaborate affair having a large number of women. Akbar's harem has approximately 5000 women. The harems of Jehangir, Shahjahan and the puritan Aurangzeb were also very large. According to Hawkins, Jehangir had "three hundred wives where foure be chief as queens."[2] According to Terry's estimates Jehangir's harem consisted of "four wives, and concubines and women beside ....enough to make up their number a full thousand."[3]

When one thinks of the women who lived inside the harem, only the picture of the king's wives, concubines, dancing and singing girls and slave and servant girls comes to one's mind. But the harem did not comprise of only the women belonging to these categories. Of course, these women did live in the harem, but other than these there were many others who also lived inside the harem. They were the mother, step-mothers, foster mothers, aunts, grandmothers, sisters, daughters and other female relatives of the king. Even the male children lived inside the harem till they grew up. Then, there were the ladies-in-waiting, slave and servant girls and a number of women officials and guards who were appointed by the emperor for taking care of the various needs of the harem. There were eunuch guards also guarding the surrounding areas of the harem quarters. Female fortune tellers also lived inside the harem. Some women and eunuchs acted as spies and they kept the emperor informed about the activities of the harem women. Women usually came into the harem through marriage, birth, purchase, appointment or as gifts.

Lifestyle

The lives of the harem ladies were governed by strict rules of *purdah*. These ladies usually did not have the liberty to move out of the harem as they liked. If at all they went out, their faces were well hidden behind veils. But inside the harem they could move around as they pleased. They were also provided with various kinds of luxuries and comforts. The daily life in the harem was full of gaiety and mirth. At least, this is the picture that foreigners like Bernier and Manucci, who once in a while had access to the harem as physicians, give in their accounts. They led lives of great comfort, luxury and materialistic pleasure. These ladies lived in grand apartments luxuriously furnished, with lovely gardens, fountains, tanks and water channels attached to them.[4] They wore beautiful and expensive clothes made from the finest material[5] and adorned themselves with jewellery from head to toe.[6] They rarely went out, but when they did, most of the times the ladies of rank travelled in style and comfort in richly decorated *howdahs* on elephant backs[7] and palanquins.[8]

The daily needs of the emperor and his harem inmates were

fulfilled to a great extent by the imperial departments. Their food came from the imperial kitchen called the Matbakh. The Akbar Khana provided drinking water and wine.[9] During summers ice-cold water was supplied to the imperial household. The Maywa Khanah provided fruits to the household.[10] Rikab Khanah or the bakery was in charge of supplying bread.[11] The imperial *karkhanas* provided the royal ladies with beautiful dresses, jewellery, household articles and fancy articles.[12]

The Diet

The diet of the Mughals comprised of a variety of rich and delicious dishes. The imperial kitchen known as the Matbakh[13] was elaborately organised. The Mughal emperors used to spend one thousand rupees daily in order to meet the expenses of the royal kitchen.[14] Cooks from different countries were employed in the royal kitchen and they prepared a number of tasty dishes everyday. The emperor took his meals in the harem. According to Abul Fazl, "the food allowed to the women of the seraglio commences to be taken from the kitchen in the morning, and goes on till night."[15] Varieties of fresh and dry fruits formed a part of the diet of the Mughal ladies like the royal men.[16] Chewing, betel (*pan*) formed an essential everyday habit of the royal ladies. It coloured the lips and teeth red and this was considered a thing of beauty[17] in those days. Betel was also presented to visitors as a mark of honour.[18]

Recreation and Pastime

Since the harem ladies rarely went outside the palace, most of their time was spent inside the seraglio. The harem staff had their respective duties to perform. The royal ladies mostly spent their time by adorning, decorating and beautifying themselves. Various arrangements were made for their recreation inside the harem. There were female superintendents of music and dance[19] and a number of lady singers and dancers. The ladies played many indoor games. Sometimes they read books like *Gulistan* and *Bostan*[20] of Shaikh Sadi Shirazi. Some of the royal ladies went a step ahead than the others and did great works like building monuments and gardens, composing works of literary value, participating in trade and commerce and sometimes even taking part in contemporary politics.

Status and Position

On the whole, the life of a Mughal lady revolved round the emperor. All the harem ladies did not enjoy equal position. Their status and the position of authority and respect in the harem was determined by the place they had in the emperor's life or in his heart. Their mutual relationship amongst themselves was usually friendly and cordial. But jealousies were prevalent though it was not shown directly. Everyone tried their best to please the emperor and nobody wanted to show her bad qualities like jealousy, quarrelsome nature or short tempered attitude. To give the king or prince his first male child was a great honour and competition in this regard often resulted in a woman's trying to miscarry the pregnancies of other women around her.[21] Worries or unpleasantness were usually kept away from them. Death was not usually mentioned throughout the palace. When a lady fell ill she was shifted to the Bimar Khanah. Only the death of very prominent harem ladies was mourned.

The more important position a lady occupied, the more privileges she enjoyed. If she was childless, she was allowed to bring up the child of some other loyal lady as her own. Maham Begam, one of Babar's principle wives and the mother of Humayun had lost four children after Humayun's birth. She was given Hindal and Gulbadan, the children of another wife Dildar Begam and she brought them up.[22] The childless first wife of Akbar, Ruqqaiah Sultan Begam was given Prince Salim's son Khurram after the child was born.[23] She brought him up with a lot of love and care as revealed by Jehangir in his memoirs when he wrote, "My father had given my son Khurram into her charge, and she loved him a thousand times more than if he had been her own.[24] Shahjahan's second son Prince Shuja was brought up by Nur Jahan Begam[25] as per Jahangir's wishes.

The Status of Mother

During the Mughal age, the first lady of the realm was usually the emperor's mother and not his chief queen, except in the case of Nur Jahan and Mumtaz Mahal. Only after the death of the Queen Mother did the chief consort of the emperor take her place. All the Mughal emperors starting from Babar, showed great respect to their mothers. The Babar Nama and Gulbadan Begam's Humayun Nama have many instances which reveal the great honour and respect shown to the mothers by the emperors. After the coronation ceremonies it was the mother whom the emperor first visited. So was the case on other days of rejoicing like festivals and birthdays. Abul Fazal said that when long fasts came to an end, the first dishes of meat went to Akbar from his mother's place.[26] Once when Akbar's mother was travelling in a palanquin from Lahore to Agra, Akbar was travelling with her. At one place he took the palanquin upon his own shoulders and carried her from one side of the river to another.[27] At one place in the Tuzuk-i-Jahangiri, Jehangir reveals his love and respect for his mother in these words:

> On the same day Her Majesty the revered Maryam-Zamani (his mother) came from Agra, and I acquired eternal good fortune from the blessing of waiting on her. I hope that the shadow of her bringing up and affection may be perennial on the head of this suppliant.[28]

Foster Mothers and Nurses

In the Mughal household there were found quite a few foster mothers besides the real mothers. Because of many political and other crisis that arose from time to time, the child many a time was separated from the real mother and therefore was looked after and even breast fed by other women of the harem. There were also other nurses who were not wet nurses. All the nurses occupied high rank in the harem and were known by the name of Anagas. Akbar in his childhood was away from his mother Hamida Banu for some years because of the prevailing political conditions. Some of these nurses of Akbar was Jiji Anaga, the wife of Shams-ud-din; Fakhr-un-Nisa, the wife of Nadim Koka; Koki Anaga the wife of Togh Begi; Piji Jan Anaga, the mother of Saadat Yar Koka; Khildar Anaga; Bibi Rupa; Bhawal Anaga, a concubine of Humayun; a lady called Hakima; and the mother of Zain Khan Koka.[29] But the most prominent of all his nurses was Maham Anaga who played an important political role during the initial years of Akbar's reign.[30] The Mughal emperors respected their foster mothers a lot. Akbar was very fond of Maham Anaga and Jiji Anaga. Jehangir in his memoirs reported the death of his foster mother, the mother of Qutub-ud-din Khan Koka in the following words.

> In the month of Zi-l-qada the mother of Qutbu-ud-din Khan Koka who had given me her milk and was as a mother to me or even kinder than my own kind mother ... was committed to the mercy of God. I placed the feet of her corpse on my shoulders and carried her a part of the way (to her grave). Through extreme grief and sorrow I had no inclination for some days to eat, and I did not change my clothes.[31]

Deference to Elder Women

Apart from their own mothers and foster mothers, the other wives of their father were also looked upon with a lot of respect by the Mughals. Jodha Bai was Jehangir's own mother. But he had great respect and affection for Ruqaiya Begam and Salima Sultan Begam also. Akbar respected Haji Begam a lot. The grandmothers, aunts and other elderly relations were also respected and well cared for. The memoirs of Babar and Jehangir and the *Humayun Nama* of Gulbadan Begam reveal many a time the esteem that the Mughal emperors had for their mothers and other elderly lady relatives. A.S. Beveridge states that, "it may be said that both Babar and Haider convey the opinion that deference to elder women was a permanent trait of their age and set."[32] These ladies too many a time, including difficult times, lent their active support to their emperor and many crisis were solved. Various incidents from the *Babar Nama* reveal the amount of respect that Babar had for the ladies of his family even if they belonged to his rival camp. From Gulbadan Begam's accounts too we have evidences proving this. In one place Gulbadan Begam wrote:

> All through the four ears that my father was in Agra he used to go on Fridays to see his paternal aunts. One day it was extremely hot, and her Highness my lady (Akam) said, "The wind is very hot indeed; how would it be if you did not go this one Friday? The begams would not be vexed. His Majesty said, Maham! It is astonishing that you should say such things! The daughters of Abu-sa'id Sultan Mirza, who have been deprived of father and brothers! If I do not cheer them, how will it be done?[33]

Gulbadan Begam goes on to say:

> To the architect, Khwaja Qasim, his Majesty gave the following order: "We command a piece of good service from you. It is this: Whatever work, even it be on a great scale, our paternal aunts may order done in their palace, give it precedence, and carry it out with might and main.[34]

The respect and affection that the Mughal emperors had for the mothers, aunts and grandmothers extended to the sisters as well. Gulbadan Begam gives many instances in her *Humayun Nama* revealing the love that Babar and Humayun had for their sisters. Babar held his elder sister Khanzada Begam in high esteem and she too underwent many a difficulties for her brother's sake. Though Gulbadan was not Humayun's own sister, Humayun loved her very much and he cared a lot for his other sisters too. If any sister met any calamity like widowhood, the brother was always there to provide her with shelter. When Gul-Chihra Begam became a widow, Humayun gave orders to bring her back to Agra.[35] Jehangir in his memoirs lovingly mentions his sisters Shukr-un-Nisa Begam and Aram Banu Begam, though born of different mothers.

Status of Girl Child

The daughters of the Mughal family or the Mughal princesses occupied places of great honour in the seraglio. The birth of a girl in those days was less welcomed than that of a boy. But the Mughal emperors loved their daughters a lot and made the best arrangements for their education and cultivation of their talents. They were brought up in great luxuries and had for themselves available all the exclusive material things that life needed. But many of them, especially after Akbar's time onwards, remained unmarried. Many writers and foreign travellers like Manucci have blamed Akbar for starting this tradition, but many scholars do not agree to this theory because Akbar got his sisters and daughters married off to eligible men. What he disapproved was marriage between first cousins.[36] Even then, by the time of Shahjahan, certain restraints on the marriage of princesses is seen. Probably this was done to limit the contenders to the throne. But Aurangzeb got some of his daughters and nieces married to first cousins. Apart from this one factor, the Mughal princesses had almost everything they wanted including the love of their fathers and brothers. Shahjahan's love for his eldest daughter Jahanara is well-known. So did Aurangzeb love his eldest daughter Zeb-un-Nisa, till she became a threat to his policies and his throne.

Emperors Wives

An extremely important place in the Mughal harem was occupied by the emperor's wives. All the Mughal emperors had many wives. But all the wives did not enjoy equal respect and facilities. Usually the chief queen and other prominent queens lived in big mahals amidst great luxuries. They had many servants who attended upon them and they got a lot of wealth and money as annual allowances from the emperor. Marriages in the Mughal family were usually settled by the parents or near relatives, but there were some love-matches too.

Babar's Queens: The wives of Babar as recorded by him and his daughter Gulbadan Begam were — Ayisha Sultan Begam, Zainab Sultan Begam, Maham Begam, Masuma Sultan Begam, Gul-rukh Begam, Dildar Begam and Bibi Mubarika, the Afghan lady.[37] Maham Begam, the mother of Humayun, was his chief queen. Some wives of Humayun were Bega (Haji) Begam, Hamida Banu Begam who was Akbar's mother, Gun-war Begam, Shad Bibi, Khanish Agha Khwarizmi and Mah-chuchak Begam.

Akbar's Queens: Some of the prominent queens of Akbar were: Ruqaiya Begam who was the daughter of his uncle Hindal and was his first wife;[38] Salima Sultan Begam who was his cousin and previously the wife of Bairam Khan, and after Bairam Khan's assassination was accepted by Akbar as his wife;[39] and the Rajput princess of Amber, Harkha on Jodha Bai, the daughter of Raja Bihari Mal, and the mother of Akbar's first son Salim.[40] Some other Rajput wives of Akbar were (i) the daughter of Kanhan, the brother of Rai Kalyan Mal of Bikaner;[41] (ii) the daughter of Rawal Har Rai of Jaisalmer;[42] (iii) the sister of Rana Udai Singh of Marwar[43] and (iv) the princesses of Merta and Dungarpur.[44] Apart from these, Akbar also married Bibi Daulat Shad, and the daughters of Abdullah Khan Mughal and Miran Mubarak Shah of Khandesh.[45]

He even got Abdul Wasi to divorce his beautiful wife so that he could marry her.[46]

Jehangir's wives: Jehangir had many wives including Hindu wives. They were Man Bai, the daugher of Raja Bhagwan Das of Amber and the grand daughter of Raja Bihari Mal, and she was the mother of Jehangir's eldest son Khusrau,[47] the daughter of Rai Singh of Bikaner;[48] Jodh Bai, or Jagat Gosain, the daughter of Mota Raja or Udai Singh and granddaughter of Raja Maldeva of Marwar and she became the mother of Khurram (Shahjahan);[49] Raj Kumari Karamsi, the daughter of Keshav Das Rathor;[50] a daughter of Jagat Singh, eldest son of Raja Man Singh,[51] a daughter of Rawal Bhim, brother of Rai Kalyan Mal of Jaisalmer;[52] Kanwal Rani, the daughter of the ruler of little Tibet;[53] and the daughter of Ram Chandra Bundela.[54] Some other wives of his were Sahib-i-Jamat, the daughter of Khwaja Hassan, cousin of Zain Khan Koka; Nur-un-Nisa Begam, sister of Muzaffar Hussain; Saliha Banu, daughter of Qasim Khan; and the daughters of Mubarak Chak and Husain Chak of Kashmir.[55] There were many more. But his chief and most prominent queen was his last wife, the beautiful talented and charismatic Nur Jahan Begam.

Shahjahan's wives: Shahjahan had as his wives among others the daughter of Mirza Muzaffar Husain Safawi, the daughter of Nur Jahan's brother Asaf Khan known as Arjumand Banu Begam, and the daughter of Shahnawaz Khan. But it is a very well-known fact that he never loved or adored anyone more than Arjumand Banu Begam, later known as Mumtaz Mahal, the lady of the Taj. Aurangzeb had four wives. Dilras Banu Begam was his chief queen though he was not much attached to her. His other wives Aurangabadi Mahal, Nawab Bai and Udipuri Mahal were inferior wives.

Secondary Wives

The daughters or relatives of Indian princes who were married to Mughal princes mostly as a part of diplomatic dealings or because of defeat of the girl's family in battles or wars against the Mughals, were generally considered as secondary wives or inferior wives. As we have seen, from the times of Akbar, practically all the Mughal emperors married Hindu princesses and princesses from other Indian States. These secondary wives known as Bais and Mahals[56] enjoyed a position lesser than the main wives. In spite of that, some secondary wives, especially some Rajput princesses came to occupy positions of great respect and honour in the Mughal household. Jodha Bai gave Akbar his first son. Man Bai's son was Khusrau and Jagata Gosain was the mother of Shahjahan.

Concubines

Apart from their legal wives, the Mughal emperors and princes had a number of concubines. These concubines were not really married legally but they lived as wives. The children born of these concubines were treated equally like those born of the legal wives. These concubines were known as Kaniz, Sarark and Paristar.[57] Manucci mentions some names given to concubines in the Mughal times like Nazuk Badan (Delicate bodied), Badam Chasm (Almond eyed), Sukh Dain (giver of Repose), Kutuhal (Joyous), Singar (Adorned), Piyar (Loving), Mahan (Proud), etc.[58] Emperor Akbar seems to have made a rule that the concubines of the Mughal emperors were to be named after the places they belonged to. Thus we get names like Akbarabadi, Fatehpuri, Aurangabadi, Zainabadi and Udipuri.[59]

Concubines in spite of their inferior status, were not always treated as inferiors or with disrespect. Sometimes they even came to occupy more important places than some legally married wives. From the times of Babar we find all the Mughal emperors having many concubines in their harems. Two of Babar's concubines, Gulnar Aghacha and Nargul Aghacha,[60] who were Circassian slaves gifted to him by Shah Tahmasp, became recognised ladies of the royal household. Gulnar Aghacha even accompanied Gulbadan Begam to Mecca for the Haj.[61] One of the Humayun's concubines by the name of Bhawal Anaga was one of Akbar's wet nurses.[62] Akbar had many concubines, some of whom became the mothers of his children. His daughter Shahzada Khanum born of Bibi Salima[63] and Shukr-un-Nisa Begam and Aram Banu Begam, both born of Bibi Daulat Shad,[64] were all born of concubines. Two of his three sons, Murad and Daniyala too were born of concubines.

Two of Jehangir's sons, Jahandar and Shahryar, were born of concubines in 1605 A.D.[65] Two prominent concubines of Shahjahan were Akbarabadi Mahal also known as Aizunissa and Fatehpuri Mahal. Waris mentions the names of Akbarabadi Mahal and Fatehpuri Mahal as the two favourite slave-girls of Shahjahan.[66] They took great care of Shahjahan and his children during his days of imprisonment. Aurangzeb, who was extremely strict in almost all matters was not so where his favourite concubine Udipuri Mahal, whom some sources mention as his wife, was concerned. He was also very fond of a slave girl called Zainabadi,[67] or Hira Bai, in his youth, whose untimely death took her away from his life. These concubines, however, were not always faithful to their masters. Udipuri Mahal was originally a concubine in Dara's household, but later she gladly went over to Aurangzeb.[68] Sometimes they even betrayed their masters. But this was not the case always. Many a times they remained faithful too. Rana-i-dil was a concubine of Dara, but she refused to go over to Aurangzeb even after Dara's execution.[69]

Apart from the categories of ladies living in the Mughal harem already mentioned, the harem also had a number of women in charge of the harem administration, women guards, female servants and slave girls. There were also dancing and singing girls who provided entertainment to the harem inmates. They usually were known as Kanchanis.[70] They were fine performers and practised no profession other than singing and dancing.[71] Some important royal ladies of the Mughal harem had their own personal singing and dancing girls. Babar had once gifted a female dancer to each of his important Begams.[72] Many of these women lived inside the harem and some came from outside to provide entertainment to the harem ladies.

Slave and Servant Girls

Though the slave and servant girls occupied quite low positions in the harem, the chief women servants or ladies-in-waiting of the important harem ladies enjoyed a much better place and sometimes had a lot of power in their hands. Many important duties connected to the emperor, his chief queen or his children were assigned to them and they carried out their duties with utmost sincerity and dedication. The memoirs of the Mughal emperors and Gulbadan Begam's *Humayun Nama*, and other accounts of that time mention some such women servants known for their service and loyalty. A certain Atun-mama served Babar's mother Qutluq-Nigar Khanum[73] and Bachaka Khalifa was a head woman-servant of Babar's household.[74] Jehangir speaks highly of such a head servant by the name of Aqa Aqayam in his memoirs.[75] During Shahjahan's time we come across the efficient and loyal lady-in-waiting of Mumtaz Mahal, Sati-un-Nisa.[76] She was an educated lady and tutored Princess Jahanara. She helped Mumtaz Mahal, and later Princess Jahanara in carrying out their duties and was extremely trusted by the Emperor, the Empress and the Princess.

Titles Given to Royal Ladies

Some of the very important royal ladies of the Mughal harem were given titles as a mark of honour and privilege. About the giving of titles, Manucci said that the "kings are very choosy about giving names to suit the persons receiving them."[77] The mothers of the Mughal emperors were held in highest respect and most of them were given lofty titles. Akbar's mother Hamida Banu Begam had the title of Maryam Makani[78] meaning "Mary of both Worlds". Jehangir's mother Jodha Bai got the title of Maryam-uz-Zamani[79] meaning "Mary of the Universe". Shahjahan's mother Jagat Gosain was called Bilqis Makani[80] meaning "the Lady of Pure Abode".

Though the mothers of the Mughal emperors received lofty titles, the favourite queens, and the most loved sisters and daughters too were recipients of such titles. Jehangir gave the title of Shah Begam to his first wife Man Bai after she gave birth to his eldest son Khusrau.[81] In 1611 A.D. after Jehangir married Mehrunnisa, he bestowed on her the title of Nur Mahal meaning "the Light of the Palace", and in 1616 A.D. during the 11th New Year's feast after his accession, he changed it to Nur Jahan[82] meaning "Light of the World". Bernier too mentions these titles of Nur Jahan Begam.[83] Nur Jahan Begam later also received the title of Padshah Begam.[84] Shahjahan's favourite wife Arjumand Banu Begam was given the title of Mumtaz Mahal.[85] Bernier calls her Tage Mehalle.[86] She also enjoyed the titles of Malika-i-Jahan[87]

(Queen of the World) and Nawwab Mahd' Ulya (Her Majesty the Queen).[88]

Shahjahan's favourite daughter Jahanara Begam was popularly known as Begam Saheb.[89] She also had the title of Nawwab' Ulya (Her Royal Highness).[90] Later she was given the most honourable title of Padshah Begam.[91] After her death she was bestowed with the title of Sahibat-uz-Zamani meaning "Mistress of the Age."[92] Aurangzeb's second daughter Zinat-un-Nisa Begam also enjoyed the title of Padshah Begam.[93]

Living Quarters of Harem Women

The splendid lifestyle of the Mughals is evident even today from their still existent palaces and forts. The ladies of the royal harem lived in exquisitely beautiful and grand quarters provided for them by their emperor. The residences of these ladies were called Mahals and also as Shabistan-i-Iqbal or Shabistan-i-Khas. But the Mahal where the ladies lived usually formed a part of the palace which itself was a part of the fort complex. The grand living quarters of the royal Mughal ladies are seen in the forts of Delhi, Agra, Fatehpur Sikri and Lahore. In Fatehpur Sikri we even find separate Mahals for the royal ladies like the Mahal of Birbal's daughter; Maryam's Mahal which belonged to Jehangir's mother and also known as Sonahla Makan or "Golden House" and the palace of the Rumi or Turkish Sultana belonging to Ruqqaiah Sultana Begam, Akbar's first wife.[94] Even then, the Mahal formed only a small portion of the palace building inside the fort. For example, the Rang Mahal or Imtiyaz Mahal, Moti Mahal and Hira Mahal of the Red Fort in Delhi were meant for the harem ladies, but they formed only a small part of the entire Red Fort complex as seen even today. So all the inmates of the harem were not provided with separate and spacious dwellings though Abul Fazl says that Emperor Akbar had provided a separate apartment to his 5000 women.[95] Since the forts and palaces of Agra and Fatehpur Sikri do not reveal so many living quarters which could have housed 5000 women, we can say that only the very special royal ladies of the harem had their separate dwellings. But living spaces were provided for all harem inmates. The ladies of rank in the harem also had separate lodgings for their "slaves, of whom there may be 10, or 20, or 100, according to her fortune".[96] However, the ladies enjoying such special privileges were very few. Even when they had separate apartments, they did not live in them all alone. There were always many maids and ladies-in-waiting, slave girls and dancing and singing girls and musicians surrounding them. The lodgings of these harem ladies usually occupied the inner portion of the palace. The servants, slave-girls, dancing girls and singing girls were provided humble dwellings in an area just within the main gate of the fort and this enclosure was known as the Chowk.[97] Some important harem ladies also had their own palaces outside the fort. In Agra near the Jamuna river are found palaces which belonged to Akbar's wife Ruqaiya Sultan. Begam and Shahzadi Begam a sister of Jehangir.[98] Nur Jahan and Jahanara Begam had their palaces in Agra, Lahore and Kashmir.[99]

Many of the foreigners visiting the Mughal cities and forts have talked in details about the women's living quarters in these forts. All of them were extremely interested to find out about the interior of these forts and palaces. Since no outsiders or male persons were usually allowed inside these palaces and harem quarters, most of the information they got about the mahals were that what they heard from the local people or from the eunuchs or servant women who lived inside these mahals or had regular access to these quarters. Bernier confirms this by saying—

> It would afford me pleasure to conduct you to the Seraglio... But who is the traveller that can describe from ocular observation the interior of that building? I have sometimes gone into it when the King was absent from Delhi, and once pretty far I thought, for the purpose of giving my professional advice in the case of a great lady so extremely ill that she could not be moved to the outward gate, according to the customs observed upon similar occasions; but a Kachemire shawl covered my head, like a large scarf down to my feet, and an eunuch led me by the hand, as if I had been a blind man. You must be content, therefore, with such a general description as I have received from some of the eunuchs.[100]

Bernier goes on to describe the harem quarters of the Delhi fort as told to him by the eunuchs. He says:

> They inform me that the Seraglio contains beautiful apartments, separated, and more or less spacious and splendid, according to the rank and income of the females. Nearly every chamber has its reservoir of running water at the door; on every side are gardens, delightful alleys, shady retreats, streams, fountains, grottoes, deep excavations that afford shelter from the sun by day, lofty divans and terraces, on which to sleep coolly at night. Within the walls of this enchanting place, in fine, no oppressive or inconvenient heat is felt.[101]

Other foreigners like William Finch[102] and De Laet too give vivid descriptions of the women's quarters in the Forts of Agra and Lahore. De Laet, describing the Mahals inside the Agra Fort says:

> The fortress, which stands on rising ground, is a wonderful place, and is most beautiful to look at from all view points, especially from the river bank; for on that side are galleries with golden windows, from which the king is wont to look at elephant fights. Behind these galleries lies the audience chamber, which is called the Gussal-can (Ghusl-khana)... Beneath are situated the women's apartments (called the Mahal) belonging to Nourzian Begum, the favourite wife of the last emperor Ziangier (Jehangir).The rest of the fort is occupied by various buildings, the most important of which are women's apartments, such as that of Mariam Makany (actually Jahangir's mother Mariam-uz-Zamani), the wife of Achabar and mother of Ziangier: there are also the three palaces in which the king's concubines are accommodated of which one is called Lethevar (i.e., Sunday), the second Mongel (i.e., Tuesday) and the third Zenisser (i.e., Saturday): for on these days the king is wont to visit the said palaces.There is also a fifth palace for women, in which live foreign concubines of the king. This is called the Bengaly Mahal.[103]

Not only the structures of these Mahals were grand, but they were very well furnished too. They were usually made of fine marbles, engraved with gold and gems and elegantly decorated. The floor was covered with rich embroidered Persian carpets, thick and soft. The bases of the columns of the halls were decorated with hollow silver pedestals in which different sweet perfumeries were burnt. There were gorgeous tapestries, elegant and richly decorated furnitures, beautiful mirrors, chandeliers, itardans, flowerpots, golden lamps and finest works of art decorating the walls.[104]

These apartments also had to themselves attached beautiful gardens with a variety of flower trees and plants, orchards, fountains, pools, water channels, artificial waterfalls and tanks. The tanks and pools were used as a part of decoration and also for providing bathing facilities to the ladies. These tanks were therefore usually large and quite deep to provide privacy. Water was supplied to these tanks and fountains from spring-fed wells beautifully "wrought up with firm stones, laid in fine plaster."[105] Water was drawn everyday by oxen turning large wheels with many small buckets.[106]

On the whole, the Mughal ladies lived amidst splendour and luxury. Irrespective of what the foreign travellers tell us in their accounts, the beauty and splendour of these palaces and mahals is evident to our eyes even today when we see for ourselves these grand and splendid edifices on our visit to the Mughal forts of Delhi, Agra, Fatehpur Sikri and Lahore. Even the Mughal gardens in Kashmir, Lahore, Agra and Delhi had beautiful quarters for the harem ladies where they rested and stayed on their visits to these royal gardens.

Sources of Wealth and Expenses of Royal Ladies

The royal ladies of the Mughal harem had a lavish lifestyle. The important harem ladies owned a lot of wealth and money which they spent as they wished. The question that arises in our minds is that — how could the royal ladies spend such large amounts or rather, what were the sources of their income and wealth?

The Mughal ladies of rank, the queens and princesses, received allowances and maintenance grants to meet their personal expenditure and wants. As Manucci says:

> These queens and princesses have pay or pensions according to their birth or the rank they hold. In addition, they often received from the king special presents in cash,

under the pretext that it is to buy betel, or perfumes, or shoes.[107]

Apart from their regular allowances some important ladies of the Mughal household owned vast jagirs bestowed upon them by the emperor. Soon after his accession, Humayun paid a visit to his mother, sisters and other ladies of his seraglio and he gave them jagirs and confirmed their mansabs.[108] The royal ladies from time to time continued to receive *jagirs* from the respective emperors. During Jehangir's time a lot of *jagirs* were given to the royal ladies. Jehangir mentions in his memoirs that he "increased the allowances of all the veiled ladies of my father's harem from 20 per cent to 100 per cent, according to their condition and relationship",[109] after his coming to the throne in 1605 A.D. The maximum number of *jagirs* during his time were owned by Nur Jahan Begam. The *jagir* of Ramsar situated about 20 miles south-east of Ajmer[110] and the *pargana* of Boda (Toda), the annual revenue of which was two lakh of rupees,[111] belonged to Nur Jahan. Beni Prasad comments: "If she (Nur Jahan) could have been admitted to the order of mansabdars, her *jagirs* would have entitled her to the rank of 30,000."[112] Nur Jahan also had the right of collecting octroi duty at Sikandarabad[113] on the merchandise coming there from the eastern parts of the country and Bhutan. She had her own *vakils* who supervised her *jagirs* and kept the necessary records of her property. Shahjahan too bestowed a lot of *jagirs* on his ladies and Manucci says that during his reign all the ladies of rank had their own nazirs who looked after their *jagirs*, properties and incomes.[114] The largest number of *jagirs* were given by Shahjahan to his eldest daughter Princess Jahanara. Some of her *jagirs* were that of Achchol[115] (later called Begamabad as Qazwini states and Sahababad as Lahori states), Bachchol, Safipur,[117] Dohraha,[118] Farjahara[119] and Panipat.[120]

The royal ladies also received special gifts in cash and kind on special occasions. Gulbadan Begam informs us that after Babar's victory against Ibrahim Lodi at Panipat, he told Khwaja Kilan Beg to take valuable presents and curiosities of Hind to his "elder relations, sisters and each person of the harem."[121] His further orders were,

To each begam is to be delivered as follows: one special

> dancing-girl of the dancing-girls of Sultan Ibrahim, with one gold plate full of jewels — ruby and pearl, cornelian and diamond, emerald and turquoise, topaz and cat's eye — and two small mother-o'- pearl trays full of ashrafis, and on two other trays Shahrukhis, and all sorts of stuffs by nines — that is, four trays and one plate.[122]

Gifts and Offerings

Akbar used to give valuable gifts to his harem ladies on special occasions like that on the Nauroz day.[123] Jehangir too continued this tradition. When Shahjahan as a prince became victorious in his Deccan campaigns, he give Nur Jahan offerings worth 200,000 rupees and 60,000 rupees to his other mothers and begams.[124] On his accessions to the Mughal throne, Shahjahan bestowed 60 lakhs of rupees on the high-ranking ladies of his seraglio.[125] He awarded 2 lakhs of ashrafis and 6 lakhs of rupees to Mumtaz Mahal, and 4 lakhs of rupees were given to Princess Jahanara.[126] On the occasion of the first Nauroz festival after his accession, Shahjahan gave Mumtaz Mahal "various kinds of precious gems and jewelled ornaments worth 50 lakhs of rupees", and to Princess Jahanara he gave similar articles worth 25 lakhs of rupees.[127] He also gave a sum of 25 lakhs of rupees to the other princes and princesses.[128] Out of the total 180 lakhs of rupees awarded on that day, 160 lakhs "were awarded to Her Majesty the Queen and the royal Princes and Princesses..."[129] On the birth of his son Prince Daulat Afza, Shahjahan gave many gifts to the Queen.[130] As a part of the festivities connected to his lunar weighing at the completion of the 46th year of his age, Shahjahan gave two lakhs of rupees to Jahanara Begam.[131] Jahanara Begam, who was a very privileged royal princess, was given ornaments and jewelled articles worth 10 lakhs as a part of the celebrations after her recovery from severe burns after eight months in Shawwal, 1054 A.H. The Emperor also bestowed on her 130 unbored pearls for a dast-band (bracelet), the value totalling 5 lakhs of rupees. He also gave to her a *sar-band,* on which was strung a large diamond with a pearl pendant. Its value came to a lakh of rupees.[132] Aurangzeb also gave gifts to his harem ladies on special occasions. On his accession to the throne he gave a lot of presents to his Begams.[133]

Aurangzeb's sister Roshanara Begam received five lakh rupees in cash and kind[134] for her active support to him in the war of succession. His four daughters got 4, 2, 1.6 and 1.5 lakhs respectively[135]. Once when a son was born to Aurangzeb's son Prince Muhammad Azam by Dara's daughter Jahanzeb Banu Begam or Jani Begam in 1081 A.H., Aurangzeb gave the mother a necklace of pearls worth Rs. 10,000 with a Samaran of the value of Rs.7,000.[136] Once in 1094 A.H. when Aurangzeb visited the Yatishkhana of Prince Muhammad Azam in the Fort, he bestowed a pearl necklace and an ear-drop of ruby worth Rs. 14,000 on Jahanzeb Banu Begam, a pearl necklace worth Rs. 19,000 on Giti Ara Begam (daughter of the Prince), and a jewelled Kara, worth Rs. 12,200 on Bijapuri Mahal.[137]

Besides the gifts given by the emperor and royal princes, some very important ladies of the Mughal royal family received gifts from the foreign merchants and ambassadors who tried to please them in order to gain the emperor's favours. Once in 1608 A.D. William Hawkins, the English Ambassador, presented some valuable jewels to Jahangir's sister Shakurunnisa Begam. He wrote:

> ... knowing the custom of these Moores that without gifts and bribes nothing would either go forward or be accomplished, I sent my broker to seek out for jewels fitting for the king's sister.[138]

Coryat too once gave a ruby studded gold whistle to Jehangir which he gave to one of his ladies.[139] Sir Thomas Roe in his accounts mention many occasions when he gave costly and rare presents to the all powerful Nur Jahan Begam to gain royal favours. Among them were an English coach, a mirror chest and toys.[140] Many foreign merchants and agents tried to please Jahanara Begam too by giving her costly gifts. Tavernier mentions giving her presents.[141] The English merchants and ambassadors tried to please her with gifts like broad cloth, embroidered cloth, mirrors, perfumed oils, cabinets, etc.[142]

It is quite evident that the royal Mughal ladies had a lot of wealth in their hands. The more important the place she occupied in the emperor's life, the wealthier she was. As a result they earned lakhs and lakhs of rupees apart from the gold, silvers, gems, jewellery and other costly articles they owned. On special occasions their annual allowances were increased by their loving husbands or doting fathers and brothers. On Shahjahan's accession ten lakh rupees were fixed as the annual allowance of Mumtaz Mahal. Jahanara Begam's annual allowance was fixed at six lakh rupees.[143] After the death of Mumtaz Mahal, the half of her property consisting of gold and silver, gems and jewelled articles, and all sorts of goods, worth upward of rupees one crore (100 lakhs) was given to Princess Jahanara.[144] Also her annual allowance of six lakh rupees was raised to ten lakh rupees.[145] Manucci estimated Jahanara Begam's income to 30 lakh rupees annually apart from the precious stones and jewels owned by her.[146] Totally it amounted to nearly three million rupees.[147] At the time of her death she divided her property and jewels among her nieces, but her finest jewels and greater share of her money went to Jani Begam, Dara's daughter.[148] To very prominent royal ladies an annual maintenance allowance was given by the next emperor after their emperor husband's death. Shahjahan continued to give Nur Jahan Begam an annual maintenance allowance of two lakh rupees when he came to the throne.[149]

This vast wealth that the royal ladies of the Mughal harem accumulated were spent by them in various ways. Apart from their daily needs, these ladies spent a lot of money in getting for themselves fine silks, brocades and muslins from which they got stitched beautiful garments. Then, they were extremely fond of gems and jewellery and often bought rare gems from different places that they had access to. They also were fond of buying rare objects of decoration or anything that they took a fancy for. Some of the royal ladies built buildings, palaces, tombs, gardens, mosques, sarais and even market places from their own purses. Many of them donated large sums in charity to the poor and needy. Some of the prominent royal ladies invested large sums in profitable trade. Apart from all this, the Mughal queens and princesses, often entertained guests and arranged for feasts and banquets. Sometimes these feasts were arranged in a very grand and lavish manner. On special occasions like birthdays, marriages, coronations and victories, they gave costly gifts to their dear ones.

Humayun's mother Maham Begam on the occasion of Humayun's accession to the throne in 1530 A.D. arranged for a grand feast and gave special robes of honour to about seven thousand persons.[150] Nur Jahan Begam was well known for arranging grand feast and bestowing costly gifts on others. When Prince Khurram (Shahjahan) came back from his successful Rajputana campaign, he was presented a rich dress of honour a jewelled sword, a horse and saddle and an elephant by Nur Jahan Begam.[151] Again in 1617 A.D. as a part of Khurram's success in the Deccan campaign Nur Jahan gave a grand feast of celebration and presented him costly dresses of honour along with other costly gifts including a waistband studded with pearls, a sword with jewelled shoulder-belt and a *phul katara*. His children, his harem ladies and even his servants received valuable gifts. She spent almost 30,000 rupees on this occasion.[152] Many a times she also made to her husband Jehangir many valuable offerings. Once Nur Jahan bought two large pearls for 60,000 rupees from a merchant who had got those from Turkey. She offered them to Jehangir.[153] On important days like the weighing ceremonies of her husband, she gave robes of honour to the *amirs* and nobles. Mumtaz Mahal too many a times offered valuable objects in the form of Peshkash to her husband Shahjahan.[154] Once Shahjahan's aunt Shukrunnisa Begam presented to him precious stones (*lals*) worth four lakh rupees when she came from Akbarabad to congratulate Shahjahan on his victory of Balkh.[155] On his solar weighing ceremony in 1066 A.H., Shahjahan's secondary wife Akabarabadi Mahal offered to him a ring set with a diamond priced at 30,000 rupees.[156] Jahanara Begam often presented valuable gifts to many including her father Shahjahan. Once on his weighing ceremony she gave him a pearl costing 31 *sarakh* and 40 thousand rupees.[157] She also gave away gold and silver for distribution amongst the poor. During one of Shahjahan's lunar weighing ceremony, she made an offering of an enamelled bedstead costing 40,000 rupees.[158] During Aurangzeb's coronation, Jahanara Begam and the other harem ladies sent him costly presents including jewels.[159] Once in 1070 A.H. when Jahanara Begam paid a visit to Aurangzeb on the occasion of his 44th Lunar weighment, she offered him a string of pearls and 5 rubies worth Rs. 2,80,000[160] and again in Shawwil 1072 A.H. she sent him jewels and jewelled articles.[161]

Organisation and Administrative set-up of the Mughal Harem

The Mughal harem was not just a beautiful marble and red sand-stone enclosure decorated lavishly, with beautiful women residing in it. It was much more than that. It was an institution and had an administrative set up which was organised in similar basis like that of the outside administration of the emperor's household. They were a set of officials, all women, who were entrusted with the various harem duties. There were female guards responsible for the security of the harem inmates. Eunuchs were stationed just outside the harem enclosure as guards. Manucci gives a detailed description of the harem officials and servants. He says:

> Ordinarily there are within the palace 2000 women of different races. Each has her office or special duties, either in attendance on the king, his wives, his daughters, or his concubines. To maintain order among this last class, each one is assigned her own set or rooms, and matrons are placed over them. Each has usually attached to her ten or twelve women servants, who are selected from the above named women. In addition to these matrons, there are the female superintendents of music and their women players. Among them are some who teach reading and writing to the princesses, and usually what they dictate to them are amorous verses... Just as the king has his officers outside, he has the same among the fair sex within the palace. Among these ladies are some who occupy the same offices that are held by grandees outside: and it is by the mouth of these illustrious persons, when the king does not come forth, that the officials outside receive the orders sent them from within. All the persons employed in these offices are carefully selected; they have much wit and judgement, and know all that is passing in the empire. For the officials outside are required to send written reports into the palace of all that the king ought to know. To these reports the women officials reply as directed by that prince. And to carry this out there are eunuchs who take out and bring back the sealed letters written from one side to the other on these matters.[162]

The female officers of the harem were divided into three categories: the high (Mahin banu), the middle (Paristaran-i-hudur) and the low.[163] The internal harem administration was in charge of women officials called Matrons or Daroghas. These Daroghas were appointed by the emperor and it was a very honourable post. Abul Fazl says that Emperor Akbar had elevated many of them to higher ranks of service in the harem from the dust of obscurity because of their merit.[164] Most of these matrons were well educated, intelligent and capable ladies and even belonged to high families. Nur Jahan's mother Asmat Banu Begam once occupied this place in the royal harem and Jehangir writes about her: "Of the amiable qualities of the matron (Qadbanu) of the family of chastity, what can I write?[165] It was the duty of these daroghas to make sure that all the women did their duties properly and also to keep order in the harem.[166]

Another important post in the harem was that of the Mahaldar. They were selected from among the Daroghas.[167] She was like a female major domo and even acted as a spy in the interest of the emperor.[168] She informed the king about the activities of the prominent personalities in the harem. Reports of the news-writers, Waqia-Nawis (public news writer) and Khufyan-Nawis (secret news writer) were read out to the king by them. They also sent the replies to these reports as per the king's direction.[169] During Jehangir's time this post was given to a certain lady by the name of Dil-Aram who had nursed Nur Jahan in her childhood. Previously it was held by Haji Koka.[170] Sati-un-Nisa had this post in Shahjahan's time.[171] In Aurangzeb's time a lady called Hamida Banu was appointed as Mahaldar of the harem of Muhammad Muazzam Bahadur Shah.[172]

In the next grade of harem staff came the supervisors whose duty was to keep control over the maid servants and the dancing girls.[173] They were also supposed to report to their appropriate superiors about all that went on inside the harem.[174] Each of these supervisors or matrons of the second category was in charge of a group of subordinates.[175] These matrons had names like Niyaz Bibi Banu, Qadir Bibi Banu, Gul Sultan Banu, Simtan Banu, Mihr Nigar Banu, Hira Bai Banu, Naval Bai Banu, Manik Banu, etc., and these names were given to them by the emperor.[176]

Another category of harem officials was that of the Tahwildars, who were in charge of the accounts of the harem. It was their duty to keep a check on the harem expenditure and to give away the salaries and allowances to the harem inmates. When a harem woman wanted anything within the limit of her salary, she applied to the Tahwildar. The Tahwildar then sent a memorandum to the writer who checked it, and the General Treasurer made the payment in cash.[177] The female store-keepers of the harem were known as Ashrafs, and they were incharge of supplies, and accounts.[178]

The low category of harem staff consisted of the slaves and the servant girls. They were usually known as *bandis*, and also as Khawas or Paristar.[179] Their duty was to serve the emperor, the princes and important harem ladies. Sometimes they were even used to satisfy their masters' physical needs. The important and high ranking ladies of the harem usually had ten to twelve women servants to look after their personal needs.[180] These *bandis* enjoyed no freedom or rights and their importance in the harem lied only when it came to serve the important inmates of the harem. According to Manucci some of the names of these slave girls were Gulal, Naiki, Chambaili, Subhati, Achanak, Rangmala, Kishmish, Pistah, Koil, etc.[181] When Manucci visited the Mughal court, he found that usually Kashmiri women were employed to stand at the doors of the chambers and their duty was to "carry away and bring back anything that was necessary."[182] These women remained unveiled. Strict discipline was enforced on the harem staff, especially on the slaves and servants by the higher officials.

Security of the Mughal Harem

The royal seraglio of the Mughals was well guarded. Inside the harem only women were employed as guards. They were brave, active and faithful and armed with bows and arrows and short daggers. Usually Habshi and Tartar women,[183] and also Urdubegis were appointed in this post.[184] The most trustworthy and efficient of them were in charge of looking after the safety and security of the emperor's chamber.[185] Over all these guards was a chief armed woman who supervised their activities. Bibi Fatima held this post in Humayun's harem.[186] The women guards like the male ones were allotted different places of duty inside the harem from time to time in a day,[187] probably to prevent internal plottings and conspiracies. Beyond the limit of these female guards, eunuchs were appointed to guard the Zenana from outside the harem enclosure. They were called Khwaja Saras.[188] The word eunuch is derived from the Greek word 'eunoukhos' which literally means bed chamber attendant.[189] Manucci says that these eunuchs were responsible for preventing all illict foods, beverages and drugs from entering the harem.[190] The senior eunuchs also had a number of other eunuchs under them. Manucci says - "there is always one set above everything that goes on in the Mahal."[191] The senior eunuchs were known as Nazirs.[192] The chief Nazir had the title of Itimad or Aitbar Khan. They were given great responsibilities by the emperor, and were men of importance. Some of them were even given *mansabs* or made commanders of armies or governor of Subahs. They amassed a lot of wealth too. Rajput guards, from Akbar's time onwards, were stationed some distances from the eunuch guards. On the gates of the palace porters were posted. On all the four sides many nobles, Ahadis and other troops were also stationed.[193] The gates of the Mahal were very well guarded. These gates closed at sunset and torches were kept burning throughout the night.[194] Outsiders and strangers were never allowed to step inside the Mahal and if any such person was caught, the punishments were very severe. Even female visitors were sent inside after a lot of scrutiny. The female guards of the harem had to send all the reports of the harem activities to the Nazir who finally gave all the reports to the Itimad Khan who passed it on to the emperor.

Many important harem ladies had their own staff who looked after their properties. Nur Jahan's officials are mentioned in the Tuzuk-i-Jahangiri.[195] Hakim Hamam and the son of Hakim Kashi served as Diwans in the Sarkars of Mumtaz Mahal.[196] Ishaq Beg was Mir-i-Saman of Mumtaz Mahal and later had this post under Jahanara Begam.[197] Afterwards he was promoted by her to the position of Diwan and got the title of Hakikat Khan.[198] In 1681 A.D. Saiyed Ashraf became the Mir-i-Saman of Jahanara Begam and got the title of Khan.[199] Sadullah Khan was appointed as Mir-i-Saman of Zinat-un-Nisa Begam.[200]

All the harem officials were given high salaries. During Akbar's time the matrons got upto 1028 to 1610 rupees a month. Lower than that the officials were paid 20 to 51 rupees. The lowest staff got 2 to 40 rupees.[201] The emperor also gave them lots of presents and costly gifts on special occasions. The salaries of the harem officials increased in course of time and by Aurangzeb's time the juniors got 300 to 500 rupees and the lowest staff got 50 to 200 rupees in a month.[202]

Religious Life

While talking about the life of Mughal ladies, the usual picture that comes to one's mind is a life spent in pleasure and merriment surrounded by all the luxuries and comforts that life could offer. Any serious aspect is not usually associated with their lives. But, amidst all the merriment and enjoyment, there was a serious side of their lives as well, like their interest in religious activities.

The ladies belonging to the Mughal royal family were introduced to the doctrines of Islam quite early in their lives. Religious education was a must in the learning process of the princesses and other ladies connected to the royal family from an early age. Learning the Quran was considered of highest importance and almost all the Mughal princesses had good knowledge of it. Aurangzeb's eldest daughter Princess Zeb-un-Nisa became a Hafiz at the age of seven when she learnt the Quran by heart.[203] Aurangzeb's two other daughters Zinat-un-Nisa and Badr-un-Nisa also learnt the Quran by heart.[204]

The Mughal harem had in it women from many cultural and religious backgrounds. There were many Hindu women including Rajput ladies. The Mughal emperors, especially Akbar, allowed his Hindu ladies to practise their own faith inside the harem. Akbar's first Rajput wife Jodha Bai, the princess of Amber is known to have kept up her Hindu ways of worship even after her marriage to a Muslim king. In Agra fort, the Jahangiri Mahal bears testimony of Sun worship, fire and Havan Kund.

Festivals Celebrated

Because of the liberal religious policies of the Mughal emperors like Akbar, both Muslim and Hindu festivals started being celebrated at the Mughal court. The Mughal emperors celebrated Muslim festivals like Id-ul-Fitr[205], Id-e-Qurbaan[206]. Shabb-i-Barat,[207] Barawafat[208] and Muharram which was later banned by Aurangzeb[209].They also adopted and started celebrating Persian festivals like Nauroz[210] and Gulab Pash[211]. The Hindu festivals celebrated by them were Dussehra[212], Diwali[213], Holi[214], Raksha Bandhan[215], Janamashtami and Shivaratri[216]. In the celebration of these festivals the Mughal ladies also participated in the gaiety and festivities. They sometimes even arranged feasts on such occasions. Nur Jahan Begam arranged grand feasts on the occasion of Shab-i-Barat[217]. Offering of special prayers also formed an essential part of the festival days. Special Prayers of thanks were also offered on other occasions like victories in wars, campaign, coronations, etc. We know from Gulbadan Begam's accounts that the ladies of Babar's harem offered prayer of thanks when the news of Babar's victory at Panipat reached them through a certain Khwaja Kilan[218].

Death Rites

Death ceremonies and the celebration of death anniversaries also formed an important part of the religious activities of Mughal ladies. Many contemporary writers like Lahori, Qazwini, Inayat Khan, Waris and other mention in their accounts the observance of such ceremonies connected to death. Usually forty days of mourning followed a death and then certain rites were performed. The celebration of the death anniversaries of Mumtaz Mahal is described in details by Qazwini, Lahori and Inayat Khan.[219]

Haj Pilgrimage

The Mughal ladies sometimes went on pilgrimages to holy places and to the shrines of holy men. During the time of Humayun and with his permission Sultanam, the wife of Nizam-ud-din Khalifa Barlas, went on a pilgrimage to Mecca. Gulbarg Begam accompanied her.[220] During Akbar's time, the royal ladies of the Mughal harem went for pilgrimages quite a few times. First Bega Begam or Haji Begam, widow of Humayun went on a pilgrimage to a holy places and Akbar made all the necessary arrangements for it[221]. In the year 1575 A.D. Akbar once again made the necessary arrangements when some prominent ladies of his harem went on the Haj pilgrimage to Mecca, starting in October 1576 A.D.[222] Some of these ladies were his aunt Gulbadan Begam. Akbar's wife and Bairam Khan's widow Salima Sultan Begam, Sultanam who was the widow of Akbar's uncle Askari, Gulnar Agha who was a wife of Babar. Haji Begam and Gul-izar Begam who were the daughters of Kamran and Gulbadan Begam's step nieces, Gulbadan's own grand daughter Um-Kulsum, a certain Gul-nar aghacha from Babar's household and another lady called Bibi Saru-qad or Saru-i-sahi of Babar's household[223]. The journey was a tedious one in spite of the efficient arrangements made by Akbar. The party came back to India in April 1582 A.D.[224] In the course of this time Gulbadan Begam and the ladies performed the Haj thrice. On the journey back home the ladies visited the shrine of Khwaja Muin-ud-din Chisti at Ajmer[225].

Pilgrimages to Shrines and Tombs

In the later years we do not come across any reference of Haj pilgrimage undertaken by the Mughal ladies. But they continued their pilgrimages to the shrines of holy men. Some Mughal ladies accompanied Akbar to the shrine of Khwaja Muin-ud-din Chisti at Ajmer when Akbar went there on foot[226]. Pilgrimages were also undertaken to the tombs of late emperors and other members of the Mughal royal family. Jehangir in his memoirs makes a mention of quite a few such times. Once in 1619 A.D. the harem ladies visited "the enlightened shrine of Humayun" in Delhi and then visited the shrine of Shaikh Nizam-ud-din Chisti[227]. In 1607 A.D. Akbar's widow Ruqaiya Begam went for a pilgrimage to the mausoleum of her father Hindal in Kabul[228]. Jahanara Begam, who had a great inclination towards spirituality and mysticism, often visited the tomb of the Chisti saint Shaikh Nizamuddin Aulia in Delhi. After her death she was even buried in a simple marble tomb near the tomb of her favourite saint Shaikh Nizamuddin Aulia. When she recovered from her severe burns in 1644 A.D. Jahanara Begam went on a pilgrimage to the shrine of Khwaja Muin-ud-din Chisti at Ajmer[229].

Sufi Belief

Princess Jahanara was a deeply religious minded person. She was a believer in Sufism. Quite early in her life, when she was around twenty-seven years of age, under the influence of her brother Dara, Jahanara became a member of the Qadiriya Sufi order[230]. Dara had turned towards Sufism after meeting the great Sufi mystic Main Mir of Lahore. On a visit to Kashmir, at Dara's initiative Jahanara came in contact with saint Mulla Shah[231] who taught her the benefits of meditation. She had certain spiritual visions too. Jahanara wrote many Risalas (pamphlets) on the subjects of mysticism and spirituality[232]. In her *Risala-i-Sahibiya* she speaks of her spiritual visions and experiences.[233] She also wrote a book called 'Munis-ul-Arwah' which was a biography of the Sufi saint of Ajmer, Khwaja Muin-ud-din Chisti and some of his descendants.[234] Aurangzeb's eldest daughter Princess Zeb-un-Nisa's verses reflect these thoughts and sentiments.

Charitable Works

Some Mughal ladies engaged themselves in a lot of charitable works. They helped poor people especially needy women, gave large amounts in alms on special occasions, built rest houses and *sarais* and constructed educational centres and mosques for the use of people. Maham Begam, mother of Humayun seems to have constructed in 1561 A.D./969 A.H. a masjid called Din Panah near the fort of old Delhi.[235] Nur Jahan Begam built the Pathar Masjid, also known by the names of Shahi Masjid and Nau Masjid at Srinagar, though this mosque was never used by the people for the purpose for which it was built. It was used as a store-house later[236]. Three of Shahjahan's secondary wives, Akbarabadi Mahal, Fatehpuri Mahal and Sarhindi Mahal built mosques in Delhi.[237] At Akbarabadi Mahal's request Shahjahan once performed the Id prayers in her newly completed mosque[238]. The mosque of Akbarabadi Mahal was destroyed in 1857 A.D. but the Fatehpuri and Sarhindi mosques are still found in Delhi. Jahanara Begam built a mosque costing 40,000 rupees in Kashmir for Mulla Shah at her own expense[239]. This mosque was surrounded by large buildings for the habitation of the poor and this was constructed at a further cost of 20,000 rupees[240] Jahanara Begam also built the

Jami Masjid at Agra. It stands outside the Agra Fort on the north-west direction. It was completed after five years of work in 1648 A.D. and had cost five hundred thousand rupees[241] Jahanara Begam also built a Rabat (monastery)[242]. Princess Zinat-un-Nisa, the second daughter of Aurangzeb built the Zinat-ul-Masjid in Delhi. It is said that Zinat-un-Nisa asked her father to give her the amount of her dowry and she used it to build this mosque[243].

Other than building mosques, the Mughal ladies gave large amounts as alms and charities on special occasions. Some ladies gave charity as a regular basis also. Humayun's widow Haji Begam gave regular alms to five hundred poor and needy people during her days of widowhood[244]. Nur Jahan Begam was extremely charitable and was widely known for her generosity. If she got to know about any orphan and poor girl of marriageable age, she arranged for her wedding[245]. About five hundred girls were helped by her in this way and thousands more were the recipients of her generosity in some way or the others[246]. She also made the required arrangements for many people to go for pilgrimages to holy places. Shahjahan's wife Mumtaz Mahal and his daughter Jahanara Begam were also known for their charitable works. Jahanara Begam patronised scholars and distributed large sums of money to poor and needy people.[247] Aurangzeb's daughter Princess Zeb-un-Nisa also patronised scholars and learned men. Her sister, Princess Zinat-un-Nisa was also extremely bountiful and charitable.[248] She built caravan *serais* for the benefit of poor travellers.[249]

The Purdah System

Since ancient times a veiled woman has always been associated with respectable and aristocratic families in India as in many other oriental and occidental countries and cultures of the world. Some scholars are of the view that the concept of strict veiling of women which we know by the term 'purdah system' have come to India with the coming of Islam to this land,[250] while some others opine that women in ancient India, especially of royal or noble birth, were not unknown to purdah or veiling as is known from the two great epics: *Ramayana* and *Mahabharata*, certain vedic literatures like *Brahama Purana* and even from Bana's *Harsha Charita* and Kautilya's *Arthashastra*.[251] Though veiling of women as a mark of respectability existed in ancient India, the Epics and other literatures of those times reveal that the women of those days enjoyed considerable freedom of movement, speech, learning and sometimes even the liberty of choosing their own husbands. These things certainly could not have been possible with strict *purdah* prevailing in the society as they were no longer possible in the Hindu society after the coming of the Muslims to this country.

When Islam came into existence in Arabia during the days of the Holy Prophet, women were not excluded from social activities of the outdoor life.[252] They even participated in political activities and public meetings though not in warfare.[253] In the days of early Islam, the *burqa* or *chadar* was not prevalent. The women did put on *jilbab* or over-garment, drawn over the face to keep away bad eyes of some people, but they moved about freely.[254] These things however began to change under the later Umayyad Caliphs when the pre-Islamic forces of tribalism, racial pride and narrow loyalties and interests began to appear once again.[255] Slaves and women were oppressed greatly. Unrestricted polygamy, concubinage and male jealousy to conceal his innumerable wives and concubines from public eyes naturally resulted in *purdah* as a system side by side with the establishment of the harem system.[256] With these came the degradation of the Muslim women which then probably reached the lowest level. Her position in society became that of an exchangeable commodity. It was under such social conditions that the Ulema and other religious interpreters misinterpreted the Quranic injunctions and started believing that women were not supposed to move freely without completely covering themselves and such other things that implied strict *purdah*.[257] With the rise of the Abbasid Caliphate things became worse.[258]

It is quite natural that when these Muslims from Western and Central Asia came to India, their narrow ideas about keeping women in seclusion also came with them, and the Hindus were also influenced a great deal in this regard. With the defeat of the Hindus at the hands of Muslim invaders and the subsequent establishment of the Muslim rule in India, the Hindus felt a greater need to save the honour of their womenfolk and in the process maintain their social and cultural integrity.[259] Thus, the *zenana* and the *purdah* in its strict form came into the Hindu society, especially in the higher castes and aristocratic families.[260]

During the Mughal times in India, we find *purdah* being imposed on women quite vigorously. Even a liberal king like Akbar issued the order that "if a young woman was found roaming about the streets and bazaars of the town and while doing so did not veil herself or allowed herself to be unveiled .. she was to go to the quarters of the prostitutes and take up the profession.[261] Not only the contemporary native accounts but also the foreigners who came to India during the Mughal times have mentioned, some times even in details, the prevalence of *purdah* in strict sense among the Mughal ladies. De Laet observed "The Mahumetan women do not come out into public unless they are poor or immodest; they veil their heads.."[262]

Whenever the royal ladies moved outside their palaces they put on veils, usually white in colour, which covered their faces.[263] Royal women seldom travelled on foot. They mostly travelled in covered palanquins[264] with servants and eunuchs surrounding them on all sides.[265] At the entrance of the residence, male palanquin-bearers were replaced by females to carry the palanquins further inside.[266] The royal ladies also travelled in covered *howdahs*[267] on elephant backs, *chaudoles*[268] and sometimes in carriages covered on all sides to maintain *purdah*[269]. When a royal lady rode an elephant, the animal was made to enter a tent near the palace-gate and the *mahout* covered his face with a cloth so that he was unable to see the princess when she entered into the covered *howdah*.[270] Whether the ladies travelled in palanquins or *chaudoles* or *howdahs* or carriages, proper care was taken to hide them from the view of the people outside,[271] and they became "almost inaccessible to the sight of man."[272]

Not only outside their palaces but within the palaces too the Mughal women lived in strict seclusion. Eunuchs and palace guards saw to it that strangers never got the chance to enter the women's apartments. Even female guests had to take permission of the concerned authority before entering the harem quarters. No one at the court was allowed to see the women housed there except the emperor and a few select relatives.[273] The men having this special privileges included the fathers and brothers of the royal ladies living inside, but they too could meet the women only in the presence of her husband.[274] Therefore it was a great honour for

Nur Jahan Begam's father Etimad-ud-Daulah when Jehangir decreed that "the ladies of the harem (were) not to veil their faces from him."[275]

About Jehangir and his wives, Roe writes: "No man enters his house but eunuchs; his women are never scene; ..."[276] Pietro Della Valle, while describing the Mughal emperor's lodgings says: "What 'tis with in side I know not, for I enter'd not into it..."[277] According to Terry he never had sight of those women[278] as "none (are) admitted, strangers or others, to have a sight of those houses, while the King's wives and women are there, which must not be seen by any but by himself, and his servants and eunuchs."[279] Bernier and Manucci, as physicians were sometimes allowed inside the Mughal Harem, but even they were not allowed to see much of the women or the apartments inside. Manucci writes:

> It is the custom in the royal household, when a physician is called within the mahal, for the eunuchs to cover his head with a cloth, which hangs down to his waist. Then they conduct him to the patient's room, and he is taken out in the same manner.[280]

Bernier too speaks of the same custom. Bernier gives this as the reason why he could not observe much of what was inside the seraglio.[281] Once Roe had a glimpse of two wives (or women) of Jehangir's harem, "whose curiosity made them break little holes in a grate of reede that hung before to gaze on me."[282] But such incidents were too rare for any outsider and almost all of them knew nothing of the women of the seraglio except a few stories of them popular with the common people living outside.

From the core of the strict *purdah* system that was prevalent in the Mughal times and in the Mughal harem, we do find the name of Nur Jahan Begam who "broke the purdah convention and did not mind to come out in public."[283] According to Hamilton, Emperor Shahjahan was sorry for the women who were kept confined in the seraglio and therefore:

> "He turned his thoughts to break those sordid Chains, and introduce the Ladies to a free Air, and reckoned his Court, which he then kept at Agra a great City, to be the most proper part for the stage to act it first upon".[284]

We do not know what good the *purdah* system did for the

women of those times other than branding them as belonging to respectable, royal, aristocratic or noble families. The practise of seclusion in a family might have also reflected the high economic standing.[283] The lord of the house too had a lot of free time at hand which he spent in the "pursuit of pleasure with his women"[286] The harem therefore became the ultimate mark of social status and for the king, "the real symbol of his imperial sovereignty"[287]. This system of keeping the women in seclusion however did a lot of harm to the all round development of their personalities, especially in the field of education. Higher education became a difficult matter for them even when they desired it.[288] We do come across educated ladies in Mughal times like Gulbadan Begam, Salima Sultan Begam, Nur Jahan, Jahanara, Zeb-un-Nisa and some others. But the majority of women in those days were deprived of this opportunity which became the privilege of a very few, and that too those belonging to aristocratic and royal families where tutors could teach the girls inside the Zenana. Even paintings of Mughal ladies were rare in those times because of strict purdah.[289] From the time of Nur Jahan, due to her influence at the Mughal court, women became more popular as the subject matter of painting.[290]

Love Life of Mughal Ladies

A life without love is no life at all. Love has always been love, and humans have always endeavoured to get love in any form possible. In fact, there can be no being who does not want love. But sometimes that which we consider as love can be a mere illusion, a shadow, a mirage of our fantasy or our deepest desire. Since all of us strive to get love, it is nothing strange that the ladies of the Mughal harem too craved to get love. In fact, love was what they craved for most and seldom got.

The Mughal women lived under a lot of restrictions. They seldom moved out of the harem quarters. Even when they went out their faces were well hidden behind veils. The seraglio was well guarded and totally hidden from the eyes of outsiders and strangers. According to William Finch, the rooms where the harem ladies resided had no doors.[291] If there were doors they were fastened from outside.[292] If such was the case then a watch could be kept over the activities of the harem ladies quite easily.

The ladies of the Mughal harem were expected to be the epitomes of chastity and virtue. The contemporary Persian chroniclers like Abul Fazl, Qazwini, Lahori, Inayat Khan, Khafi Khan and others refer to the royal ladies as the chaste and virtuous daughters or wives of someone. It was quite all right for the Mughal men to enjoy as many women as they could, but when it came to their wives, daughters and other female relatives, such things were not only strictly forbidden but were also unimaginable. To Manucci, "...all Mahomedans are very fond of women who are their principal relaxation and almost their only pleasure"[293]. Although the men could seek any forms of pleasure for themselves and could have any number of wives and concubines, their ladies were never allowed any such pleasure and were expected to show complete fidelity to their men. Edward Terry writes:

> Not withstanding this polygamie, the hot jealousies of the lustfull Mahometans are such that they will scare endure the brothers or fathers of their beloved wives or women to have speech with them, except in their presence; and Time, by this restraint, hath made it odious for such women to have the reputation of honesty to be seen at any time by strangers. But if they dishonour their husbands beds or, being unmarried, are found incontinent, professing chastity rather than they shall want punishment, their own brothers will be their executioners...[294]

Though it be a man or a woman, side by side with the want for love comes a need to satisfy the physical desires. In the medieval times, as in many other ages, a man's needs in this regard were never considered evil, but a woman was not supposed to feel that way about any other person other than her husband. Lots of measures were taken by the Mughal emperors to prevent their ladies from coming across any sort of temptations that could have aroused their physical desires. Not only were they prevented to meet any man or go out of the harem as they willed, even things like certain vegetables and intoxicants were prevented from entering the harem. According to Thomas Coryat:

> Whatsoever is brought in the virile shape, as for instance radishes, so great is the jealousy, and so frequent the wickedness of this people, that they are cut and jagged for fear of converting the same of some unnatural abuse.[295]

Even Manucci speaks of something similar when he says "Nor do they permit into the palace radishes, cucumbers, or similar vegetables that I cannot name."[296]

What the Mughal emperors seemed to have ignored was that the women living inside their harems were also human beings with wants and desires like any others belonging to any age. These emperors had a number of wives and concubines who were expected to show complete loyalty and fidelity to them. There were hundreds of other women living inside the harem who were not the wives or concubines, mothers, sisters, daughters or other female relatives of the emperor. The laws of the harem dictated the lives of these women too and even they were supposed to lead chaste lives. But when it came to pleasing the emperor, any of these women could be used as the emperor pleased.

Marriages and Courtships

In the Mughal royal family, marriages were mainly political affairs. But that does not mean that the Mughal emperors and princes never married for love or never fell in love. Babar himself wrote in his memoirs that his marriage to Masuma-Sultan Begam (Miran-Shahi) was a love match on both sides.[297] Humayun's marriage to Hamida Banu Begam, who later became the mother of Akbar, was also a love match. Humayun who had fallen in love with Hamida Banu on seeing her, had to court her and pursue her a lot before he succeeded in getting Hamida Banu as his wife. Hamida Banu on her part was not interested in marrying Humayun basically for the reason that he was a king and therefore someone above her status. She expressed the feeling that she wanted to be the wife of someone who "shall be a man whose collar my hand can touch, and not one whose skirt it does not reach."[298] She finally agreed after a lot of persuasion and advice from elderly harem ladies.[299]

Jehangir's love for Nur Jahan is well-known. There are not enough evidences to prove the story that Jehangir when a prince fell in love with the young Mehrunisa and Akbar's knowledge of it forced him to arrange the marriage of this beautiful and talented daughter of Ghiyas Beg with a Persian youth at the court by the name of Sher Afghan, and that Jehangir after coming to the throne planned the killing of Sher Afghan to get back Mehrunnisa. But, contemporary native and foreign accounts do more than confirm the fact that Jehangir fell head over heels in love with Mehrunnisa when as a widow she came back to Agra and took up employment in Akbar's widow Ruqaiya Begam's household. After courtship and persuasion Jehangir married her in 1611 A.D. After that Nur Jahan gained extreme powers in administration and became the virtual ruler of Jehangir's life as well as his kingdom. Nur Jahan too loved Jehangir and Jehangir confirms this by saying about her: "I did not think anyone was fonder of me."[300] Her affectionate care even led him to diminish his excessive drinking, to abstain from unwholesome diet and to take proper remedies.[301] During the medieval age, a woman was considered old on attaining the age of thirty. When Jehangir fell in love with Nur Jahan and married her, she was not only above this age but was also the mother of a daughter. Even though she was extremely beautiful, cultured and talented, to love and marry a lady at that age during those days by someone who never had a scarcity of beautiful women around him, was certainly a matter of the heart. Many foreign travellers have talked about the love of Jehangir and Nur Jahan in their accounts and the importance she had in his life.[302]

May be Jehangir loved Nur Jahan most but she was certainly not the only love of his life. In his memoirs he speaks of the love that he bore for his first wife Man Bai (who had the title of Shah Begam), the mother of his eldest son Khusrau and mourns her suicidal death. He writes:

> What shall I write of her excellences and goodness? She had perfect intelligence and her devotion to me was such that she would have sacrificed a thousand sons and brothers for one hair of mine... In consequence of her death, from the attachment I had for her, I passed some days without any kind of pleasure in life or existence, and for four days... I took nothing in the shape of food or drink.[303]

Jehangir's love for a dancing girl in Akbar's harem by the name of Anarkali has become a love legend popular even today. Emperor Akbar was so much against the whole affair that he is said to have buried Anarkali alive, "enclosed quick within a wall in his moholl, where she dyed..."[304] When Prince Salim became Emperor Jehangir, he built a lovely tomb in her memory in Lahore. About it Finch says:

> ...and the King (Jehangir), in token of his love, commands a sumptuous tomb to be built of stone in the midst of a foure-square garden richly walled, with a gate and divers room over it.[305]

Finch calls Anarkali a wife of Akbar's, but that cannot be accepted as the truth. Considering the respect that the Mughals showed to their mothers and even their step mothers, if Anarkali was one of Akbar's wives, Jehangir could not have had an affair with her how much ever inclined he might have been towards her. She must have been a concubine, dancing-girl or a slave-girl in Akbar's harem.

Jehangir's eldest son Prince Khusrau loved his wife so much that he refused to marry Nur Jahan's daughter Ladli Begam. When Khusrau was in captivity, his wife left the life of luxury of the palace and lived with him in captivity sharing his days of misery. Nur Jahan told him "that if he would marry Nurmahal's daughter he should be immediately set free."[306] Khusrau's wife also urged him to accept this offer. But Khusrau adamantly refused this offer again and again. A life of captivity along with his beloved wife was more welcome to him than having another wife and a life of freedom.[307] Without doubt he loved his wife extremely.

The love that Shahjahan bore for his beloved wife Arjumand Banu Begam has been immortalised by the greatest symbol of conjugal love in the world — the Taj Mahal, which is her mausoleum. Shahjahan had many wives and concubines. Roe even says that he had an inclination towards his beautiful and dynamic step-mother Nur Jahan.[308] But Shahjahan never loved anyone as much as he loved Arjumand Banu Begam whom he married on 10th May, 1612 A.D.[309], when she was nineteen, and gave her the title of Mumtaz Mahal. She became the mother of his fourteen children, and died in 1631 A.D. at Burhanpur in the Deccan after giving birth to the fourteenth child. She was his constant companion in joy and sorrow and underwent a lot of difficulties in sharing her husband's difficult times, but never left his side. Her untimely death left Shahjahan a broken man. Qazwini describes his condition in details. He says that Shahjahan shed so much tears that pretty soon he came to need spectacles resulting out of excessive weeping. For two years after that he gave up listening to musical performances, indulging in pastimes and wearing good clothes and jewellery. His beard which hardly had any grey hair before now turned almost grey.[310] Other court chroniclers like Lahori too speak of similar state that became of Shahjahan after Mumtaz's death.[311]

The love that Shahjahan bore for his wife seemed to have been inherited by his son Dara Shukoh, who had great love for his wife Nadira Begam. Nadira Begam too like Mumtaz Mahal, had shared Dara's days of happiness and misery and was his constant companion. In Hansen's words:

> For 27 years Nadira Begam had been far more than a wife and a consort; she had been companion, counsellor, disciple, a substitute mother filling the gap of Mumtaz Mahal's early death.[312]

Nadira Begam's untimely death of 6th June, 1659 A.D. left Dara miserable and totally shattered.

The otherwise strict and stone-hearted Aurangzeb was not so where his youngest and most loved concubine Udipuri Mahal was concerned. In the words of Sir Jadunath Sarkar, "She retained her youth and influence over the Emperor till his death, and was the darling of his old age."[313] Before this too, Aurangzeb as a prince, during his viceroyalty of the Deccan, had met and fallen in love with a young slave girl by the name of Hira Bai, surnamed Zainabadi. Her sweet voice and unparalled beauty had charmed Aurangzeb to a very great extent. Her early death ended this love story soon.[314]

From the few instances discussed here, it can be clearly seen that all Mughal ladies were not devoid of love. But love touched the lives of very few women. There were so many wives and concubines for one man and it was not possible for any man to give attention to all of them. Usually the ones they loved most got all their love and attention. Sometimes the wives got their husband's attention because the husband felt that it was his duty to do so. Babar speaks of his first wife Ayisha Sultan Begam towards whom he did not have love, saying:

> Though I was not ill disposed towards her, yet this being my first marriage, out of modesty and bashfulness, I used to see her once in 10, 15, or 20 days. Later on when even my first inclination did not last, my bashfulness increased. Then my mother Khanum used to send me, once in a month or every 40 days, with driving and driving, dunnings and worryings.[315]

But all the ladies did not even have the chances of Ayisha-Sultan Begam. After the age of thirty they were considered aged. Terry confirms this by saying that the men of that age did not come "near their wives or women, after they exceed the age of thirty years."[316] Though some of the royal ladies were lucky enough to get their husband's love, it was never the case that they happened to be the only women in their husband's life. The Mughal emperors and princes did have some special women they loved and cared for, but they also had a number of other women like concubines, dancing-girls and slave girls whom they could use for their pleasure as they liked. Then, there were the Mughal princesses, many of whom were never given in marriage, probably because no man was considered worthy enough to marry them, and also may be to limit the contenders for the throne. Whatever might have been the reason, these princesses had to remain satisfied with the material luxuries and the love of their fathers and brothers. About the condition of these women Pelsaert says:

> These wretched women wear, indeed, the most expensive clothes, eat the daintiest food, and enjoy all worldly pleasures except one, and for that one they grieve saying they would willingly give everything in exchange for a beggar's poverty.[317]

Under all these circumstances it is not a very strange thing that the ladies of the Mughal harem seeked other forms of physical pleasure. Though these women were guarded strictly, yet they managed to enjoy the company of other men inside the harem. In some way or the other a man's touch meant a lot to them. The physicians who came into the harem for treating ailing women were the most accessible ones. When a doctor came to examine a lady, there used to be a curtain separating them and the doctor used to feel the pulse of the lady and diagnose the ailment. Manucci, who went inside the harem sometimes as a physician, mentions the times when as the doctor he put his hand inside the curtain, the ladies used to "lay hold of it, kiss it, and softly bite it. Some out of curiosity, apply it to their breast, which had happened to conceal what was passing from the matrons and eunuchs then present, and not arouse their suspicion."[318]

Apart from the physicians, the ladies of the harem sometimes had other men brought inside the harem. The help of the eunuchs and maids were greatly needed for this. In the darkness of nights outside men used to be smuggled inside the harem. Sometimes these men were not total strangers, but those connected to the palace. Then there were the Khanzadas whose mothers belonged to the seraglio, and therefore they had more liberty in the palace than total outsiders and were more accessible to the harem ladies. Great risks were involved in such matters and the punishment was death if the emperor found out about it. But this did not stop the practise. Lights burned all nights in the palaces but they were not bright enough to illuminate all the areas well. This certainly helped these love-sick ladies of the harem. Even eunuchs were sometimes enjoyed for the satisfaction of physical pleasure. As a result many love affairs between eunuchs and harem women came to be established. K.S. Lal states that:

> ...some eunuchs were born inter-sexual, with characteristics of neither sex fully developed due to hormonal or genetic disturbances. Some others were hermaphrodite who combined characteristics of both sexes... But such cases are rare... The vast majority of eunuchs were strong men who were subjected to castration.[319]

Some eunuchs were very handsome. Roe mentions an affair between a gentel woman of Normalls and a eunuch.[320] The story of one of the principal eunuchs of Akbar by the name of Didar Khan, who fell in love with a scrivner's sister and got killed by the scrivner, is quite popular.[321] At later times, during the reign of Muhammad Shah (1719-1748 A.D.) his queen carried on an affair with the head eunuch Javed Khan.[322]

Manucci and Bernier speak of the love escapades of Shahjahan's daughters, Jahanara and Roshanara. About the love adventures of Mughal princesses Bernier wrote:

> What I am writing is a matter of history, and my object is to present a faithful account of the manners of this people. Love adventures are not attended with the same danger in Europe as in Asia... but in this part of the world, few are the instances in which they are not followed by some dreadful and tragical catastrophe.[323]

About Princess Jahanara, Bernier speaks of two incidents. He says:

> Begam-Saheb, although confined in a Seraglio, was guarded like other women, received the visits of a young man of not very exalted rank, but of an agreeable person. It was scarcely possible, surrounded as she was on all sides by those of her own sex whose envy she had long provoked, that her conduct should escape detection. Shah-Jehan was appraised of her guilt, and resolved to enter her apartments at an unusual and unexpected hour. The intimation of his approach was too sudden to allow her the choice of more than one place of concealment. The affrighted gallant sought refuge in the capacious cauldron used for the baths. The King's countenance denoted neither surprise nor displeasure; he discoursed with his daughter on ordinary topics, but finished the conversation by observing that the state of her skin indicated a neglect of her customary ablution, and that it was proper she should bathe. He then commanded the Eunuchs to light a fire under the cauldron, and did not retire until they gave him to understand that his wretched victim was no more.[324]

Manucci also speaks of the same incident but he says that this youth jumped into a stove when he heard Shahjahan coming.[325]

Relating another incident about Princess Jahanara, Bernier says:

> Begam-Saheb formed another attachment, which also had a tragical termination. She chose for her Kane-Samen, or steward, a Persian, named Nazerkan, a young nobleman remarkable for grace and mental accomplishments, full of spirit and ambition, and the favourite of the whole court. Chah Hestkan (Shaista Khan), the Uncle of Aurangzeb ventured to propose him for Begam-Saheb's husband: a

> proposition which was very ill received by the Mogol. He had indeed already entertained some suspicion of an improper intercourse between the favoured Nobleman and the Princess and did not long deliberate on the course he should pursue. As a mark of distinguished favour the King presented the betel, in the presence of the whole court, to the unsuspecting youth, which he was obliged immediately to masticate, agreeably to the custom of the country... Little did the unhappy lover imagine that he had received poison from the hand of the smiling monarch... He died before he could reach home.[326]

Both Bernier and Manucci relate the incident how Roshanara Begam once allowed two men into her apartments at night. This story was told to them by a Portguese lady who had access to the harem frequently. When Aurangzeb found out about it and caught them red-handed, he seems to have let them go, but the eunuchs superseded his orders and the two men were thrown down from the top of the palace walls. Aurangzeb punished the eunuchs severely for the lack of security at the entrances of the seraglio.[327] Manucci goes on to say that again sometime later, Roshanara Begam kept nine youths secretly in her apartments for her pleasure. When Aurangzeb's daugher Fakhr-un-Nissa Begam (Badr-un-Nisa Begam) discovered it, she asked Roshanara to give at least one of them for her pleasure. Roshanara refused and Fakhr-un-Nissa reported this to her father Aurangzeb. He then ordered a search and the nine men were caught. They were announced to others as thieves and the Kotwal Sidi Faulad "destroyed them in less than a month by various secret tortures. Already angered at the misconduct of his sister Aurangzeb shortened her life by poison."[328]

Such stories are many in the Mughal annals. Emperor Shahjahan, well known for his love for Mumtaz Mahal, seems to have led a licentious life after her death. Manucci said that the only thing that Shahjahan seemed to have cared for was "the search for women to serve his pleasure."[329] He had great intimacy with the wives of his nobles Jafar Khan and Khalilullah Khan. It seems they became so notorious that whenever they passed, the mendicants and beggars cried out in loud voice to Jafar Khan's wife, calling her Shahjahan's breakfast and they called Khalilulah

Khan's wife as the Luncheon of Shahjahan.[330] Almost all the foreigners who came to the Mughal capital at that time speak of Shahjahan's affairs with many women. Some of them like Bernier even say that he had incestuous connection with his daughter Jahanara Begam. About this he writes:

> Begam-Saheb, the eldest daughter of Shah-Jehan, was very handsome, of lively parts, and passionately loved by her father. Rumour has it that his attachment reached a point which it is difficult to believe, the justification of which he rested on the decision of the Mullas, or doctors of their law. According to them it would have been unjust to deny the King the privilege of gathering fruit from the tree he had himself planted.[331]

Even present day scholars like Vincent Smith accept this theory. He comes to the conclusion that "the unpleasant accusation against Shahjahan and his daughter, even if it be not conclusively proved, certainly is not disproved. Although it may be reasonably regarded as improbable, it cannot be dismissed summarily as incredible."[332] Somehow Manucci does not accept this as the truth. He says:

> It was from this cause (Shahjahan's great affection for Jahanara) that the common people hinted that she had intercourse with her father, and this has given occasion to Monsieur Bernier to write many things about this princess, founded entirely on the talk of low people. Therefore it is incumbent on me, begging his pardon, to say that what he writes is untrue.[333]

Whether Manucci sincerely disbelieved this story or tried to disbelieve it because of his great liking for Begam Saheb cannot be said. But as such this story cannot be accepted as true. The origin of this gossip lay in the great love and trust that Shahjahan had for Jahanara and the manner in which she reciprocated this love. As it has already been said, the Mughals had a strong sense of family ties and great regard for family members and there could never have existed such relationships between fathers and daughters, mothers (even step-mother) and sons and brothers and sisters.

The love that Dara had for his sister Jahanara has been interpreted by some historians, especially westerners, to be something more than a brotherly or sisterly affection, something like an "unholy union of brother and sister."[334] Dara and Jahanara had much in common like believing in Sufi ideology and having the same bent of mind and spirit. They were very much fond of each other. She even seems to have said, "I love my brother Dara Shikoh extremely both in form and spirit. We are, in fact, like one soul in two bodies and one spirit in two physical forms. The Mughal kings and princes might have enjoyed any number of women they could, but they gave due respect to the ladies related to them. The fact that Dara and Jahanara were very fond of each other cannot be concluded as any romantic attachment between them.

The ladies of the Mughal harem led unhappy lives as far as satisfaction of physical desires or love was concerned. They spent long hours and innumerable days waiting for the love they rarely got. The number of those lucky ones who got it was very few. Frustrated, they took recourse to intoxicants or searched for lovers elsewhere. Great risk lay in this and even if they got a lover, their fathers or brothers made it sure that the unfortunate man ceased to live and the whole matter was hushed down. All the Mughal ladies did not indulge in adultery or extra-martial affairs. But we cannot blame the ones who did so. After all, they did so to find love and as the famous saying goes - 'Everything is fair in love and war.'

REFERENCES

1. Manucci, *Memoirs of the Mughal Court*, ed. Michael Edwardes (London : 1963), p. 33.
2. Hawkins in Foster ed. *Early Travels in India* (London : 1921), p. 101.
3. Terry in *Early Travels in India*, p. 406.
4. Bernier, *Travels in the Moghul Empire*, tr. Constable and Smith (New Delhi : 1983), pp. 267-68; William Finch in *Early Travels in India*, p. 151; De Laet, *The Empire of the Great Mogol*, tr. J.S. Hoyland (New Delhi : 1974), pp. 39-40; N.L. Mathur, *Red Fort and Mughal Life* (New Delhi : 1964), pp. 38-39.
5. K.S. Lal, *The Mughal Harem* (New Delhi : 1988), p. 122; S.N. Dar, *Costumes of India and Pakistan* (Bombay) : 1969), p. 45.
6. Abul Fazl, *Ain-i-Akbari*, Vol. III, tr. H.S. Jarrett, pp. 343-44.
7. Roe, *The Embassy of Sir Thomas Roe to India*, ed. William Foster, (London : 1926), Vol. II, p. 321; Terry in *Early Travels in India*, p. 405; Bernier, p. 372.
8. Manucci, *Storia* .... Vol. I, p. 212.

9. *Ain-i-Akbari*, Vol. I, p. 57.
10. *Ibid.*, p. 68.
11. *Ibid.*, p. 64.
12. *Ibid.*, pp. 93-101.
13. *Ibid.*, Vol. I, p. 59.
14. Manucci, *Storia...*, Vol. II, p. 332.
15. *Ain-i-Akbari* (tr.), Vol. I, p. 59.
16. *Ibid.*, pp. 68-71.
17. M.S. Commissariat, *Mandelslo's Travels in Western India* (London : 1931), p. 46; Herklots, *Islam in India* (London etc.: 1921), p. 330.
18. Roe, Vol. II, p. 421; Tapan Kumar Ray Chaudhary, *Bengal Under Akbar and Jehangir* (Calcutta : 1953), p. 202.
19. Manucci, *Memoirs of the Mughal Court*, p. 33.
20. Manucci, *Storia ...*, Vol. II, p. 331.
21. Terry in *Early Travels in India*, p. 487; Pelsaert, *Jahangir's India, The Remonstrantie of Francisco Pelsaert*, tr., Moreland and Geyl (Delhi : 1972), p. 66.
22. A.S. Beveridge in Gulbadan Begam's *Humayun Nama* (New Delhi : 1983), p. 8.
23. Mutamid Khan, *Iqbal Nama-i-Jahangiri* (Text), (Calcutta : 1865), p. 251; *Tuzuk-i-Jehangiri* tr. Rogers and Beveridge, Vol. I, p. 48.
24. *Tuzuk-i-Jahangiri* (tr.), p. 48.
25. *Ibid.*, Vol. II, p. 45.
26. *Ain-i-Akbari* (Text), Vol. I, p. 26; tr., Vol. I, Blochmann, pp. 61-62.
27. Coryat quoted in K.S. Lal, *The Mughal Harem*, p. 24.
28. *Tuzuk-i-Jahangiri* (tr.) Vol. II, p. 68.
29. Abul Fazl, *Akbar Nama*, Vol. III, tr. H. Beveridge (Calcutta : 1939), pp. 109-10, 130-31.
30. *Akbar Nama*, Vol. II, tr. Beveridge (Calcutta : 1912), p. 230.
31. *Tuzuk-i-Jahangiri* (tr.), Vol. I, pp. 84-85.
32. A.S. Beveridge in *Humayun Nama*, p. 20.
33. Gulbadan Begam, *Humayun Nama* (tr.), p. 97.
34. *Ibid.*, pp. 97-98.
35. *Humayun Nama* (tr.), p. 115.
36. *Akbar Nama* (tr.), Vol. III, p. 677.
37. A.S. Beveridge in *Babar Nama*, Vol. II, pp. 711-12 (translator's note).
38. *Humayun Nama* (tr.) pp. 274-75.
39. *Ain-i-Akbari* (tr.), Vol. I, p. 321 & n.
40. *Akbar Nama* (tr.), Vol. II, pp. 242-43.
41. *Ibid.*, p. 518.
42. *Ibid.*, pp. 518-19.
43. Tod, *The Annals and Antiquities of Rajasthan* (London, etc. : 1920), Vol. II, p. 26.
44. *Akbar Nama* (tr.), Vol. II, pp. 278 & 295.
45. *Ain-i-Akbari* (tr.), Vol. I, p. 322.
46. Badauni, *Muntakhab-ut-Tawarikh*, Vol. II, tr. Lowe, pp. 59-60.
47. *Akbar Nama* (tr.), Vol. III, pp. 677-78; *Tuzuk-i-Jahangiri* (tr.), Vol. I, p. 15.
48. *Akbar Nama* (tr.), Vol. III, p. 749; Badauni (tr.), Vol. II, p. 364.
49. *Akbar Nama* (tr.), Vol. III, pp. 677-678; *Tuzuk-i-Jahangiri* (tr.), Vol. I, p. 19.

50. *Tuzuk-i-Jahangiri* (tr.), Vol. I, pp. 18-19.
51. *Ibid.*, pp. 144-45.
52. *Ibid.*, pp. 325-26.
53. *Akbar Nama* (tr.), Vol. III, pp. 117, 647 & 921.
54. *Tuzuk-i-Jahangiri*, Vol. I, p. 160; Beni Prasad, *History of Jahangir*, p. 30.
55. Beni Prasad, *History of Jahangir*, p. 30.
56. Sarkar, *History of Aurangzib*, Vol. I, p. 61.
57. K.S. Lal, *The Mughal Harem*, p. 29.
58. *Ibid.*, p. 29.
59. Jadunath Sarkar., *Akham-i-Alamgiri* of Hamid-ud-din, Khan Bahadur (Calcutta : 1949), p. 41.
60. *Babur Nama*, tr., A.S. Beveridge, p. 712 (Translator's notes); *Humayun Nama* (tr.), p. 225.
61. *Akbar Nama* (tr.) Vol. III, pp. 205-206.
62. *Ibid.*, pp. 130-31.
63. *Tuzuk-i-Jahangiri* (tr.), Vol. I, p. 34.
64. *Ibid.*, p. 36.
65. *Ibid.*, p. 20.
66. Waris quoted in B.P. Saksena, *History of Shahjahan of Dihli*, p. 337.
67. J. Sarkar, *History of Aurangazib*, Vol. I, p. 65.
68. *The Mughal Harem*, p. 30.
69. *Ibid.*, p. 30.
70. *Ain-i-Akbari* (tr.), Vol. III, p. 272.
71. Bernier, p. 273; John Ovington, *A Voyage to Surat in the Year 1689*, ed, H.G. Rawlingson, (London : 1929), p. 257.
72. *Humayun Nama* (tr.) p. 95.
73. *Ibid.*, p. 208.
74. *Ibid.*, p. 212.
75. *Tuzuk-i-Jehangiri* (tr.), Vol. II, p. 110.
76. Jadunath Sarkar, *Studies in Mughal History*, pp. 21-25.
77. Manucci, *Storia...*, Vol. II, p. 315.
78. *Akbar Nama* (tr.), Vol. III, p. 815.
79. *Tuzuk-i-Jahangiri* (tr.), Vol. I, p. 76.
80. Qazwini, *Padshah Nama*, ff. 13a, 49a.
81. *Tuzuk-i-Jahangiri* (tr.), Vol. I, p. 55.
82. *Ibid.*, p. 319.
83. Bernier, p. 5.
84. K.S. Lal, *The Mughal Harem*, p. 71.
85. Lahori, *Badshahnama*, tr. in Elliot and Dowson, Vol. 7, p. 27; Bernier, p. 5 n.
86. Bernier, p. 5.
87. E.B. Findly, *Noorjahan...* (New York: 1991), p. 94; K.S. Lal, *The Mughal Harem*, p. 84; R. Misra, *Women in Mughal India*, p. 60.
88. Inayat Khan, *The Shah Jahan Nama*, tr. & ed., Begley and Desai, p. 3.
89. *The Shah Jahan Nama* (tr.), pp. 3-4; Jadunath Sarkar, *History of Aurangzib*, Vol. III, p. 58.
90. *The Shah Jahan Nama* (tr.), p. 3.
91. Manucci, *Storia...*, Vol. II, p. 127; Jadunath Sarkar, *History of Aurangzib*, Vol. III, p. 58.

92. Jadunath Sarkar, *History of Aurangzib*, Vol. III, p. 58; Mustaidd Khan, *Maasir-i-Alamgiri* (text), p. 213.
93. R. Misra, *Women in Mughal India*, p. 60.
94. Fergusson, *History of Indian and Eastern Architecture*, Vol. II (Delhi: 1967), p. 293.
95. *Ain-i-Akbari* (tr.), Vol. I, p. 46.
96. Pelsaert, *Jahangir's India, The Remonstrauite of Francisco Pelsaert*, tr. W.H. Moreland & P. Geyl, p. 64.
97. Finch in Foster ed., *Early Travels in India*, p. 183.
98. K.S. Lal, *The Mughal Harem*, p. 45.
99. *Ibid.*, p. 45.
100. Bernier, p. 267.
101. *Ibid.*, pp. 267-68.
102. William Finch in *Early Travels in India*, pp. 151, 163-64.
103. De Laet, pp. 39-40.
104. N.L. Mathur, *Red Fort and Mughal Life*, pp. 38-39.
105. Edward Terry in *Early Travels in India*, p. 287.
106. Pelsaert, p. 66.
107. Manucci, *Storia*... Vol. II, p. 341.
108. *Humayun Nama* (tr.), p. 25.
109. *Tuzuk-i-Jahangiri* (tr.), Vol. I, p. 10.
110. *Ibid.*, p. 342.
111. *Ibid.*, p. 380.
112. Beni Prasad, *History of Jehangir*, p. 194.
113. De Laet, p. 41; Pelsaert, p. 4.
114. Manucci, *Storia...*, Vol. II, p. 328.
115. Qazwini, *Padshah Nama*, f. 620a; Lahori, *Badshah Nama*, Vol. I, Part II, p. 51 and Vol. II, Part I, p. 209.
116. Lahori, Vol. I, Part II, p. 51 and Vol. II, Part I, p. 209; Qazwini, f. 626a.
117. Lahori, Vol. II, Part II, p. 426.
118. *Ibid.*, Vol. I, Part II, p. 51 and Vol. II, Part I, p. 207.
119. *Ibid.*, Vol. II, Part II, p. 582.
120. Md. Saleh Kambu, *Amal-i-Saleh*, Vol. III, p. 109; Inayat Khan, *The Shahjahan Nama* (tr.), p. 447.
121. *Humayun Nama* (tr.), pp. 94-95.
122. *Ibid.*, p. 95.
123. Nizamuddin Ahmad, *Tabqat-i-Akbari*, tr. B. De., Vol. II, pp. 559-60.
124. *Tuzuk-i-Jahangiri* (tr.), Vol. I, p. 399.
125. Inayat Khan, *The Shah Jahan Nama* (tr.), p. 19.
126. *Ibid.*, p. 18.
127. *Ibid.*, p. 22.
128. *Ibid.*
129. *Ibid.*
130. *Ibid.*, p. 23.
131. *Ibid.*, p. 191.
132. Lahori, Vol. II, Part II, pp. 396-97.
133. Mustaid Khan, *Maasir-i-Alamgiri* (text), p. 14; Khafi Khan, *Muntakhab-ul-Lubab*, Vol. II, p. 77.

134. Sarkar, *History of Aurangzib, Vol. I and II, p.* 385 (Vol. II).
135. *Ibid.*, p. 385.
136. *Maasir-i-Alamgiri* (text), p. 105.
137. *Ibid.*, p. 235.
138. William Hawkins in *Early Travels in India*, p. 94.
139. Coryat in *Early Travels in India*, p. 267.
140. Foster, ed., *The Embassy of Sir Thomas Roe to the Court of the Great Mughal*, Vol. II, pp. 324, 364, 396, 426, 458.
141. Tavernier, *Travels in India*, ed. William Crooke (London: 1925), Vol. I, p. 141.
142. Foster, ed., *The English Factories in India* (1646-50), (Oxford: 1906-8), p. 304.
143. *The Shah Jahan Nama* (tr.) p. 18.
144. *Ibid.*, p. 71.
145. Qazwini, ff. 240 and 449.
146. Manucci; *Storia...*, Vol. I, p. 216.
147. *Ibid.*, p. 216.
148. *Ibid.*, Vol. II, p. 256.
149. Lahori, Vol. I, Part I, pp. 96-97.
150. *Humayun Nama* (tr.), p. 114.
151. *Tuzuk-i-Jahangiri* (tr.), Vol. I, p. 278.
152. *Ibid.*, p. 397.
153. *Ibid.*, Vol. II, p. 237.
154. Qazwini, f. 364.
155. Khafi Khan, Vol. I, p. 646.
156. Lahori, f. 105a.
157. *Amal-i-Saleh*, Vol. III, p. 199.
158. *The Shah Jahan Nama* (tr.), p. 505.
159. *Maasir-i-Alamgiri* (text), p. 19.
160. Abdul Aziz, *Arms and Jewellery of the Indian Mughals* (Lahore: 1947), p. 119.
161. Abdul Aziz, *The Imperial Treasury of the Indian Mughals* (Delhi: 1972), p. 546.
162. Manucci, *Memoirs of the Mughal Court*, ed. Michael Edwardes (London: 1963), pp. 33-34.
163. M.A. Ansari, *Social Life of the Mughal Emperors* (New Delhi: 1983), p. 69.
164. *The Mughal Harem*, p. 52.
165. *Tuzuk-i-Jahangiri* (tr.), Vol. II, p. 216.
166. *Ain-i-Akbari* (tr.), Vol. I, p. 46.
167. K.S. Lal, *The Mughal Harem*, p. 52.
168. R. Misra, *Women in Mughal India*, p. 78.
169. *The Mughal Harem*, p. 52.
170. Mutamid Khan, *Iqbal Nama-i-Jahangiri* (text), p. 56.
171. Jadunath Sarkar, *Studies in Mughal India* (Calcutta & Cambridge: 1919), p. 24.
172. Jadunath Sarkar, *Ancedotes of Aurangzib* (Calcutta: 1949), pp. 58-59.
173. *The Mughal Harem*, p. 52.
174. *Ibid.*, p. 53.
175. *Ain-i-Akbari* (tr.), Vol. I, p. 46.
176. *The Mughal Harem*, p. 53.
177. *Ain-i-Akbari* (tr.), Vol. I, p. 46; Manucci, *Storia ....*, Vol. II, pp. 330-31.
178. Ila Mukherjee, *Social Status of North Indian Women* (Agra: 1972), p. 36.

179. *The Mughal Harem,* p. 31.
180. Manucci, *Memoirs of the Mughal Court,* p. 33.
181. Manucci, *Storia...,* Vol. II, p. 338.
182. *Ibid.,* p. 352.
183. R. Misra, *Women in Mughal India,* p. 79.
184. *The Mughal Harem,* p. 56.
185. *Ain-i-Akbari* (tr.), Vol. I, pp. 46-47.
186. A.S. Beveridge in *Humayun Nama,* p. 40.
187. Foster in Roe, *The Embassy of Sir Thomas Roe to the Court of the Great Mogul* (London: 1899), Vol. I, p. 253 n.
188. *The Mughal Harem,* p.-56.
189. *Ibid.,* p. 56.
190. Manucci, *Storia...,* Vol. II, p. 328.
191. *Ibid.,* p. 350.
192. *Ibid.*
193. *Ain-i-Akbari* (tr.), Vol. I, pp. 46-47; Manucci, *Storia....* Vol. I, p. 288.
194. Manucci, *Storia* ... Vol. II, p. 352.
195. *Tuzuk-i-Jahangiri* (tr.), Vol. II, p. 192.
196. Qazwini, *Padshah Nama,* fol. 458.
197. *Ibid.,* fol. 449.
198. Lahori, Vol. II, Pt. I, p. 142.
199. J. Sarkar tr., *Maasir-i-Alamgiri,* p. 127.
200. R. Misra, *Women in Mughal India.* p. 65.
201. *Ain-i-Akbari* (tr.), Vol. I, p. 46.
202. Manucci, *Storia...,* Vol. II, p. 330.
203. Magan Lal, tr. *The Diwan of Zeb-un-Nissa* (London: 1913), p. 8; Mustaidd Khan, *Maasir-i-Alamgiri,* tr. in Elliot & Dowson, Vol. 7, p. 196.
204. Jadunath Sarkar, *History of Aurangzib,* Vol. 1 & 2, p. 39 (Vol. 1).
205. *Babur Nama* (tr.), Vol. I, pp. 235-36; *Akbar Nama* (tr.), Vol. III, p. 109; *Tuzuk-i-Jahangiri* (tr.), Vol. I, pp. 45-46; *Maasir-i-Alamgiri,* tr. Jadunath Sarkar, pp. 18, 25, 36.
206. *Akbar Nama* (tr.), Vol. II, p. 51; Md: Yasin, *A Social History of Islamic India,* pp. 53-54.
207. *Ain-i-Akbari* (tr.) Vol. III, p. 353; *Tuzuk-i-Jahangiri* (tr.), Vol. I, pp. 385.
208. Md. Yasin, *A Social History of Islamic India,* pp. 58-59.
209. Tavernier, *Travels in India,* tr. & ed. V. Ball (London : 1925), Vol. II, p. 177.
210. *Ain-i-Akbari* (tr.) Vol. I, p. 286; (Badauni (tr.) Vol. II, pp. 348-349., *Tuzuk-i-Jahangiri* (tr.) Vol. I, p. 48, DeLaet, pp. 100-101; Manrique, Vol. II, pp. 195-200; J.P. Guha ed., *India in the 17th Century, Vol. II, The Voyages of Thevenot and Careri* (New Delhi; 1976), p. 85; P.N. Chopra, *Some Aspects of Society and Culture During the Mughal Age,* p. 81.
211. *Akbar Nama* (tr.) Vol. II, p. 23-24; *Tuzuk-i-Jahangiri* (tr.), Vol. I, pp. 265, 295, 379n.
212. *Akbar Nama* (tr.), Vol. III, p. 831; *Tuzuk-i-Jahangiri* (tr.) Vol. I, p. 252 & Vol. 2, p. 176.
213. *Tuzuk-i-Jahangiri* (tr.), Vol. I, pp. 244, 268, *Ain-i-Akbari* (tr.) Vol. I, p. 226.
214. *Ain-i-Akbari* (tr.), Vol. I, p. 210, *Tuzuk-i-Jahangiri* (tr.), Vol. I, p. 246.

215. *Tuzuk-i-Jahangiri* (tr.), Vol. I, p. 246.
216. *Ibid.*, Vol. I, p. 361.
217. *Ibid.*, Vol. I, pp. 22, 94.
218. *Humayun Nama* (tr.), p. 8 (Introduction).
219. *The Shah Jahan Nama* (tr.), pp. 95, 299, etc.
220. *Humayun Nama* (tr.), pp. 159, 230.
221. *Akbar Nama* (tr.), Vol. II, pp. 366–67.
222. *Ibid.*, Vol. III, p. 570 n.
223. *Ibid.*, pp. 205-206.
224. *Ibid.*, Vol. III, pp. 569 - 70.
225. *Humayun Nama* (tr.), p. 75; Badauni (tr.), Vol. II, p. 320.
226. *Akbar Nama* (tr.), Vol. II, pp. 476–77.
227. *Tuzuk-i-Jahangiri* (tr.), Vol. II, p. 108.
228. *Ibid.*, Vol. I, p. 110.
229. *Amal-i-Saleh*, Vol. II, p. 422.
230. Aziz Ahmed, *Studies in Islamic Culture in the Indian Environment* (Oxford : 1964), p. 138; W. Hansen, *The Peacock Throne* (Great Britain: 1973), p. 147.
231. *The Peacock Throne*, p. 151.
232. R. Misra, *Women in Mughal India*, p. 90.
233. *Ibid.*, p. 93.
234. R.C. Mazumdar ed., *The Mughal Empire*, p. 14.
235. Kabir Kausar and Inamul Kabir, *Biographical Dictionary of Prominent Muslim Ladies*, (New Delhi : 1982), p. 193.
236. Gorham, *Indian Mason's Marks of the Moghul Dynasty* (London : 1911), p. 19; E.B. Findly, Noorjahan..., pp. 238 - 39.
237. Maheshwar Dayal, *Rediscovering Delhi, The Story of Shahjahanabad* (New Delhi: 1982), p. 71.
238. M.A. Ansari, *Social Life of the Mughal Emperors*, p. 122.
239. *Shah Jahan Nama* (tr.), p. 458; Khafi Khan, Vol. I, p. 706.
240. *Shah Jahan Nama* (tr.), p. 458.
241. Lahori, Vol. I, Pt. II, p. 252; James Fergusson, *History of Indian and Eastern Architecture*, Vol. 2, (New Delhi: 1967), pp. 318-320; Sayad Md. Latif, *Agra, Historical and Descriptive* (Calcutta : 1896), pp. 184-88.
242. Lahori, Vol. II, Pt. II, p. 469.
243. Jadunath Sarkar, *History of Aurangzib*, Vol. I, p. 70.
244. Monserrate, *Commentarius*, tr. J.S. Holyland, (London etc. : 1922), p. 96.
245. *Iqbal-Nama-i-Jahangiri*, tr. in Elliot and Dowson, Vol. 6, p. 405.
246. *Tatimma-i-Wakiat-i-Jahangiri*, tr. in Elliot and Dowson, Vol. 6, p. 399.
247. *The Mughal Harem*, p. 95.
248. *Maasir-i-Alamgiri* (text), p. 323.
249. R. Misra, *Women in Mughal India*, p. 110.
250. A.S. Altekar, *The Position of Women in Hindu Civilization* (Varanasi : 1938), p. 206; R.C. Mazumdar ed., *Bharatiya Vidya Bhavan's History and Culture of the Indian People* (Bombay: 1974), p. 699; D.N. Roy, *The Spirit of Indian Civilization* (Calcutta: 1938), pp. 162-64.
251. S.M. Jaffar, *Some Cultural Aspects of Muslim Rule in India* (Delhi: 1972), pp. 197-200.

252. Mazhar ul Haq Khan, *Purdah and Polygamy* (Delhi : 1982), p. 28.
253. *Ibid.*, p. 28.
254. *Ibid.* p. 29.
255. *Purdah and Polygamy*, p. 31.
256. *Ibid.*, p. 32.
257. *Ibid.*, pp. 33-34.
258. *Ibid.*, p. 35.
259. D.N. Roy, *The Spirit of Indian Civilization*, pp. 161-63.
260. *Ibid.*, p. 163.
261. *Muntakhab-ut-Tawarikh* (tr.), Vol. II, tr. Lowe, pp. 404-406; R.C. Mazumdar ed., *The Mughal Empire*, p. 699.
262. De Laet, p. 81.
263. Della Valle, pp. 44-45.
264. R.C. Mazumdar ed., *The Mughal Empire*, p. 699.
265. Bernier, p. 413; Manucci, *A Pepys of Mogul India*, tr. W. Irvine (London : 1913), p. 107; M.S. Commissariat, *Mandelslo's Travels in Western India*, (London : 1931), p. 51.
266. Tavernier, *Travels in India*, tr. V. Ball (London : 1899), p. 125.
267. Roe, Vol. II, p. 321.
268. Bernier, p. 371; Peter Mundy Vol. II, pp. 190-91.
269. De Laet, p. 81; Della Valle, p. 24; Mandelslo, p. 66; Terry in *Early Travels in India*, p. 404.
270. Manucci, *Storia...*, Vol. II, pp. 333-34.
271. Monserrate, *The Commentary*, p. 79.
272. Bernier, p. 373.
273. Roe, Vol. I, p. 32; Vol. II, p. 457.
274. Terry in *Early Travels in India*, p. 283.
275. *Tuzuk-i-Jahangiri* (tr.), Vol. I, p. 351.
276. Roe, Vol. II, p. 270.
277. Della Valle, p. 97.
278. Terry in *Early Travels in India*, p. 203.
279. *Ibid.*, p. 180.
280. Manucci, *A Pepys of Mogul India*, p. 203.
281. Bernier, p. 267.
282. Roe, Vol. II, pp. 282-83.
283. P.N. Chopra, *Some Aspects of Society and Culture During the Mughal Age* (Agra : 1955), p. 106.
284. Foster ed., *A New Account of the East India by Alexander Hamilton* (London : 1930), p. 99.
285. Findly, *Noorjahan...*, p. 90.
286. *Ibid.*, p. 90.
287. *Ibid.*, p. 90.
288. F.E. Keay, *Indian Education in Ancient and Later Times* (London: 1983), p. 80.
289. P. Pal, *Court Paintings of India, 16th to 19th Centuries* (New York : 1983), p. 44.
290. P. Pal, *Court Paintings of India, 16th to 19th Centuries*, p. 44.
291. William Finch in *Early Travels in India*, p. 151.
292. *The Mughal Harem*, p. 179.

293. Manucci, *Storia...*, Vol. II, p. 342.
294. Edward Terry in *Early Travels in India*, p. 320.
295. Thomas Coryat in *Early Travels in India*, pp. 278-79.
296. Manucci, *Storia...*, Vol. II, pp. 350-51.
297. *Babur Nama* (tr.), Vol. I, p. 306.
298. *Humayun Nama* (tr.), p. 151.
299. *Ibid.*, p. 151.
300. *Tuzuk-i-Jahangiri* (tr.), Vol. I, p. 266.
301. Beni Prasad, *History of Jahangir*, pp. 321-322.
302. De Laet, pp. 181-182; Della Valle, pp. 53-54.
303. *Tuzuk-i-Jahangiri* (tr.), Vol. I, pp. 55-56.
304. Finch in *Early Travels in India*, p. 166.
305. *Ibid.*, p. 166.
306. Della Valle, pp. 56-57.
307. *Ibid.*, pp. 56-57.
308. Roe, Vol. II, p. 289.
309. Qazwini, *Padshah Nama*, fol. 48b.
310. Qazwini, *Padshah Nama*, foll, 232b and 233a.
311. Lahori, *Badshah Nama*, Vol. I, p. 386.
312. W. Hansen, *The Peacock Throne*, p. 359.
313. Jadunath Sarkar, *History of Aurangzib*, Vol. I, p. 64.
314. *Ibid.*, pp. 65-66.
315. *Babur Nama* (tr.), Vol. I, p. 120.
316. Terry in *Early Travels in India*, p. 387.
317. Pelsaert, p. 66.
318. Manucci, *Storia...*, Vol. II, p. 353.
319. *The Mughal Harem*, p. 188.
320. Roe, Vol. I, p. 190.
321. Bernier, pp. 130-31.
322. *The Mughal Harem*, p. 189.
323. Bernier, p. 12.
324. *Ibid.*, pp. 12-13.
325. Manucci, *Storia...*, Vol. I, p. 210.
326. Bernier, pp. 13-14.
327. Bernier, pp. 132-33; Manucci, *Memoirs of the Mughal Court*, pp. 32-33.
328. Manucci, *Memoirs of the Mughal Court*, pp. 109-10.
329. Manucci, *Storia...*, Vol. I., p. 195.
330. *Ibid.*, p. 194.
331. Bernier, p. 11.
332. V.A. Smith quoted in B.P. Saksena, *History of Shah Jahan of Dihli*, p. 339.
333. Manucci, *Storia...*, Vol. I. pp. 208-209.
334. W. Hansen, *The Peacock Throne*, p. 151.

Two

Adornment of the Mughal Harem: Education and Beauty

After discussing the socio-religious life of the Mughal ladies, here is an account of the cultural aspects connected to the life of the Mughal women, like the manner in which the Mughal women got education, the types of clothes and jewellery they wore, the cosmetics they liked to use while dressing themselves up, the pleasures and pastimes they indulged in and the feasts and festivals that were celebrated by the Mughals.

Learning and Education

Women's education, both among Hindus and Muslims were not encouraged during the medieval times. The strict rules of *purdah* and seclusion made their education a matter of great difficulty.[1] At the primary level, the Muslim girls usually were imparted education in the same school with the boys,[2] or in separate *madrasas* and *maktabs*[3] meant for them. But once they grew up, the scope of education became limited to the daughters of the rich, noble and royal families. Therefore, the middle and lower class women usually remained uneducated.

The Mughal emperors who were themselves men of literary tastes, took keen interest in education of their children including their daughters, the princesses of the royal household.[4] Though Emperor Akbar hiself had very less formal education, he was very much interested in educational process as a whole, and also that of the royal princes and ladies. He made proper arrangements for imparting education to the ladies of the imperial seraglio. It is said that he set apart some chambers at his Fatehpur Sikri palace in order to establish a girls' school there, and also appointed some mistresses to work in it.[5] Monserrate, who came to Akbar's court says: "He (Akbar) gives very great care to the education of the Princesses... (who) are taught to read and write and are trained in other ways by matrons."[6] About Aurangzeb, Bakhtawar Khan writes: "The Emperor has given a very liberal education to his fortunate and noble children... The ladies of the household also, according to his orders have learnt the fundamental and necessary tenets of religion..."[7] Babar, Humayun, Jehangir and Shahjahan too must have made adequate arrangements for female education and educated princesses and royal ladies.

The Mughal Princesses were imparted education inside the palaces by educated tutoresses or aged male tutors known for their literary achievements.[8] Usually, the tutoress, who was also the governess, was given the name of Atun[9], sometimes called as Atun Mama. A certain Atun Mama's mention is found in the list of the guests at the Mystic Feast mentioned by Gulbadan Begam in her *Humayun Nama*[10]. Princess Jahanara had as her tutoress the scholarly Persian lady Sati-un-Nisa, who herself recited the Quran well and had proficiency in Persian[11]. She belonged to a family of scholars and physicians. Her brother Taliba Amuli had earned the title of "Prince of Poets" at Jehangir's Court[12]. Princess Zeb-un-Nisa received her education under Hafiza Mariam Bibi[13], the wife of Mirza Shukrullah of Kashmir, whose family originally came from Naishabur in Khurassa[14]. She also had another lady teacher named Miyabai under whom she learnt Arabic, mathematics, astronomy, etc.[15]

Apart from giving training on household activities, embroidery, etc., there were quite a few subjects in which the royal ladies received tutoring during the Mughal times like prose, poetry, humanities, theology and the study of languages like Persian and Arabic.[16] The language of everyday use inside the harem was Turki for the Mughal women and Hindi or other regional languages for the Hindu ladies and the ladies from other Indian provinces.[17] Having a good command over Persian, which was the language of poetry and literature, and was considered as an accomplishment.[18] The women competed among themselves in various fields of learning to please the emperor[19]. About the educational system of Mughal ladies, Manucci says:

Among them are some who teach reading and writing to

> the princesses, and usually what they dictate to them are amorous verses. Or the ladies obtain relaxation in reading books called 'Gulistan' and 'Bostan', written by an author called Sec Sadi Chiragi (Shekh Sa'di Shirazi)[20].

Religious education was a must in the learning process of the royal princesses as was in the case of the royal princes, and learning the Quran thoroughly was considered of prime importance. Mehrunnisa, the daughter of Ghiyas Beg, a Persian noble at the Mughal Court, was taught the Quran[21], when as a child she lived and moved around with the royal ladies and princesses at Agra. Later she became Jehangir's most loved wife Nur Jahan. It is said that Zeb-un-Nisa, the scholarly daughter of Aurangzeb, became a 'Hafiz' at the age of seven, when she learnt the Quran by heart.[22] Her proud father Aurangzeb, to celebrate the occasion, feasted the whole army in the great maidan at Delhi, gave 30,000 gold mohurs to the poor and kept the public offices closed for two days.[23] Zeb-un-Nisa received as a reward a sum of 30,000 asharfis.[24] Aurangzeb's second daughter Zinat-un-Nisa too had indepth knowledge of the doctrines of Islam[25], and Badr-un-Nisa, Aurangzeb's daughter by Nawab Bai also learnt the Quran by heart.[26]

The Mughal times did witness quite a few royal Mughal ladies who were not only educated themselves, but have left behind them works of literary value or influences with long time effects. Babar's mother Qutluq-Nigar Khanum was an educated and accomplished daughter of Yunus Khan, the Chagtai Chief in Central Asia, and descendent of the great Mongol Chengiz Khan[27]. Herself being a scholar's daughter she was educated in Turki and Persian.[28] Qutluq-Nigar Khanum and her mother Aisan-daulat had a great influence in shaping Babar's life at an early age which became the guiding force of his later life activities. Babar is even said to have inherited much of his intellectual and artistic faculty from his mother.[29] Babar's daughter Gulbadan Begam will always be remembered as the author of her brother Humayun's biography, the *Humayun Nama*, which she wrote according to the wish of Emperor Akbar during his reign, so that the composition of the *Akbar Nama* of Abul Fazl be made easy.[30] During Akbar's time, his nurse Maham Anaga and his wives Ruqaiya Begam and Salima

Sultan Begam were all educated women.[31] Akbar's mother Hamida Banu Begam is also known to have been an educated women.[32] Salima Sultan Begam is even said to have composed verses,[33] and was probably that wife of Akbar who wrote under the pen-name of 'Makhfi' (the concealed one).[34] Empress Nur Jahan was not only accomplished in various fields like riding, shooting, embroidery, etc., but was also a highly cultured and educated woman of that time, one of her various preoccupations being writing poetry.[35] Mumtaz Mahal, wife of Shahjahan's too wrote poetry.[36] Jahanara and Roshanara, the beautiful daughters of Shahjahan were educated ladies and Jahanara produced literary works of great value. She wrote beautiful verses[37] and a biography of the great Sufi saint, Khwaja Moin-ud-Din Chisti of Ajmer, called *Munis-ul-Arwah*.[38] As we have already seen, Aurangzeb gave good education to all his children including his daughters. His eldest daughter Zeb-un-Nisa, not only received good tutoring, but became a reknowned poetess of her times. She could also write the different kinds of Persian hand like nastaliq, maskh and shikasta beautifully,[39] Zinat-un-Nisa, the second daughter of Aurangzeb, also composed verses.[40]

The Mughal women spent much of their personal allowances in giving active support to the spread of education, establishing educational institutions, lending patronage to learned men, maintaining libraries and collecting books. We come to know that out of the nine copies that were made of Bayazid's *Humayun Nama* written in obedience to Akbar's command, one was given to Gulbadan Begam.[41] Gulbadan Begam had a library of her own which had many rare works.[42] Salima Sultan Begam too collected books.[43] Zeb-un-Nisa Begam had her own library of repute,[44] and is said to have employed skilled calligraphers to copy valuable books for her.[45] Many Mughal ladies built madrasas for the benefit of the ordinary people. Maham Anaga, Akbar's nurse, herself being educated, built a madrasa at Delhi known as 'Khair'ul Manzil', with a mosque attached to it.[46] Several other Mughal ladies like Jodha Bai, Nur Jahan, Jahanara and Mumtaz Mahal, had all made sincere efforts to spread education among the common people.[47] Princess Jahanara's madrasa attached to the Jami Masjid at Agra prospered in later times too.[48] Mumtaz Mahal,[49] her daughter Jahanara[50] and Zeb-un-Nisa,[51] daughter of Aurangzeb, extended active support and patronage to scholars, poets and learned men who flocked to the Mughal court at that time. Zeb-un-Nisa encouraged compilations and translations of various works too.[52] A certain Mulla Safi-ud-Din Ardheli (Ardbeli) under her patronage translated the gigantic Arabic work *Tafsir-i-Kabir* into Persian and named it *Zeb-ut-Tafsir* after her.[53]

Thus, we see that the Mughal harem was not devoid of learned ladies who could keep pace with the learned Mughal emperors and princes of distinguished literary tastes. They received good education from learned men and ladies, maintained libraries, composed works of literary value, patronised men of letters and encouraged mass education. But, if we take into consideration the large number of women in the Mughal harem, we will find that only a few of them received higher education or contributed towards the literary field. What most of them received was limited education[54] till the primary level only, because they were married off early,[55] after which there existed very little scope for further education. Even then it cannot be denied that considering the prevailing social conditions and position of women in those days, it is indeed remarkable that these educated Mughal ladies, though not too many, could keep their mark in the literary world keeping pace with the men of that time. That certainly was a great achievement.

Methods of Beautification

Since ancient times women of various civilisations have known the use of cosmetics for beautifying themselves. Different concepts of beauty have resulted in the creation of different kinds of cosmetics of various people throughout the world. The first ancient people whose concept of beauty was similar to what we have today were the Egyptians.[56] They felt that a woman should have a good complexion, slim figure, healthy shining hair and well-defined lips, cheeks, brows, eyelids and lashes. Egyptians were great users of perfumes. Next, we come across the ancient Greeks. They also used many kinds of perfumes, got their lips painted and had their hair made blond. When the Romans conquered the Greeks, they brought back with them the "beauty doctors", thus acquiring the secrets of dying the hair, special face masks and skin foods for complexion and various other beauty treatments.[57] Ancient Roman ladies made face and body masks out of beauty clays to get smooth and clear skin, just as today's women do.

As in other parts of the world, in India too women had a deep liking for cosmetics since ancient times, as is evident from various carvings (like those of Khajuraho and others), paintings (like those of Ajanta, etc.), and mythological legends.

In the Mughal times too women were not left behind in the use of cosmetics to beautify themselves. As in all ages, it were the women more than the men of those days, who gave importance to toilet and cosmetics making their daily routine of dressing up and beautification an elaborate and complicated affair. They used different kinds of oil like *narayana* oil to massage their bodies[58] and turmeric paste, sandalwood paste, paste of *kusum* flower, pulse-flower powder, rice powder and many other things to wash their bodies.[59] It was considered a luxury to bathe with water drawn from wells or tanks because the common people went to the rivers and tanks for bathing.[60] Abul Fazl says that oils extracted from certain sweet smelling flowers were used for the skin and hair.[61] Manucci also speaks of 'scented oils distilled from different flowers'.[62]

Great emphasis was laid on hair care and hair decoration. Hair dyes, methods for curing baldness and removing unwanted hair were also used.[63] Sometimes hair was washed with *amlaki* fruits also.[64] Long hair were considered a mark of beauty.[65] Manucci reported - "Their hair is always very well dressed, plaited and perfumed with scented oil.[66] Women decked their heads with jewels and flowers like marigold and jasmine.[67] Some elegant styles of coiffure in those days were even named after birds, e.g., Santhali, *lotan*, etc.[68]

Like their men, the Mughal women were very fond of perfumes. A detailed account of various kinds of scents and oils and their prices is given by Abul Fazl in the *Ain-i-Akbari*[69]. There was a special perfumery department under Akbar known as the Khushbu Khana. Jehangir writes in his memoirs about a new kinds of perfume prepared from rose petals by Nur Jahan's mother

Asmat Banu Begam, who called it as Itr-i-Jehangiri.[70] Jehangir writes: "It is of such strength in perfume that if one drop be rubbed on the palm of the hand it scents a whole assembly, and it appears as if many rosebuds had bloomed at once".[71] As a reward the Emperor presented a string of pearls to the inventress.[72] According to Monserrate, certain parts of the city of Lahore were full of fragrance because of scents and scented oils prepared there.[73]

The Mughals were very fond of chewing betel leaf. The Mughal women's habit of chewing this leaf had reached such a proportion that it is said that Jahanara Begam[74] and Princess Zeb-un-Nisa[75] spent the entire revenue of the port of Surat on providing betel for the entire household during their respective times. This leaf when chewed colour the lps red.[76] The frequent use of betel leaf discoloured the teeth which turned red, but was considered one of the beauties of Indian women.[77] In *lakha*, a form of lip-dye, rolls of betel leaves filled with a solution of catechu and the essence of *kevre* blossoms were preserved overnight in a piece of damp cloth (chhana) to be chewed early in the morning after treating the lips with black *missi* powder.[78]

Apart from this, the women used collyrium for the eyes,[79] antimony to darken the eyebrows and eyelashes,[80] and *mehndi* and *mahawar* to colour their hands and feet.[81] Manucci writes:

> All women in India are in the habit of scenting their hands and feet with a certain earth, which they call *mehndi*, which colours the hand and feet red, in such a way that they look as if they had on gloves.[82]

Manucci further comments that this was done because the hot climate of India prevents the women from wearing either gloves or stockings. Married Hindu women used vermillion (*sindur*) in the parting of their hair and as a dot in the middle of their forehead.[83]

According to Abul Fazl, there are sixteen constituents by which a woman is adorned:

> Bathing, anointing with oil, braiding the hair, decking the crown of the head with jewels, anointing with sandal-wood unguent, wearing various kinds of dresses, sectarial marks of caste, and often decked with pearls and golden ornaments, finting with lamp-black like collyrium, wearing

ear-rings, adorning with nose-rings of pearls and gold, wearing ornaments round the neck, decking with garlands of flowers and pearls, staining the hands, wearing a bell hung with small bells, decorating the feet with gold ornaments, eating pan, and finally blandishments and artfulness.[84]

Other than literary accounts, quite a few Mughal paintings too reveal the various methods used by Mughal ladies to beautify themselves, as it does regarding the other aspects of their lives. As an example we have a later Mughal painting showing a lady colouring her feet.[85]

The various methods of beautification that have been discussed so far certainly reveal the high level of beauty consciousness of the Mughal ladies. This elaborate routine of beautification might have consumed most of their time in a day. Foreign travellers like Manucci even felt that the Mughal ladies did nothing much with their lives other than decorating themselves and engaging themselves in such other frivolous activities.[86] But, this certainly was not the case with all of them, and there were quite a few Mughal ladies of the royal household who engaged themselves in various constructive activities, as can be seen from other aspects of their lives. One such remarkable lady was Zeb-un-Nisa, the highly educated daughter of Aurangzeb, who had no interest in toilet accessories or jewellery to decorate herself.[87] Why she did not take a liking for these things is not known clearly. Probably all her interests revolved round learning and education which left her with little time or interest for other things.

Jewellery and Ornaments

Jewellery has been an obsession with women of all ages and times. Ornaments are worn not only for the purpose of attracting the attention of others around but also as a distinctive mark of status, rank and dignity. Indian women, too, have shown a great liking for jewellery since times immemorial. Both Hindus and Muslims have given religious significance to the use of ornaments. Hindus consider gold ornaments auspicious.[88] A touch of gold on the woman's body is considered to be auspicious. Muslims lay emphasis on holy amulets and ornaments with stone-settings, and their basic intention in wearing ornaments is to secure protection against evil eye.[89]

Women in India were accustomed to the use of ornaments for their very childhood. The noses and ears of girls were pierced through at an early age. Gold or silver or brass ornaments, according to the means of the parents were put in these holes which, it seems grew wider and wider with age.[90] Almost every child had a gold or silver chain with bells tied around their waist and anklets round the legs.[91] The widows, however, discarded all ornaments.[92]

Indian women's fascination and deep liking for ornaments were in no way less during the Mughal age. Various contemporary sources, accounts of foreign travellers and Mughal paintings reveal the fact that the Mughal ladies loaded themselves with a large variety of ornaments. Most of the travellers agree that ornaments were "the very joy of their hearts".[93]

Head Ornaments

The Mughal ladies decorated every part of their bodies from head to toe with different types of ornaments. Abul Fazl speaks of thirty-seven different kinds of ornaments worn by women in his *Ain-i-Akbari*.[94] The five head ornaments he speaks of are Sis-phul which was a raised bell-shaped piece of gold or silver, hollow and embellished from inside with attachments fastened to the hair over the crown of the head; Mang was worn on the parting of the head; Kotbiladar, which consisted of five bands and a long centre-drop was worn on the forehead; Sekra, mainly used in marriage ceremonies and other special occasions, consisted of seven or more strings of pearls linked to studs and hung from the forehead in such a manner as to conceal the face; and finally the Binduli, which was smaller than a (gold) mohar and worn on the forehead.[95] Adding to the list of head ornaments, Manucci says:

> Upon the middle of the head is a bunch of pearls which hangs down as far as the centre of the forehead with a valuable ornament of costly stones formed into the shape of the Sun, or Moon, or some star or at times imitating different flowers.[96]

This ornament was probably similar to the Mang. Manucci

further speaks of a little round ornament worn on the right side of the head, in which a small ruby was inserted between two pearls. Women sometimes wore turbans which often had in them "a valuable aigrette surrounded by pearls and precious stones."[97]

Ear Ornaments

All women wore pierced earring or pendants usually made of gold, silver or copper which hung down from the ears almost touching the shoulder.[98] Bauli was worn in the upper part of the ear while *kundala* was for the lower part.[99] Sometimes women of those days wore several small rings of gold or silver in holes bored around the rim of the ear.[100] Abul Fazl speaks of certain ear ornaments like Kuntila, a tappering shaped earring; Karnphul (ear flower) shaped like the flower of the Magrela; Pipal-patti, crescent-shaped, worn as a bunch of eight or nine in each ear; Champakali, smaller than the red rose, worn on the shell of the ear; and Mor-Bhanwar, which was a ear-pendant shaped like a peacock.[101] All these ear ornaments had valuable stones set in them.[102]

Nose Ornaments

Nose ornaments were not known in India in the ancient times. The pre-Muslims literatures do not refer to Nath or nose ornament. The fashion of wearing nose ornaments was brought into India probably by the Muslim invaders from the north-west[103]. Even after their introduction, nose ornaments took sometime to become popular in the Mughal harem as known from the Persian miniature paintings,[104] and was certainly not in the height of fashion during the Mughal age.[105] However, its presence in the Mughal harem is known from various sources. Abul Fazl mentions in the *Ain-i-Akbari* nose ornaments like the Besar, which was a broad piece of gold to the upper ends of which a pearl was attached and at the other a golden wire which is clasped on to the pearl and hung from the nose by gold wire; Phuli, which was like a bud, the stalk of which was attached to the nose; Laung, which had the shape of a clove; and Nath, which was a golden circlet with a ruby between two pearls, or other jewels, worn in the nostril.[106] There was another nose ornament known as the *nakmachi*.[107]

Necklaces

Various kinds of necklaces mostly made of gold and silver and studded with gems and pearls were worn by the Mughal women. Guluband[108] consisted of five or seven rose-shaped buttons of gold strung on to silk and worn round the neck. Har[109] was a necklace of strings of pearls interconnected by golden roses. Hans[110] was another type of necklace. Some other necklaces contained five to seven strings of gold beads.[111] Sometimes, the Mughal women also had three to five rows of pearls hanging from their neck, coming down as far as the lower part of the stomach.[112] Round their necks they also had strings of pearls or precious stones, and over these a valuable ornament having in its centre a big diamond, or ruby, or emerald or sapphire, and round it huge pearls.[113] These necklaces of jewels were worn like scarvers or both shoulders, added to three strings of pearls on each side.[114]

Hand Ornaments

In Abul Fazl's list of bracelets, we have the Kangan[115] which were of different designs, surmounted with small knobs;[116] Gajrah,[117] a bracelet of gold and pearls; Jawe,[118] consisting of five golden barley corns strung on silk, and fastened on each wrist; Chur,[119] a bracelet worn above the wrist; Bahu,[120] like the Chur but a little smaller; and Churin,[121] thinner than the bracelet and worn in a bunch of seven or more. Sometimes the bracelets were in the form of pearl bands which went round the wrist nine or twelve times.[122] Manucci found these an obstruction for feeling the pulse as these covered the wrist completely.[123]

Arms without ornaments were not considered a good omen.[124] The upper part of the arms above the elbows were ornamented with armlets, called Bazuband,[125] usually two inches wide, inlaid with precious stones and having small bunches of pearls hanging down.[126] Tad[127] was a hollow circle worn on the arm just below the Bazuband.

The Mughal women were also fond of wearing rings of various designs on their fingers, usually one for each finger and they were studded with precious stones like diamonds and sapphires.[128] On their right thumb there was always a ring where in place of a stone there was a little round mirror (arsi), having pearls around it.[129] The reason for this, Manucci tells us, was that the Mughal women were very fond of looking at themselves in these tiny mirrors quite often.[130] Abul Fazl also speaks of the Anguthi (finger-ring) which were of different kinds.[131]

Waist Belts

On the waist the women wore some sort of waist belt of gold, two fingers wide, and studded with precious stones.[132] Abul Fazl also mentions a similar gold belt called the Kati-mekhla and another type called the Chhudr-Khantika, which had golden bells strung on gold wire and twisted round the waist.[133] Manucci tells us that at the end of the strings which tied up their drawers there were bunches of pearls made up of fifteen strings five fingers in length.[134]

Ankle/Foot Ornaments

Among the various kinds of ankle-ornaments worn by the Mughal ladies, we come across the three gold rings called Jehar.[135] The first was called Chura, consisting of two hollow half-circlets which when joined together formed a complete ring; the second called Dundhani was the engraved form of the first; the third was called Masuchi which was like the second but differently engraved.[136] Then we have the Pail[137] or anklet called Khalkhal in Arabic. These produced a jingling sound when its wearer moved about.[138] Ghunghru, consisting of small golden bells, usually six on each ankle and strung upon silk was worn between the Jehar and Khalkhal.[139] Bhank was a triangular and square ornament for the instep.[140] Bichhwah, another ornament for the instep was shaped like half a bell.[141] Anwat was an ornament for the great toe.[142] Writing about foot ornaments Hamilton says:

> They wear also Rings on their Toes, and Shekels on their Legs...made hollow, and some Glass Beads loose in them, that when they move the Leg they make a Noise like a rattle Snake.[143]

The large number of ornaments worn on their feet did not permit wearing a shoe which was consequently dispensed with,[144] at least inside the four walls of their palaces.

So far we have seen various kinds of ornaments, usually made of gold and studded with precious gems, worn from head to toe by the Mughal ladies. These ornaments undoubtedly reveal the excellent craftsmanship of the goldsmiths and jewellers of those times who certainly remained very busy.[145] These also helps us to get an idea of the Mughal grandeur and wealth. The best and the costliest ornaments made by the goldsmiths and jewellers were for the king and the royal ladies.[146] Abul Fazl says that their delicacy and skill is such that the cost of the work is ten *tolahs* (about 120 grams) for each *tolah* of gold.[147]

The royal ladies had no difficulty in affording these costly ornaments because of their rich allowances, personal sources of income and gifts they got from the emperors and from others. According to Manucci, all these princesses owned six to eight sets of jewels in addition to others worn according to their fancy.[148] They were also very fond of exhibiting their jewellery, and Manucci himself came across such situations several times when they used their ornaments, brought in great trays of gold, to open up a conversation.[149] Sir Thomas Roe who once had a glimpse of Jehangir's "two principal wives", one of them probably Nur Jahan, found them so gorgeously dressed that he said - "If I had no other light, their diamonds and pearls had sufficed to show them."[150]

It will be wrong to assume that the royal Mughal ladies were concerned only with decorating themselves with these costly jewels and ornaments. There were some of them who were creative enough to bring out new patterns in jewellery. Abul Fazl mentions one of Akbar's queens who contributed in this field, though he does not give her name.[151] Begam Nur Jahan is also famed to have invented new patterns for gold ornaments.[152]

Dress of Mughal Women

The Mughal Women's concept of beauty did not confine itself to jewellery and cosmetics alone, but extended to various kinds of costly, brightly coloured, richly designed and brocade patterned dresses. With the arrival of the Mughals in India, we find the coming of Iranian and Central Asian fashions in dresses too. Before this the Indian women never wore stitched dresses or covered their upper-bodies with a separate garment. But with the coming of the Mughal culture came a totally different concept in women's as well as in men's clothing.

It will be wrong to assume that the gorgeous dresses worn by the Mughal ladies inside the harems were confined within its four walls. There were quite a few opportunities for frequent contacts between the Indian and the Mughal ladies. Noble and royal women of both communities had mutual social gatherings. Muslim and Hindu festivals were publicly celebrated amidst great splendour where ladies also took part.[153] Royal laides sometimes entertained Hindu officials and their wives at their residences.[154] The Mughal Emperors many a time organised fancy fairs called Meena Bazaar[155] which were exclusively for women with the exception of the Emperor and some royal princes. Rajput women also participated in these.[156] It is, therefore, quite natural that the Hindu women connected to the Mughal court and other Rajput ladies of high rank and birth belonging to the Rajput dependencies of northern India adopted "that distinctively Mogul style of dress which has been immortalised in the old Kangra school of painting."[157] These various fashions in dress of the Mughal period "are so well known that a Mughal miniature painting can be dated often within five years with no auxiliary method than that of costume history."[158]

Usually, the Mughal women inside the harem wore short tight bodice tops with the midriff showing, ankle-length loose pants under a thin long skirt and a large veil covering their heads but not their faces as is evident from contemporary paintings.[159]

When the Mughals first came to India, their women wore long gowns, caps and trousers.[160] Kartiji, an inner garment was worn beneath the gown "as a short bodice reaching to the hips."[161] Another jacket worn over the dress like a vest was called *nimtana*.[162] Gulbadan Begam in her *Humayun Nama,* while describing Mirza Hindal's marriage, mentions 'nine-jackets *(nimtana)* with garnitures of jewelled balls' and four shorter jackets (*kartiji*) with `ball trimmings' among the articles of dowry for the bride Sultana Begam.[163]

Bodice, Jacket and Breaches

The garment to drape the upper part of the body has been described by Stavorinus[164] and Grose[165] as a pair of hollow cups or cases. Stavorinus writes - "They support their breasts and press them upwards by a piece of linen which passes under the arm and is made fast on the back".[166]

The bodice were sometimes "brocade lined with pearls and kept together with a beautifully wrought clasp in diamonds and emeralds."[167] The use of this garment was greatly popularised in India under the influence of the Mughal culture with its fashion of close-fitting garments for women. The bodice in its latest form is said to have been brought into fashion by one of Aurangzeb's daughters.[168]

Some of the ladies wore half smocks reaching the waist, which were made of fine cotton or silk through which their skin was quite visible.[169] While going out they put on a waist-coat over the smocks, the sleeves of which reached till the middle of the arm[170] and covered the rest of the arm with ornaments.

Breeches (trousers) were common among Mughal ladies which usually reached the ankle.[171] These breaches which did not differ much from those of men, were tied at the naval by means of a silver or silk string running through them, which hanged down to the knees or even lower.[172] These breaches were in tapering shape and slowly the tight ones began to be considered fashionable and more and more ladies started preferring those.[173] The breeches were made of silk or brocade, mostly white or red in colour, or striped with all sorts of colours.[174]

Apart from the bodice, jacket and close-fitting trousers, the Mughal ladies wore the *jagulfi*, "a sort of empire-gown fastening at neck and waist, opening between the fastening and permitting a glimpse of the breasts and with long tight wrinkled sleeves and long flowing skirt" reaching down to the ankles.[175] This garment in course of time was adopted by the Rajput and other women as an imitation of it or with modifications. Sometimes a short under petticoat was worn below the skirt of the outer robe, usually slit open in front. According to Abul Fazl, instead of drawers, some ladies wore *lehnga* stitched on both sides and fastened with a belt, which appeared to be a short under-petticoat and with it no chemise was worn. Over the *lehnga* is worn the common shalice or petticoat.[176] In the 16th and 17th centuries, stripes, were very popular patterns for these skirts.[177] Under the Mughal influence long skirts became the fashion even if it meant hiding the foot-ornaments.[178]

Mughal women did not wear gloves or stockings, probably for the many different varieties of hand and foot ornaments used by them. According to Manucci, gloves and stockings were not used by them because of the hot climate of this country.[179] Women of aristocratic or royal families put on shoes of various designs and beautiful slippers covered with golden and silver flowers, usually red in colour and without backs.[180]

Head Cover

Both Hindu and Muslim ladies covered their heads with an *orhni* or *dupatta* which Manucci describes as a sheet of gold cloth of different types and colours.[181] This cloth "hung down on both sides as low as the knees"[182] and was sometimes made of white calicos. Sometimes the Mughal ladies covered their heads with a shawl or mantilla made of the finest materials and dyed in delicate colours.[183] Gulbadan Begam in the *Humayun Nama* mentions the *taq*, a type of cap worn by unmarried girls, and the *lachak*, which was a kerchief folded cross ways and tied under the chin by two corners, used by married women.[184] Both the *taq* and the *lachak* were probably meant only for princesses and daughters of nobles. Sometimes the royal women wore turbans[185] some of which had in them "a valuable agirette surrounded by pearls and precious stones.[186]

Whenever the Muhammaden ladies went out they covered themselves from head to toe with white shrouds or *burqas*.[187] During the winter season the Mughal women wore the same clothes but covered themselves from top of the other garments "with a woollen cabaye (qaba, a long open gown), of fine Kashmir make."[188] Above all those, they put on fine shawls so delicate and fine that they could go through a small finger-ring.[189]

Materials Used

The garments of Mughal ladies were made of the finest muslins, silks, velvets and brocades. The muslins used for their clothes were of three types: Ab-e-Rawan (running water), Baft Hawa (woven air) and Shabnam (evening dew).[190] Muslins called Shabnam were brought from Dacca and were famous as Dhaka *malmal*. Some of the Dacca muslins used for their dresses were so fine that they became invisible to the eye when made to float on water.[191] A lot of silk was brought from China and Persia and also from parts of India like Banaras, Bengal and Orissa to make beautiful dresses for the royal ladies who had great love for silk. Some of the other well-known fabrics used by the Mughal ladies were Satin, Kimkhab, Katan, Tasser, Tafta, Ambari, Atlas, etc. Imported velvet, both plain and brocaded, called Makhmal was also used.[192]

Inayat Khan in his *Shah Jahan Nama* also speaks of the delicate fabrics used for the dresses of the royal ladies, which were also perfumed with fragrant oils.[193] He says that this was the reason why Jahanara's garments once caught fire so easily from a burning lamp and caused her severe burns.[194] Manucci elaborately talks about the fine and scented dresses of Mughal ladies. According to him these women normally wore two to three garments in a day, perfumed with the essence of rose, each weighing about one ounce, costing forty to fifty rupees each without the gold lace added to them.[195] They changed their clothes several times a day and even slept in these clothes.[196] Each day new garments were worn and the old ones given away to the servants.[197] Pelsaert also considered these garments as the most expensive of anything available.[198] Costly dresses and fine garments not only revealed the rank and position of the Mughal women, but also the extent of the Emperor's affection towards them.[199]

Fashions and Designs

The Mughal ladies were not just content with wearing beautiful, costly and decorative garments. Some of them like Nur Jahan Begam went a step forward and introduced new fashions and designs in dress and jewellery, laces, brocades, gowns and carpets, some of which like *dudami* and *panchatolia, badhah, kinari* and *farsh-i-chandani* are still well known.[200]

When it came to colours, the Muslim women preferred white dresses, either plain, "or wrought with gold flowers".[201] The other colour popular among both the Hindus and the Muslims was red. Sometimes the garments were made of "certain linen stamped with works of sundry colours (in spots) but all upon red."[202]

Expert Stitching and Tailoring

Since the Mughal emperors like Akbar, Jehangir and Shah Jahan took equal amount of interest as their ladies in wearing beautiful garments, the ladies certainly had no difficulty in getting costly materials for their clothes and expert tailors to stitch these clothes. Cloth came from foreign lands and different parts of India including Southern India famed for its woven fabric.[203] Bernier speaks of "the riches and most exquisitely wrought brocades, fine linens and *alachas* or silk stuffs interwoven with gold and silver," among the presents which passed between the 'Great Mogul' and the neighbouring kingdoms.[204] Some of these items were exhibited at the fairs and festivals held in the royal seraglios.[205] Among the various Karkhanas, or manufacturing houses under the Mughal emperors, we find a separate dress and apparel making unit known as Tushak Khana and a shawl department.[206] Bernier also speaks of Kar-Kanays (Karkhanas) where embroidery was done.[207] He also says that these costly articles of dress beautifully embroidered with needle-work cost ten or twelve crowns or even more but they were only used for a few hours.[208] Akbar is said to had employed eleven thousand tailors for the manufacture of clothes for his household.[209]

For the innovative designs in dress that we find in Mughal times, we have to thank their women whose boldness sometimes made them go against the established traditions in many fields including garments. Manucci tells us of an incident through which Jahanara Begam made Emperor Aurangzeb change his mind about issuing laws barring women from wearing tight trousers like men.[210] Aurangzeb, it seems, was influenced by the Mullas in this respect. So Jahanara Begam invited the wives of the Kazi and other Mullas to her palace and treated them with wine. When they got heavily drunk Aurangzeb was called to her palace and Jahanara asked him as to why he put such restrictions on women's clothing. Aurangzeb told her that the learned men felt that wearing such dresses by women was against the Islamic Law. Jahanara then took him inside the Zenana and showed him the wives and daughters of the learned men of Faith, drunk, lying in disorder and wearing tight trousers. Jahanara told Aurangzeb that if the Muslim Law prevented wearing such garments, then how could the Mullas allow their women to wear those or drink intoxicating drinks. This changed Aurangzeb's mind about the matter.

Therefore, we can see that the contributions of the royal Mughal ladies were quite apparent in the field of dress too. The Mughal grandeur famed world wide was very well reflected in the clothes worn by the Mughal men and their ladies. Their garments revealed not only their riches and tastes but also the excellent work done by the tailors in those times. The fashions in garments introduced to our land by the Mughals have come down to us in their various modified forms which are found even today.

REFERENCES

1. S.M. Jaffar, *Some Cultural Aspects of Muslim Rule in India* (Delhi: 1972), p. 85; F.E. Keay, *Indian Education in Ancient and Later Times* (London: 1938), p. 80.
2. S.M. Jaffar, *Some Cultural Aspects of Muslim Rule in India*, p. 85; Ila Mukherjee, *Social Status of North Indian Women* (Agra : 1972), p. 94.
3. S.M. Jaffar, *Some Cultural Aspects of Muslim Rule in India*, p. 85.
4. Yusuf Husain, *Glimpses of Medieval Indian Culture* (Bombay : 1962), p. 92.
5. E.B. Havell, *A Handbook to Agra and the Taj* (London : 1904), p. 116.
6. Antonio Monserrate, Commentarius, tr. J.S. Hoyland (London : 1922), p. 202; F.E. Keay, *Indian Education in Ancient and Later Times*, p. 80; N.N. Law, *Promotion of Learning in India During the Muhammadan Rules*. (London : 1915), p. 202.
7. Bakhtawar Khan's *Mir-at-i-Jahan Numa* tr. in Elliot and Dowson's *The History of India as Told by Its Own Historians*, Vol. 7, p. 162.
8. S.M. Jaffar, *Some Cultural Aspects of Muslim Rule in India*, p. 85; N.L. Mathur, *Red Fort and Mughal Life* (New Delhi : 1964), p. 44; Jadunath Sarkar, *Studies in Mughal India* (Calcutta : 1919), p. 301.
9. *Babur Nama*, tr. A.S. Beveridge, p. xxvii (Preface); Manucci, *Storia do Magor*, (tr.) W. Irvine (London: 1907), Vol. II, p. 331; Ila Mukherjee, *Social Status of North Indian Women*, p. 95.
10. Gulbadan Begam, *Humayun Nama*, tr. A.S. Beveridge, p. 121.
11. Jadunath Sarkar, *Studies in Mughal India*, p. 21.
12. *Ibid.*, p. 21.
13. Sarkar, *Studies in Mughal India*, p. 79.
14. *Ibid.*, p. 79.
15. Magan Lal (tr.), *The Diwan of Zeb-un-Nisa*, p. 8 (Introduction).
16. Sarkar, *Studies in Mughal India*, p. 301.
17. E.B. Findly, *Noorjahan, Empress of Mughal India* (New York : 1993), p. 122.
18. *Humayun Nama* (tr.), p. 79 (Introduction).
19. Findly, *Noorjahan...*, p. 112.
20. Manucci, *Storia...*, Vol. II, p. 331.
21. Padmini Sengupta, *The Story of Women in India* (New Delhi : 1974), p. 134.

22. Magan Lal (tr.)., *The Dewan of Zeb-un-Nisa,* p. 8 (Introduction).
23. *Ibid.,* p. 8.
24. Mustaidd Khan's *Maasir-i-Alamgiri* tr. in Elliot and Dowson, Vol. 7, p. 196; Jadunath Sarkar, *History of Aurangzib* (Vol. I & II), pp. 37-38 (Vol. I); Maharani Sunity Devee, *The Beautiful Mogul Princesses,* p. 55.
25. Mustaid Khan, *Maasir-i-Alamgiri,* tr. Jadunath Sarkar (Calcutta: 1947), p. 323.
26. Sarkar, *History of Aurangzib* (Vol. I & II), p. 39 (Vol. I).
27. *Babur Nama* (tr.), Vol. I, pp. 17-19.
28. *Babur Nama* (tr.), p. xxviii (Preface), S.M. Edwardes, *Babur, Diarist and Despot,* (New Delhi : 1977), pp. 19-20.
29. S.M. Edwardes, *Babur, Diasist and Despot,* p. 19.
30. *Humayun Nama* (tr.), p. 76 (Introduction).
31. S.C. Raychaudhuri, *Social, Cultural and Economic History of India* (Medieval Age), pp. 62, 128.
32. Yusuf Husain, *Glimpses of Medieval Indian Culture,* p. 92.
33. Ila Mukherjee, *Social Status of North Indian Women,* p. 99.
34. Sarkar, *Studies in Mughal India,* p. 301.
35. Khafi Khan, *Muntakhab-ul-Lubab,* Vol. I, pp. 270-71; P. Thomas, *Indian Women Through the Ages* (Bombay: 1964), p. 323.
36. Ila Mukherjee, *Social Status of North Indian Women,* p. 100.
37. S.M. Jaffar, *Some Cultural Aspects of Muslim Rule in India, pp.* 195-196; N.N. Law, *Promotion of Learning in India...,* pp. 203-204.
38. P. Thomas, *Indian Women Through the Ages,* p. 323.
39. Sarkar tr., *Maasir-i-Alamgiri, p.* 322; Sarkar, *Studies in Mughal India,* p. 79.
40. Macnicol ed., *Poems by Indian Women,* p. 79.
41. A.S. Beveridge in Gulbadan Begam's *Humayun Nama,* p. 76.
42. F.E. Keay, *Indian Education in Ancient and Later Times,* p. 80; N.N. Law, *Promotion of Learning in India,* pp. 201-202.
43. A.S. Beveridge in Gulbadan Begam's *Humayun Nama,* p. 76.
44. Magan Lal tr., *The Diwan of Zeb-un-Nisa,* p. 13.
45. *Ibid.,* p. 13.
46. S.K. Banerjee, *Humayun Badshah* (Calcutta : 1983), Vol. II, p. 324; Yusuf Hussain, *Glimpses of Medieval Indian Culture,* p. 82; F.E. Keay, *Indian Education in Ancient and Later Times,* pp. 80-81; N.N. Law, *Promotion of Learning in India.,* p. 202.
47. Ila Mukherjee, *Social Status of North Indian Women,* p. 97.
48. Yusuf Husain, *Glimpses of Medieval Indian Culture,* p. 86.
49. Ila Mukherjee, *Social Status of North Indian Women,* p. 102.
50. *Ibid.,* p. 103.
51. Mustaid Khan's *Maasir-i-Alamgiri* tr. in Elliot & Dowson, Vol. 7, p. 196; Magan Lal tr., *The Diwan of Zeb-un-Nisa,* p. 9; Sarkar, *Studies in Mughal India,* p. 79.
52. Mustaid Khan's *Maasir-i-Alamgiri* tr. in Elliot and Dowson, Vol. 7, p. 196.
53. Mustaid Khan's *Maasir-i-Alamgiri* tr. in Elliot and Dowson, Vol. 7, p. 196; Sarkar, *Studies in Mughal India,* p. 79.
54. P.N. Chopra, *Some Aspects of Society and Culture During the Mughal Age* (Agra: 1955), p. 156.
55. *Ibid.,* pp. 156-57.
56. *Competition Success Review,* February, 1995, p. 58.

57. *Ibid.*
58. T. Raychaudhuri, *Bengal Under Akbar and Jehangir,* (Calcutta : 1953), p. 194.
59. A.L. Srivastava, *Akbar the Great,* Vol. III (Agra : 1982), p. 199.
60. T. Raychaudhuri, *Bengal Under Akbar and Jehangir,* p. 194.
61. Abul Fazl, *Ain-i-Akbari,* Vol. I, tr. H.Blochmann, pp. 78-79.
62. Manucci, Memoirs of the Mughal Court, tr. Michael Edwardes (London : 1963), p. 35.
63. G.A. Herklots (tr.), *Islam in India* (London : Edinburgh, etc. : 1921), p. 305; A.L. Srivastava, *Akbar the Great,* Vol. III, p. 199.
64. T. Raychaudhuri, *Bengal Under Akbar and Jehangir,* p. 194.
65. M.S. Commisariat, *Mandelslo's Travels in Western India,* (London : 1931), p. 50.
66. Manucci, *Memoirs of the Mughal Court,* p. 36.
67. P.N. Chopra, *Some Aspects of Society and Culture During the Mughal Age,* p. 22; E.B. Findly, *Noorjahan...,* p. 112; T. Raychaudhuri, *Bengal Under Akbar and Jehangir,* p. 194.
68. T. Raychaudhuri, *Bengal Under Akbar and Jehangir,* p. 194.
69. *Ain-i-Akbari* (tr.), Vol. I, pp. 78-81.
70. *Tuzuk-i-Jahangiri* (tr.), p. 270.
71. *Ibid.,* p. 270.
72. *Ibid.*
73. Antonio Monserrate, *Commentarius* (tr.), J.S. Hoyland, p. 160.
74. K.S. Lal, *The Mughal Harem* (New Delhi : 1988), p. 94.
75. S.N. Dar, *Costumes of India and Pakistan,* (Bombay : 1969), p. 108.
76. Manucci, *Storia do Magor* Vol. II, p. 316.
77. M.S. Commissariat, *Mandelslo's Travels in Western India,* p. 46.
78. S.N. Dar, *Costumes of India and Pakistan,* p. 108.
79. A.S. Altekar, *The Position of Women in Hindu Civilization,* (Banaras : 1938), pp. 300-301.
80. P.N. Chopra, *Some Aspects of Social and Culture During the Mughal Age,* p. 22; A.L. Srivastava, *Akbar the Great,* Vol. III, (Agra : 1972) p. 200.
81. A.L. Srivastava, *Akbar the Great,* Vol. III, p. 200.
82. Manucci, *Memoirs of the Mughal Court,* p. 36.
83. Altekar, *Position of Women in Hindu Civilization,* p. 300; A.L. Srivastava, *Akbar the Great,* Vol. III, p. 200.
84. *Ain-e-Akbari* (tr.) Vol. III, p. 342.
85. P. Pal, *Court paintings of India, 16th to 19th Centuries* (New York & New Delhi : 1983), Painting illustrations.
86. Manucci, *Memoirs of the Mughal Court,* p. 37.
87. P.N. Chopra, *Some Aspects of Society and Culture During the Mughal Age,* p. 22; Maharani Sunity Devee, *The Beautiful Mogul Princesses* (London: 1918), p. 56.
88. Otto Rothfeld, *Women of India* (Bombay : 1928), p. 192.
89. G.A. Herklots tr., *Islam in India* (London, Edinburgh, etc.: 1921), p. 313.
90. Manucci, *Storia...,* Vol. III, p. 40; Terry in Foster ed. *Early Travels in India,* p. 323.
91. Samuel Purchas, *Early Travels in India* (Glasgow: 1864), p. 76.
92. Manucci, *Storia...,* Vol. III, p. 40; Rothfeld, *Women of India,* p. 192.
93. Manucci, *Storia...,* Vol. III, p. 40; John Ovington, *A Voyage to Surat in 1689,* ed. H.G. Rawlinson (London: 1929), p. 320.
94. Abul Fazl, *Ain-i-Akbari,* Vol. III, tr. H.S. Jarrett, p. 343.

95. *Ain-i-Akbari* (tr.), Vol. III, p. 343.
96. Manucci, *Memoirs of the Mughal Court,* p. 35.
97. Manucci, *Memoirs of the Mughal Court,* p. 35.
98. Ovington, p. 320.
99. Tapan Kumar Raychaudhuri, *Bengal Under Akbar and Jehangir,* p. 194.
100. Alexander Hamilton, *A New Account of the East India,* ed. William Foster (London : 1930), p. 97.
101. *Ain-i-Akbari* (tr.), Vol. III, p. 343.
102. Manucci, *Memoirs of the Mughal Court,* p. 35.
103. P.N. Chopra, *Some Aspects of Society and Culture During the Mughal Age,* p. 25.
104. *Ibid.*, pp. 25-26.
105. S.N. Dar, *Costumes of India and Pakistan* (Bombay : 1969), p. 193.
106. *Ain-i-Akbari* (tr.), Vol. III, pp. 343-44.
107. T. Raychaudhuri, *Bengal Under Akbar and Jehangir,* p. 194.
108. *Ain-i-Akbari* (tr.), Vol. III, p. 344.
109. *Ibid.*, p. 344.
110. *Ibid.*
111. P.N. Chopra, *Some Aspects of Society and Culture During the Mughal Age,* p. 26.
112. Manucci, *Memoirs of the Mughal Court,* p. 35.
113. *Ibid.*, p. 35.
114. *Ibid.*
115. *Ain-i-Akbari* (tr.), Vol. III, p. 344.
116. P.N. Chopra, *Some Aspects of Society and Culture During the Mughal Age, p. 27.*
117. *Ain-i-Akbari* (tr.), Vol. III, p. 344.
118. *Ibid.*
119. *Ain-i-Akbari* (tr.), Vol. III, p. 344.
120. *Ibid.*, p. 344.
121. *Ibid.*
122. Manucci, *Memoirs of the Mughal Court,* p. 36.
123. *Ibid.*
124. P.N. Chopra, *Some Aspects of Society and Culture During the Mughal Age,* p. 26.
125. *Ain-i-Akbari* (tr.), Vol. III, p. 344.
126. Manucci, *Memoirs of the Mughal Court,* p. 36.
127. *Ain-i-Akbari* (tr.), Vol. III, p. 344.
128. P.N. Chopra, *Some Aspects of Society and Culture During the Mughal Age, p. 27.*
129. Manucci, *Memoirs of the Mughal Court,* p. 36.
130. *Ibid.*
131. *Ain-i-Akbari* (tr.), Vol. III, p. 344.
132. Manucci, *Memoirs of the Mughal Court,* p. 36.
133. *Ain-i-Akbari* (tr.), Vol. III, p. 344.
134. Manucci, *Memoirs of the Mughal Court,* p. 36.
135. *Ain-i-Akbari* (tr.), Vol. III, p. 344.
136. *Ibid.*
137. *Ibid.*
138. Hamilton, p. 163; Thomas Herbert, *Travels* (London : 1677), p. 38.
139. *Ain-i-Akbari* (tr.), Vol. III, p. 344.
140. *Ibid.*

141. *Ibid.*
142. *Ibid.*
143. Hamilton, p. 97.
144. Fitch in Foster ed. *Early Travels in India,* p. 293.
145. Manucci, *Memoirs of the Mughal Court,* p. 35.
146. *Ibid.*
147. *Ain-i-Akbari* (tr.), Vol. III, p. 344-345.
148. Manucci, *Memoirs of the Mughal Court,* p. 35.
149. *Ibid.*
150. Roe, *The Embassy of Sir Thomas Roe to India,* ed. William Foster (London: 1926), Vol. II, pp. 282-83.
151. *Ain-i-Akbari* (tr.), Vol. III, p. 344-45.
152. Beni Prasad, *History of Jehangir* (Madras: 1922), p. 185.
153. S.N. Dar, *Costumes of India and Pakistan* (Bombay : 1969), p. 38.
154. *Ibid.,* p. 38.
155. Bernier, *Travels, tr.* Constable and Smith, p. 272-73, Manucci, *Storia...,* Vol. I, p. 195.
156. James Tod, *Annals and Antiquities of Rajasthan* (London: 1829-32), Vol. I, pp. 401-402.
157. S.N. Dar, *Costume of India and Pakistan,* p. 38.
158. Charles Fabri, *Indian Dress, A Brief History* (New Delhi : 1977), p. 2.
159. E.B. Findly, *Noorjahan...* (New York : 1993), p. 165.
160. S.N. Dar, *Costumes of India and Pakistan,* p. 38.
161. *Ibid.,* p. 38.
162. *Ibid.,* p. 38.
163. Gulbadan Begam, *Humayun Nama,* tr. A.S. Beveridge, pp. 127-128.
164. Stavorinus, *Voyages to the East Indies,* tr. S.H. Wilcocks (London: 1978), Vol. I, p. 415.
165. John Henry Grose, *A Voyage to the East Indies* (London: 1772), Vol. I, pp. 142-43.
166. Stavorinus, Vol. I, p. 415.
167. N.L. Mathur, *Red Fort and Mughal Life* (New Delhi: 1964), p. 46.
168. S.N. Dar, *Costumes of India and Pakistan,* p. 40.
169. *India in the 17th Century, The Voyages of Thevenot and Careri,* ed. J.P. Guha (New Delhi : 1976), p. 384.
170. P.N. Chopra, *Some Aspects of Society and Culture During the Mughal Age,* p. 12.
171. Hamilton, p. 97.
172. M.S. Commissariat, *Mandelslo's Travels in Western India,* p. 50.
173. S.N. Dar, *Costumes of India and Pakistan,* p. 39; Otto Rothfeld, *Women of India,* p. 189.
174. Della Valle, *The Travels of Pietro Della Valle in India,* ed. Edward Grey (London: 1891), p. 45.
175. A.K. Coomaraswamy, *History of Indian and Indonesian Art* (London: 1927), p. 131; G.S. Ghurye, *Indian Costume* (Bombay : 1966), p. 133: O. Rothfeld, *Women of India,* p. 190.
176. Abul Fazl quoted in S.N. Dar's *Costumes of India and Pakistan,* p. 379.
177. Charles Fabri, *Indian Dress,* p. 19.
178. S.N. Dar, *Costumes of India and Pakistan,* p. 40.

179. Manucci, *Memoirs of the Mughal Court,* ed. M. Edwardes, p. 36.
180. P.N. Chopra, *Some Aspects of Society and Culture During the Mughal Age,* p. 14.
181. Manucci, *Memoirs of the Mughal Court,* p. 36.
182. Della Valle, p. 411.
183. Rothfeld, *Women of India,* p. 190.
184. *Humayun Nama* (tr.), p. 31.
185. De Laet, *The Empire of the Great Mogul* , tr. J.S. Hoyland (New Delhi: 1974), p. 44; Manucci, *Storia...* Vol. II, p. 318.
186. Manucci, *Storia...* Vol. II, p. 318.
187. De Laet, pp. 80-81; Hamilton, Vol. I, p. 164; Mandelslo, p. 50; Tavernier, *Travels in India,* tr. V. Ball (London: 1899), Vol. III, p. 181.
188. Manucci, *Memoirs of the Mughal Court,* p. 37.
189. *Ibid.,* p. 37.
190. K.S. Lal, *The Mughal Harem,* p. 122.
191. S.N. Dar, *Costumes of India and Pakistan,* p. 45.
192. K.S. Lal, *The Mughal Harem,* p. 123.
193. Inayat Khan, *The Shah Jahan Nama,* tr. and ed. Begley & Desai (Delhi: 1990), p. 309.
194. *Ibid.,* p. 309.
195. Manucci, *Memoirs of the Mughal Court,* p. 36.
196. *Ibid.,* p. 36.
197. *Ibid.,* p. 36.
198. Pelsaert, *Jahangir's India (Remonstrantie of Francisco Pelsaert),* tr. Moreland and Geyl (Delhi: 1972), p. 66.
199. *Ibid.,* p. 66.
200. Beni Prasad, *History of Jehangir* (Madras: 1922), p. 185.
201. De Laet, p. 44.
202. *Ibid.,* pp. 44-45.
203. S.N. Dar, *Costumes of India and Pakistan,* p. 45.
204. Bernier, p. 120.
205. *Ibid.,* p. 272.
206. Abdul Aziz, *The Imperial Treasury of the Indian Mughals* (Delhi : 1972), p. 4.
207. Bernier, pp. 258-259.
208. *Ibid.,* pp. 258-259.
209. S.N. Dar, *Costumes of India and Pakistan,* p. 45.
210. Manucci, *Memoirs of the Mughal Court,* p. 94.

Three

Amusements and Festivities

The Mughal ladies apparently led very lonely lives in their harems though they had several people in the form of relatives, servants, attendants and guards, around them most of the times. But, there seemed to be a void in their lives, a void which could only be filled up by love and companionship. And this they rarely got. To fill this emptiness in their lives, they found many ways and means to entertain themselves. The Mughal emperors too made many arrangements to provide entertainment to the harem ladies.

Indoor Amusements

Chess

Chess or Shatranj, one of the most popular indoor games of all times, was a very popular one with the Mughals. It is not exactly known when this game came into existence, but it is the only game which is considered lawful by the exponents of Muslim law as it depends totally on the skill of the person playing it and not on chance.[1] Chess is played differently in different parts of the world.[2] Emperor Akbar liked the game of chess. Through it he not only tested the skill of the players but he also wanted to establish harmony and good fellow-feeling at the court.[3] Chess could be played both "two-handed and four-handed".[4] The chess-board is divided into 64 squares, eight on each of the four sides. Each player had a command over an army of sixteen men with king, queen, pawns, castles, bishops and knights.

During the Mughal times chess was a very popular indoor game played by the men as well as the ladies of the Mughal harem. Paintings of those times reveal the women's interest towards it.[5] Apart from Abul Fazl, Badauni[6] and even Manucci[7] in his accounts talk about the popularity of this game among the Mughals.

Manucci mentions a chess combat which lasted for three days and was played between Jehangir's courtier Khan-i-Khanan and Shah Shafi of Persia.[8] Aram Jan Begam, one of Jehangir's wives was a well known chess player.[9]

Chaupar

Another popular indoor game of the Mughals was Chaupar. Both the Mughal men and ladies took interest in it and this game has existed in our country since ancient times. As in the Mughal days, it was a popular pastime in the royal and aristocratic families. Chaupar is played on a cloth board which is in the shape of a cross. "Each arm of the cross is divided into 24 squares in three rows of eight each, twelve red and twelve black."[10] In the centre the arms meet in the form of four triangles to form a large black square. "The cross is called Chaupar, the arms Phansa, the square Khana."[11] On the same board three types of games were played under three different names with certain differences. They were Chaupar, Chausar and Pachisi. On this board, the game played with dice is called Phansa and that played with *cowries* called Pachisi.[12]

Emperor Akbar liked the game of Chaupar. Through this game he measured the talents of a man and taught kindness.[13] Many noblemen also took part in it and "there were often as many as two hundred players and no one was allowed to go home before he had finished 16 games, which in some cases lasted three months."[14] Among the Mughal ladies, Princess Zeb-un-Nisa is said to have been fond of the game of Chaupar.[15]

Pachisi

Pachisi was a very popular game of Indian origin. It was a favourite with the Mughal ladies. The pachisi board consisted of four triangles with their sides placed in such a manner that it formed a square in the centre. Each rectangle was divided into 24 smaller squares, each of which further consisted of three rows of eight squares each. The game was played with *gots* or *gotis* which were ivory or wooden cones of a particular colour for each player. Usually four persons played it, each one sitting opposite to one of the rectangles.[16]

The Pachisi board could be used as a carpet, beautifully sewn and ornamented. Sometimes it was played by two persons, "each taking the two opposite rectangles with eight pieces, and playing them all from the rectangle next to him."[17] The game was usually never played for money. The popularity of the game of *pachisi* in the Mughal days is seen from the boards marked out in marble squares in a quadrangle at the Fatehpur Sikri[18] and also in the Agra Fort.[19] During Akbar's time the game was played using beautiful slave girls as pieces.[20] Many Mughal paintings also reveal the popularity of the game of pachisi among the ladies of the Mughal harem.

Cards (Ganjifa)

Playing cards was another popular pastime of the Mughals. This game too has existed in our lands since the ancient times. The first reference of this game among the Mughals is found in the Babur Nama.[21] Akbar,[22] and later Shah Jahan too liked the game of cards very much. So did Emperor Jehangir.[23] Abul Fazl says that Emperor Akbar had made certain changes in this game.[24] The royal ladies also must have played this game as a pastime.

Chandal Mandal

Chandal Mandal was a game invented by Emperor Akbar.[25] The board consisted of sixteen parallelograms arranged in a circular form. Each parallelogram was divided into 24 sections, 8 of them for making a row. Total number of pieces were 64 and four dices were used, of which the four longer sides were marked with 1, 2, 10 and 12 points respectively. Sixteen players were required to play the game.[26]

Game of Dice (Gambling)

Since the ancient times, gambling has been a favourite pastime of all classes of people, especially the rich and aristocratic classes.[27] Any indoor game like Chaupar, cards, etc. played for stakes was considered as gambling. A very early reference of it is found in the *Mahabharata*. During the Mughal times too both the aristocratic classes as well as the commoners indulged in it. It is not known for sure whether the Mughal ladies too indulged in it. May be not seriously, but as a form of pleasure the Mughal ladies might have gambled.

Ankh Michauli

The Mughal ladies were very fond of playing the game of *ankh-michauli* which is an Indianised form of the game 'hide and seek'. In this one of the players' eyes were covered with a piece of rough cloth so that she was unable to see the others. The other players then hid themselves at different places and after that the player's eyes were uncovered. If she succeeded in catching any of the other players who were hiding, then the player caught was made to cover her eyes while the others hid, and then the same process was repeated. This game could be played both indoors and outdoors, but the strict rules of *purdah* and seclusion which were imposed on the Mughal ladies made them play the game of *ankh-michauli* inside their living quarters. In Fatehpur Sikri we find a section of the living quarters known to have been built for the purpose of this game.[28] Thus we can say that this game was a popular one among the Mughal ladies.

Dancing, Singing and other Sources of Entertainment Inside the Harem

The ladies of the Mughal harem were often entertained by groups of singers and dancers.[29] Other than during Aurangzeb's time, such forms of entertainments were very common. Jehangir and his women had great liking for it and during his time singers used to line up outside the palace gate for their turn.[30] There was a female superintendent of music and dance inside the harem.[31] These musical groups put up different programmes. Sometimes the emperors received dancing and singing girls as presents and used to send them to the harem for the entertainment of their ladies.[32] There were times when famous musicians and dancers performed at the Mughal Court and at such times too the royal ladies were allowed to attend the programmes, but always hidden behind veils and sitting in a covered area meant for them, from where they could see the performers, but no one saw them. Many of the harem ladies themselves could sing and play musical instruments. Manucci tells us that Jahanara Begam was much fond of singing, dancing and other forms of entertainment.[33]

Apart from music, the Mughal ladies took interest in painting also. Sometimes they passed their time in reading books especially romances and books like Sheikh Sadi Shirazi's *Gulistan* and *Bostan*.[34] Some Mughal ladies like Gulbadan Begam, Salima Sultan Begam, Nur Jahan, Jahanara and Zeb-un-Nisa composed poetry and other works of literary value. Composing verses seems to have been a favourite pastime of the royal ladies. Some Mughal women like Nur Jahan took interest in the art of decoration and dress, textile and jewellery designing. Some ladies took interest in perfumery. Pelsaert wrote that these women studied day and night to find methods of making exotic perfumes.[35] Nur Jahan's mother Asmat Banu Begam invented a perfume from rose petals and named it Itr-i-Jahangiri.[36] Some royal ladies who had the money and taste designed and funded the construction of buildings and gardens. Certain royal ladies like Nur Jahan and Zeb-un-Nisa were even skilled at the use of arms and certainly used this special skill as an engaging pastime. Apart from these individual hobbies and pastimes, the Mughal women spent some of their evenings in watching displays of fireworks. They also spent a lot of their money in getting torches lighted in hundreds and thousands.[37]

Use of Intoxicants

Many of the royal ladies, side by side with their men, loved to take various kinds of intoxicants and stimulants which elevated the spirit even though Islam puts a strict ban on this. During Jashns, feasts and evening of music and dance there was much drinking and merrymaking. Even otherwise some Mughal ladies drank wine and consumed intoxicants quite frequently. Apart from various types of wines, different kinds of intoxicants were used during the Mughal days. Some of them were opium (*afyun* or *afim*) *bhang, charas, ma'jun, ganja, hashish,* etc.[38]

Opium and hashish and a variety of wine were the most popular intoxicants in the Mughal harem. Even though the Mughal emperors tried their best to prevent intoxicants like bhang, wine, opium, nutmegs, etc., from reaching the hands of the harem ladies,[39] these ladies certainly found their own ways in getting hold of these intoxicants. Jahangir's first wife Man Bai (Shah Begam) is said to have died by swallowing a large quantity of opium.[40] The Mughal ladies also smoked water pipes or hukkas as known from contemporary paintings.

Pelsaert found the Mughal women eating during the day, efficacious preserves containing amber, pearls, gold and opium as these elevated the spirit, and at night, drinking wine. He also found the habit of drinking quite fashionable during Jehangir's time.[41] Jahanara Begam was very much fond of drinking wine, and Manucci says that she brought them from Persia, Kabul and Kashmir.[42] But the best liquor she drank was made in her own palace from wine and rose water and spiced with aromatic drugs and flavours.[43] Manucci further adds: "Many a times she did me the favour of ordering some bottles of it to be sent to my house, in sign of her gratitude for my curing people in her harem."[44] Another Mughal lady greatly addicted to drinking was Udipuri Mahal, one of the wives of Aurangzeb. Aurangzeb often found her in a dishevelled condition.[45]

Outdoor Amusements

During the Mughal times the royal ladies of the seraglio sometimes had the opportunity for outdoor recreations and amusements side by side with indoor amusements. Outdoor recreations were provided in forms of hunting expeditions, visiting palaces for sightseeing or holiday excursions to places of scenic beauty like the Kashmir valley, and in playing outdoor games like Chaugan (Polo), pigeon flying, kite flying and watching animal fights. In all these recreations the Mughal women participated in them along with their menfolk.

Hunting

As said earlier, some Mughal ladies like Nur Jahan Begam and Zeb-un-Nisa Begam[46] were skilled in the use of arms. Aasaish Banu Begam, the daughter of Murad Baksh and grand daughter of Shah Jahan is said to have been a good hunter and a perfect shot.[47] The Mughal ladies frequently went on hunting expeditions as companions of their king. Gulbadan Begam mentions some women who were able to shoot with the bow and arrow, played polo, etc.[48]

Nur Jahan Begam accompanied her husband Emperor Jehangir several times on hunting expeditions. She was a skilled shooter. Once she shot a *qarisha* (a kind of bird) weighing 19 tolas and 5 mashas.[49] At another time she shot four tigers with six shots. About this Jehangir writes:

> Until now such shooting was never seen, that from the top of an elephant and inside of a howdah (amari) six shots should be made and not one miss, so that the four beasts found no opportunity to spring or move. As a reward for this good shooting I gave her a pair of bracelets (pahunchi) of diamonds worth 100,000 rupees and scattered 1,000 ashrafis (over her).[50]

Jehangir mentions another hunting expedition where he went with his ladies. Here too Nur Jahan Begam under difficult situations killed a tiger with one shot.[51] Nur Jahan's skill with the gun was undoubtedly great but Khafi Khan gives a very interesting theory as to how she acquired such a skill and excelled even men in this field. According to him, Nur Jahan developed this skill in order to compete with a rival wife, Jagat Gosain. Once it seems, both these ladies accompanied Jehangir on a hunting expedition where they were confronted by a lion. Jagat Gosain acted swiftly, picked up a gun and killed the lion. Emperor Jehangir praised Jagat Gosain greatly and found Nur Jahan to be a coward. Thereafter Nur Jahan tried her best to develop her skill in shooting.[52]

Chaugan (Polo)

The game of *chaugan* or polo was an extremely popular one among the members of the Mughal royal family and the aristocrats of that time. Young and active royal ladies also participated in the game,[53] though strict rules of purdah might have restricted their number to just a few ladies who could really play it well. Contemporary paintings too reveal that Mughal ladies played Chaugan.[54] Abul Fazl says that the game of Chaugan revealed hidden talents and skill, both of the players and the animals (horses).[55] This game was played with 10 players, each on horse-back and five on each side (team). Each player had a chaugan or polo-stick with a curved end in hand. The game could be played in two ways as said by Abul Fazl.[56] The Mughals maintained large openfields (*maidans*) for the game of chaugan. The famous ones were at Agra and Fatehpur Sikri. Badauni mentions a place called Gharawali near Agra where Akbar used to play chaugan.[57] At Fatehpur Sikri too such fields existed.[58] The game of chaugan is said to have had a direct influence on the development of games like hockey, golf and cricket.[59]

Ishq-Baazi (Pigeon-flying)

Pigeon-flying was another popular outdoor amusement of the Mughals. So was kite flying. Akbar called pigeon-flying Ishq-baazi (love-play).[60] This amusement had been popular with the Mughals even before Akbar, but Akbar's pigeons excelled all the previous ones in breed and skill. Some of them were called Ashki (the weeper), Parizaad (the fairy), Almaas (the diamond), and Shah Sudi (Aloe Royal).[61] Home bred young pigeons were trained in the palace. Pigeons were also engaged for carrying messages from one place to another.[62]

Animal-fights

Animal fights were greatly enjoyed by the Mughals. Fights were arranged between tigers, elephants and other ferocious animals. Some fights were arranged between a tiger and a ram, or between deer and stags. Mughal emperors like Akbar, Jehangir and Shahjahan were much fond of this sort of entertainment.[63]

Combats like boxing and wrestling were also arranged between men.[64] There were a large number of Persian and Turani boxers at Akbar's court.[65] Some other forms of outdoor sports and amusements were archery, mock-fights, blind man's buff, javelin-throwing, ball-throwing, climbing trees, etc.[66]

In all these various forms of outdoor amusements and recreations, the Mughal ladies participated as spectators, because of the prevailing purdah system and also because these forms of sports and games were totally for men as participants.

Persian Festivals Celebrated by the Mughals

We have already discussed about the Muslim and Hindu festivals that were celebrated at the Mughal Court. The Mughals also adopted and celebrated certain Persian festivals which became very popular among them.

Ab-i-Pashan

This was a Persian festival held in memory of the rain which fell on the 13th day of the Persian month of Tir and put an end to the famine. It was similar to the Hindu festival of Holi, but here rose water was sprinkled instead of colours. It was introduced by Akbar to the Mughal Court.[67] The Mughal rulers celebrated this festival amidst gaiety and great elegance at the commencement of the rainy season. The members of the royal family along with the other people connected to the Mughal court and seraglio found great pleasure in sprinkling rose water over one another. As a part of the custom the emperor was presented with jewelled golden flasks containing rose water, juice of the jujube tree flower and the aroma of orange flowers.[68] This festival was called Ab-i-Pashan by some and Id-i-Gulabi (rose water festival) or Gulab Pash by some others. Contemporary Mughal paintings reveal that women also joined the Mughal men in the celebration of Ab-i-Pashan.

Nauroz

Nauroz was the Persian New Year's Day which fell on the Ist of the Persian month of Farwardin (around 20th or 21st March) when the Sun moved to Aries.[69] It was the greatest festival during the Mughal times, celebrated for nineteen days (from the Ist to 19th of Farwardin),[70] and marked the advent of spring in India. Monserrate says that it lasted for nine days.[71] The first and the nineteenth day of Farwardin were considered most auspicious and on these two days a lot of money and gifts were distributed.[72]

Nauroz was the time of merrymaking, abandon and gaiety. Preparations for the festival were made months ahead. The palaces, porticoes, gardens, private and public audience halls and even the market places were richly decorated. The common people also decorated their houses[73] and wore good clothes. Many people from the villages and small towns flocked to the capital to participate in the festivities.[74] Restrictions on gambling were relaxed during the days of the festival.[75] The common people were allowed to meet the emperor freely once a week during these days.[76] Musicians and nautch girls thrilled the audiences by their performances. Singers came from many parts, even Persia.[77]

Several foreign travellers like De Laet, Mandelslo, William

Hawkins, Sir Thomas Roe, Monserrate, Manrique, Thevenot, Bernier and Manucci, the contemporary Persian chroniclers and even Jehangir in his memoirs have given a detailed and picturesque description of the Nauroz celebrations. Jehangir writes about the Nauroz celebrations of March 11 or 12, 1606 A.D.:

> Players and singers of all bands and castes were gathered together. Dancing lulis and charmers of India whose caress would captivate the hearts of angels kept up the excitement of the assemblies. I gave orders that whoever might wish for intoxicating drinks and exhilarating drugs should not be debarred from using them.[78]

The Nauroz celebration was introduced by Akbar and continued till it was abolished by Aurangzeb on grounds of his religious orthodoxy. He is said to have substituted for it another imperial festival called Nishat Afroz Jashn, which began in the month of Ramzan and continued upto Id-ul-Fitr.[79]

Some other Special Days of Feasts and Festivities

Mina Bazaar (Khus Ruz)

On special days, especially during the Nauroz celebrations in the Mughal times, a special kind of fair known as the Mina Bazaar was held which usually lasted for eight days.[80] According to Thevenot it lasted for five days, [81] and Tod is of the opinion that this fancy fair lasted for nine days.[82] The days of the fair were termed as Khus Ruz, or the day of joy and gaiety.

The Mina Bazaar in an elaborate form was introduced at the Mughal seraglio by Akbar as a source of entertainment for the harem ladies, but it was not his own invention. These fairs were first instituted by Humayun and the first of its kind were held on boats near the king's palace after the mystic feast.[83] This custom is said to have been borrowed by the Mughals from Turkistan and Transoxiana[84] where such bazaars were held once or twice a week in every village, but there women as well as men participated in the buying and selling.[85]

The Mina Bazaar was an exclusively women's affair and not open to the general public.[86] Here beautiful stalls were set up by the royal ladies and other harem women and also the wives and daughters of the nobles, who acted as traders, to sell a variety of commodities ranging from handicrafts, jewellery, cloth, brocades, fruits, flowers, etc. Rajput ladies also participated in these.[87] Only the emperor, royal princes and privileged nobles could enter the bazaar as buyers. The commodities were sold at sky high prices and the return went for charitable purposes.[88] A lot of mock bargaining was also done. Sometimes the emperor and the princes landed up paying double for a single commodity. The women who sold these articles were very charming and beautiful, and quite skilled at the art of conversation and therefore became good sellers. Bernier gives a detailed description of the Mina Bazaar. He writes:

> A whimsical kind of fair is sometimes held during these festivities in the Mehale, or royal seraglio: it is conducted by the handsomest and most engaging of the wives of the Omrahs and principal Mansebdars. The articles exhibited are beautiful brocades, rich embroideries of the newest fashion, turbans elegantly worked on cloth of gold, fine muslin worn by women of quality, and other articles of high price. These bewitching females act the part of traders, while the purchasers are the King, the Begums or Princesses, and other distinguished ladies of the seraglio.... The charm of this fair is the most ludicrous manner in which the King makes his bargains, frequently disputing for the value of a penny.... The women, on the other hand, endeavours to sell to the best advantage, and when the King perseveres in offering what she considers too little money, high words frequently ensue, and she fearlessly tells him that he is a worthless trader, a person ignorant of the value of merchandise; that her articles are too good for him, and that he had better go where he can suit himself better, and similar jocular expressions.[89]

According to Abul Fazl, the main intention of Akbar behind holding such fairs was "to select any article which he wishes to buy, or to fix the price of things, and thus add to his knowledge. The secrets of the empire, the character of the people, the good and bad qualities of each office and worship, will then appear." After the bazaars for women, bazaars for men were also held.[90] During the time of Shahjahan these fancy fairs were even more a grander affair. Hamilton says that by letting his harem women participate in these fairs, he introduced the ladies to a free air.[91] Though the Mina Bazaar was primarily held as a part of the Nauroz celebrations, it was held at other times too. According to Abul Fazl it was held once a month.[92] During Shahjahan's time such fair were also held on the occasion of every festival.[93]

Marriage Feasts

Marriages of the emperor and other members of the Mughal royal family used to be celebrated in extreme grandeur and amidst gaiety and merrymaking. In such occasions the royal ladies had an important part to play. The royal marriages were usually arranged by the emperor, even in the case of love matches. But the entire responsibility of arranging the feasts and festivities depended on important royal ladies of the Mughal harem. Marriages were celebrated lavishly.

When these royal marriages were settled, usually betel leaves (*Pan*) were given as a mark of acceptance of the proposal by the elders of the bride's family. Then the first wedding gift or sacnaq came to the bride's home on behalf of the bridegroom. The hennabandi ceremony was performed next in which henna or *mehandi* was applied on the bridegroom's hands and feet by the harem ladies.[94] Then came the day of the actual wedding. On the day of the wedding princes and nobles went to the groom's place to offer him wedding presents. Then a magnificent procession was taken out where the groom mounted an elephant and was followed by important men, some on decorated horses and some on foot, till the procession reached the Diwan-i-Aam (Hall of Public Audience). Here the emperor himself tied on the groom's forehead the sehra made of pearls and gems. Then the marriage procession started for the bride's place where they were cordially received, and at an auspicious hour the marriage was performed by the Qazi in front of the emperor. Finally gold and silver coins and gems were showered on the newly wedded couple.[95]

In the Mughal annals we come across many important and grand marriage ceremonies. Prince Khurram's (Shahjahan) marriage with Arjumand Banu Begam (Mumtaz Mahal), the daughter of Asaf Khan and niece of Nur Jahan was such a lavish affair. This marriage was held on the night of Friday, the 9th of the month of Rabi I of the year 1021 A.H. (10 May, 1612), corresponding to the 22nd of the month of Urdibihisht of the 7th year of Jahangir's accession.[96] Before the actual wedding took place, emperor Jehangir along with his ladies paid a visit to Asaf Khan's house where a feast was arranged. Again after the conclusion of the marriage ceremonies, Jehangir paid another visit to Asaf Khan's house. Magnificient processions were taken out and gifts lavished on people. Exclusive fireworks lit the night sky. The festivities continued for about a month.[97]

Another grand Mughal royal family marriage was that of Shahjahan's eldest son Dara Shukoh with Nadira Begam, the daughter of Prince Parvez, another son of Jehangir.[98] This marriage had been settled by Mumtaz Mahal when she was alive, but she did not live to see it take place due to her untimely death. So, for this marriage Princess Jahanara took upon her the responsibility for the successful organisation of the feasts and festivities. The entire sum kept aside for this purpose was about 16 lakh rupees including both what Mumtaz Mahal had set aside for her son's marriage during her lifetime, and also what Princess Jahanara had added to it. On Jumada I, 1042 A.H. (Nov.-Dec. 1632) one lakh worth of goods and another in cash was sent to the mansion of Jahan Banu Begam, the widow of Prince Parvez, as the customary sachaq gifts to the bride. Half of the goods consisted of jewellery and the other half a valuables and dresses.[99] An exhibition of the wedding gifts was arranged in the hall of public audience at the Agra Fort on 25 January, 1633 A.D. by Jahanara Begam and Sati-un-Nisa Khanum.[100] Hundred robes of honour were given to the princes and princesses of the royal family and the wives and daughters of nobles. Other costly clothes and jewellery were also given to them.[101] The hinabandi ceremony was performed on the 21st of Shaban, 1042 A.H. (11 February, 1633 A.D.). Shahjahan gave his consent to the revival of music and dance in the harem which were earlier stopped due to Mumtaz's death.[102] The whole of Agra was illumined with lights and fireworks. Next day the marriage was performed. The total sum of money spent on this occasion armounted to 32 lakhs out of which 16 lakhs were given by Jahanara Begam alone.[103]

Once again soon Jahanara Begam played an important role in arranging the marriage of her second brother Prince Shuja with the daughter of Mirza Rustam Safawi. The ceremony was held on the night of Friday, the 23rd of Shaban, 1042 A.H. (5 March, 1633 A.D.). Rupees 1,60,000 in cash and one lakh worth of goods were sent as sachak to the mansion of Mirza Rustam.[104] On 23rd Feb. 1633 A.D. the wedding presents worth Rupees 10 lakhs were displayed by Jahanara and Sati-un-Nisa.[105]

Mughal history is quite abundant with stories of grand marriages like the ones already mentioned and many more, like that of Aurangzeb's marriage to Dilras Banu Begam and the marriage of Dara's daughter Jani Begam to Sultan Azam, son of Aurangzeb. The history is long. But the fact that these marriages did not lack in grandeur and style cannot be denied. Most of the times a royal lady took upon herself the charge of arranging the marriage feasts like Jahanara Begam did in Dara's and Shuja's marriages and also when Dara's daughter Jahanzeb Banu Begam got married to Muhammad Azam son of Aurangzeb.[106] Another of Shahjahan's daughter Gauhara Begam and a certain Hamida Banu Begam arranged the marriage feast of Zubdat-un-Nisa Begam, a daughter of Aurangzeb to Sipihr Shukoh, Dara's son.[107] Zinat-un-Nisa Begam supervised the marriage celebrations of Muizzuddin to Sayyid-un-Nisa Begam.[108] Moreover, these occasions provided a lot of enjoyment and merrymaking to the harem inmates.

Emperor's Birthday

The Emperor's birthday was another extremely joyous occasion at the Mughal Court. On this day the emperor was weighed against some precious metals and commodities in imitation of the Hindu fashion. Humayun was the first Mughal emperor to adopt this custom of weighing.[109]Akbar celebrated both his solar and lunar birthdays and on both these days the weighing ceremony formed an important part of the festivities.[110] Almost all the contemporary foreign travellers have described the weighing ceremony as part of the emperor's birthday celebrations.[111] Says De Laet:

> ...he weighs himself in a golden balance against gold, silver, precious stones, all kinds of grain, and so on. His

> weight is carefully noted and compared with that of the previous year. On the next day the king distributes all the above things as alms to the poor (or as others say, to the Bramens); but the gifts which he receives from his courtiers far exceeds in value against which he is weighed, though they are estimated to be worth L 10,000 sterling.[112]

The custom of weighing on the occasion of the emperor's birthday continued in Jehangir's and Shahjahan's times. Jehangir mentions about it in his memoirs.[113] Aurangzeb weighed himself only once a year and even this was stopped in March 1670 A.D., i.e., in his 51st year.[114]

The weighing ceremonies formed just a part of the entire birthday celebrations. There were great rejoicing everywhere. Feasts were arranged and arrangements were made for a lot of enjoyment and entertainment like singing, dancing, fireworks, gambling etc. The palaces, elephants and horses were grandly decorated. A lot was given in form of charity. The festivities continued for five days. Some courtiers gained ranks and some others jagirs. The chief ladies of the harem and also the wives of principle nobles exchanged lots of gifts amongst themselves.[115]

Coronation Festivities

Another grand festive occasion at the Mughal Court was when a new king came to the throne. Whatever might have been the method of getting the crown, the new kings did not let the coronation ceremonies lack and sort of grandeur or gaiety. This fact is clearly seen when we go through the accounts of the coronation celebration of Shahjahan and Aurangzeb. Humayun is said to have even introduced another festival to be held to commemorate the anniversary of the coronation.[116] The coronation festivities usually continued for about a week.[117] The palaces, gardens, market places and other important public places were grandly decorated. Fireworks were displayed at night.[118] Tournaments in archery were also organised.[119] Jagirs were given to the nobles and alms to the needy. The chief ladies of the harem also became the recipients of a lot of money and valuables.

During Shahjahan's coronation held on 4th February, 1628 A.D., the emperor bestowed on his wife Mumtaz Mahal a present of two hundred thousand ashrafis, and six hundred thousand of rupees and fixed 10 lakhs of rupees as annual allowance for her.[121] To his beloved daughter Jahanara Begam he presented one lakh ashrafis and four lakhs of rupees and fixed for her an annual allowance of 6 lakhs of rupees.[121] His other children also got gifts. During Aurangazeb's coronation, his sister Roshanara Begam received as gift five lakhs of rupees in cash and kind for her constant support to him. His four daughters got Rupees 4, 2, 1.6 and 1.5 lakhs respectively.[122]

Other Feast Days

Other than the occasions already discussed, the Mughals also arranged for grand feasts at certain other times. Feasts were an important part of all Mughal ceremonies, festivals and other occasions. The royal ladies of the harem always participated in these and sometimes themselves arranged for feasts.

Babar in his memoirs make a mention of such occasions when special guests were entertained like the one when gold embroidered silk dresses were presented to the servants of his daughter Masuma and his son Hindal and even dancing girls were brought for the occasion.[125] Babar's widow and Humayun's mother Maham Begam, arranged for a grand feast at Humayun's accession, when not only the bazaars but also the nobles and soldiers' quarters were lighted and decorated. With all the arrangements and lavish decorations, Gulbadan Begam says that Maham Begam "made an excellent and splendid feast."[124]

Also in Gulbadan Begam's accounts we find detailed description of the great Mystic feast where important harem ladies like Khanzada Begam and Maham Begam played an important part. Describing the Mystic House where the feast was arranged, Gulbadan writes:

> First there was a large octagonal room with an octagonal tank in the centre, and again, in the middle of reservoir, an octagonal platform on which were spread Persian (Wilayati) carpets. Young men and pretty girls and elegant women and musicians and sweet-voiced reciters were ordered to sit in the tank. The jewelled throne which my lady (Maham Begam) had given for the feast was placed

> in the forecourt of the house, and a gold embroidered divan was laid in front of it, (on which) his Majesty and dearest lady sat together.[125]

On the whole the feast was extremely grand.

Dildar Begam, another wife of Babar, arranged a grand feast in 1514 A.D., when Humayun was at Pat.[126] All the harem ladies took part in it. Gulbadan Begam also describes the circumcision feast of Akbar in Kabul when Akbar was five years old. All the bazaars were well decorated and the royal ladies celebrated it in Bega Begam's garden.[127] Akbar's nurse Maham Anaga arranged a large feast and banquet on the occasion of her son's wedding.[129] She often arranged feasts and in such occasions the harem ladies participated.[129] Nur Jahan Begam's wonderful ability to arrange feasts is quite clear from their accounts in Jehangir's memoirs.[130] Sometimes feasts were arranged for very strange happenings, like the one given by Roshanara Begam when Dara was killed in 1658 A.D.[131]

Thus, we see that during the Mughal times the royal women had a lot of ways, means and opportunities to entertain themselves. They also got lot of scope to indulge themselves in hobbies and pastimes of their choice. They played a variety of indoor games and some of them even participated in outdoor recreations like playing polo and going for hunting expeditions. Some very talented royal ladies engaged themselves in constructive works. Apart from these activities, there were a number of festive occasions where they had the chance of participating. Even an exclusive fair called the Mina Bazar was organised for the entertainment of the harem women. The royal ladies also wore beautiful clothes and jewellery, ate good food and drank exclusive wine. Many of them were addicted too intoxicating drinks and drugs.

REFERENCES

1. G.A. Herklots tr., *Islam in India* (London: 1921), p. 331.
2. *Ibid.*, pp. 331-32.
3. Abul Fazl, *Ain-i-Akbari*, Vol. I, tr. Blochmann, p. 320.
4. *Ibid.*, p. 320.
5. Pratapaditya Pal, *Court Paintings of India* (16th-19th centuries) (New York: 1983), Plates showing two ladies playing chess and another showing some ladies playing chess.

6. Badauni, *Muntakhab-ut-Tawarikh*, Vol. II (Lowe), p. 324; Vol. III (Haig), pp. 408, 467.
7. Manucci, *Storia...*, Vol. II, pp. 460-61.
8. *Ibid.*, pp. 460-61.
9. Kabir Kausar & Inamul Kabir, *Biographical Dictionary of Prominent Muslim Ladies* (New Delhi: 1982), p. 25.
10. Herklots tr. *Islam in India*, p. 335.
11. *Ibid.*, p. 335.
12. *Ibid.*, p. 335.
13. *Ain-i-Akbari* (tr.), Vol. I, pp. 315-16.
14. *Ibid.*, p. 316.
15. Rekha Misra, *Women in Mughal* India, pp. 85-86.
16. Herklots tr., *Islam in India.*, p. 333.
17. *Ibid.*, p. 334.
18. Md. Ashraf Husain, *A Guide to Fatehpur Sikri* (Delhi: 1937), p. 18.
19. R.C. Arora, *The City of the Taj* (Aligarh: 1937), p. 43.
20. S.M. Latif, *Agra, Historical and Descriptive* (Calcutta: 1896), p. 86.
21. *Babur Nama* (tr.), Vol. II, p. 584 and n.
22. Foster ed., *The Embassy of Sir Thomas Roe to the Court of the Great Moghul*, Vol. I, p. 293.
23. *Ibid.*, p. 293.
24. *Ain-i-Akbari* (tr.), Vol. I, pp. 318-19.
25. *Ibid.*, p. 316.
26. *Ibid.*, p. 316.
27. Tapankumar Raychaudhuri, *Bengal Under Akbar and Jehangir* (Calcutta 1953), pp. 193, 203.
28. Md. Ashraf Husain, *A Guide to Fatehpur Sikri*, pp. 16-17.
29. *Ain-i-Akbari* (tr.), Vol. I, p. 166.
30. Finch in *Early Travels in India*, p. 183.
31. Manucci, *Memoirs of the Mughal Court*, p. 33.
32. *Humayun Nama* (tr.), p. 95.
33. Manucci, *Storia...*, Vol. I, p. 211.
34. Manucci, *Storia...*, Vol. II, p. 331.
35. Pelsaert, *Remonstrantie*, tr. Moreland & Geyl, p. 65.
36. *Tuzuk-i-Jahangiri* (tr.), Vol. I, pp. 270-71; Vol. II, p. 115.
37. Manucci, *Storia...*, Vol. II, p. 341.
38. Herklots tr., *Islam in India.*, pp. 325-30.
39. Manucci, *Storia...*, Vol. II, p. 328.
40. *Tuzuk-i-Jahangiri* (tr.), Vol. I, pp. 19, 55-56.
41. Pelsaert, p. 65.
42. Manucci, *Storia...*, Vol. I, p. 211.
43. *Ibid.*, p. 211.
44. *Ibid.*, p. 211.
45. *Ibid.*, Vol. II, pp. 99-100.
46. Magan Lal tr. *The Diwan of Zeb-un-Nisa*, p. 14.
47. Kabir Kausar and Inamul Kabir, *Biographical Dictionary of Prominent Muslim Ladies*, p. 3.
48. *Humayun Nama* (tr.), pp. 120-21.
49. *Tuzuk-i-Jahangiri* (tr.), Vol. I, p. 348.
50. *Ibid.*, p. 375.

51. *Ibid.*, Vol. II, p. 104.
52. Khafi Khan quoted in Findly, *Noorjahan...*, p. 116.
53. *Humayun Nama* (tr.), pp. 120-21.
54. Binyor, *The Court Painters of Grand Mughals*, Plate vii, p. 18.
55. *Ain-i-Akbari* (tr.) Vol. I, p. 309.
56. *Ibid.*, pp. 309-310.
57. Badauni, Vol. II, tr. Lowe, p. 69.
58. *Ain-i-Akbari* (tr.), Vol. II, p. 191.
59. Encyclopaedia Britanica, Vol. 22, pp. 11-12.
60. *Ain-i-Akbari* (tr.), Vol. I, p. 310.
61. *Ibid.*, p. 311.
62. Manucci, *Storia...*, Vol. I, p. 65; Vol. II, p. 467.
63. A.L. Srivastava, *Akbar the Great*, Vol. III (Agra: 1972), p. 211.
64. *Ibid.*, p. 212.
65. *Ibid.*, p. 212.
66. *Ibid.*, p. 212.
67. *Akbar Nama* (Pr.),Vol. II, p. 13; (tr.) Vol. II, pp. 23-24.
68. *Tuzuk-i-Jahangiri* (tr.), Vol. I, pp. 265, 295 and 379 (n); Md. Saleh Kambu, *Amal-i-Saleh*, p. 374; Lahori, *Badshah Nama*, Vol. I, p. 204.
69 *Ain-i-Akbari* (tr.) Vol. I, p. 286.
70. *Ibid.*, p. 286.
71. Monserrate, *Commentarius*, pp. 175-76.
72. *Ain-i-Akbari* (tr.), Vol. I, p. 286.
73. Manrique, *Travels*, tr. & ed. Luard & Hosten (Oxford: 1927), Vol. II, p. 193.
74. Monserrate, *Commentarius*, pp. 175-76.
75. Badauni, Vol. II, tr. Lowe, pp. 348-49.
76. P.N. Chopra, *Some Aspects of Society and Culture During the Mughal Age*, p. 81.
77. *Ibid.*, p. 81.
78. *Tuzuk-i-Jahangiri* (tr.), Vol. I, p. 48.
79. Jadunath Sarkar tr., *Maasir-i-Alamgiri*, p. 14.
80. Manucci, *Storia...*, Vol. I, p. 195.
81. Thevenot, *Indian Travels*, ed. Sen, p. 71.
82. Tod, *The Annals and Antiquities of Rajasthan*, Vol. I, p. 401.
83. Gulbadan Begam, *Humayun Nama* (tr.), p. 126.
84. Syed Ameer Ali, 'Islamic Culture Under the Moguls', *Islamic Culture*, 1927, p. 509.
85. P.N. Chopra, *Some Aspects of Society and Culture During the Mughal Age* (Agra: 1955), p. 88n.
86. Syed Ameer Ali, 'Islamic Culture Under the Moguls', *Islamic Culture*, p. 509.
87. Tod, *Annals and Antiquities...*, Vol. I, pp. 401-402.
88. *Ibid.*, pp. 401-402.
89. Bernier, pp. 272-73.
90. *Ibid.*, p. 273.
91. Alexander Hamilton, *A New Account of the East Indies*, ed. William Foster (London: 1930), p. 99.
92. *Ain-i-Akbari* (tr.), Vol. I, p. 287.
93. Bernier, p. 273.
94. Lahori, *Badshah Nama*, Vol. I, Pt. II, pp. 266-68; Vol. II, pp. 137, 305.
95. N.L. Mathur, *Red Fort and Mughal Life* (New Delhi : 1964), pp. 42-43.
96. Qazwini, *Padshah Nama*, fol. 486.

97. Qazwini, *Padshah Nama*, ff. 48b-49b; *Tuzuk-i-Jahangiri* (tr.), Vol. I, pp. 224-25.
98. Lahori, *Badshah Nama*, Vol. I, pp. 452-60.
99. Inayat Khan, *The Shah Jahan Nama* (tr.), p. 90.
100. B.P. Saksena, *History of Shahjahan of Dihli*, p. 311; Jadunath Sarkar, *Studies in Mughal India*, p. 24.
101. *The Shah Jahan Nama* (tr.), p. 90-91.
102. *Ibid.*, p. 91.
103. B.P. Saksena, *History of Shahjahan of Dihli*, p. 312.
104. *The Shah Jahan Nama* (tr.) p. 93.
105. Sarkar, *Studies in Mughal India*, p. 24.
106. Md. Saqi Mustaidd Khan, *Maasir-i-Alamgiri*, tr. Jadunath Sarkar, p. 47.
107. *Ibid.*, p. 77.
108. *Ibid.*, p. 152.
109. Khwand Amir, *Qanun-i-Humayuni*, p. 76.
110. *Ain-i-Akbari*, Vol. I (tr.), pp. 276-77.
111. Bernier, p. 272; De Laet, *The Empire of the Great Mogol*, pp. 101-102; Della Valle, *Travels, ed.*, Grey, p. 459; Mandelslo, *Travels in Western India* (Commissariat), p. 42; Manrique, *Travels* (Luard & Hosten), Vol. II, pp. 200-204; Manucci, *Storia*, Vol. II, p. 348; Roe, Vol. II, pp. 378-380; Tavernier, Travels in India (V. Ball), p. 112.
112. De Laet, p. 101.
113. *Tuzuk-i-Jahangiri* (tr.), Vol. I, p. 77.
114. P.N. Chopra, *Life and Letters Under the Mughals*, (New Delhi : 1976), p. 87.
115. Manucci, *Storia...*, Vol. II, p. 345.
116. Khwand Amir, *Qanun-i-Humayuni*, pp. 19-20.
117. Ovington, *A Voyage to Surat in the Year 1689*, ed. H.G. Rawlingson, p. 178-79.
118. Ovington, pp. 178-79.
119. Khwand Amir, *Qanun-i-Humayuni*, pp. 19-20.
120. *The Shah Jahan Nama* (tr.), p. 18; Qazwini, *Padshah Nama*, ff. 121-32; Lahori, *Badshah Nama*, Vol. I, pp. 82-99.
121. *The Shah Jahan Nama* (tr.), p. 18.
122. Jadunath Sarkar, *History of Aurangzib*, Vol. I & II, (Calcutta: 1973), p. 385 (Vol. II).
123. *Babur Nama* (tr.), Vol. II, p. 633.
124. *Humayun Nama* (tr.), p. 113.
125. *Ibid.*, p. 118.
126. Jauhar Aftabchi, *Tazkirat-ul-Waqiat*, tr., Charles Stewart (London : 1832), p. 30.
127. *Humayun Nama* (tr.), p. 179.
128. *Akbar Nama* (tr.), Vol. II, pp. 204-205.
129. *Ibid.*, p. 221.
130. *Tuzuk-i-Jahangiri* (tr.), Vol. I, p. 385; Vol. II, pp. 199, 214.
131. Manucci, *Storia...*, Vol. I, p. 359.

Four

Mughal Ladies in Contemporary Politics

The Mughal age was an era marked by many distinctive features and developments in almost all fields of art, architecture, learning, economy, and polity. In the political field, their rule of about two hundred years is just a droplet in the bucket of Indian history, but, during their rule, the Mughal presence was felt heavily from the northern parts to the southern parts of India and from the eastern to the western parts. In fact, the Mughals were the first ruling class in the country whose domain touched almost the entire India. They ruled the country efficiently and provided stable governance in the areas under them. They crushed rebellions with ease and set up an efficient administrative system. Most of the Mughal rulers were men of indomitable courage and proved their worth as efficient rulers.

As in all other fields, in the political field too, the Mughal women tried to keep pace with their menfolk. Some of these Mughal women were just not satisfied with leading a life of luxury and pleasure inside the harem. Their activities were not only confined to beautifying themselves, indulging in the pleasure of life and trying to please the emperor in their own ways. The ladies of the Mughal harem went a step forward, and in each period, right from the time of Babar to Aurangzeb, and even during the time of the later Mughals too, we come across politically ambitious women, or women who directly or indirectly influenced the political course of events of those times.

Since many hundreds of years the Central Asian women have played an active part in war and politics. It is said that they accompanied their menfolks to the war fields, where they looked after the comforts of the warriors and sometimes even took part in the combat themselves. In the army of Taimur there were many dauntless and daring women warriors, efficient in the use of bows, spears and swords.[1] The same could be said about women in Chengiz Khan's time too.[2] When the leader of the tribe died, his widow could assume all the rights of her husband, and could even act as regent to her son if he was a minor.[3]

The Women Behind Babar

Babar's family which had the assimilation of the blood and traditions of Chengiz Khan and Taimur, gave their women many opportunities to directly or indirectly participate in the political affairs of that time. But, the right to sovereignty was denied to them.[4] In the *Babur Nama*, we come across an instance when once Shah Begam of Badakhshan wrote to Babar that she being a woman could not become a sovereign, but her grandson Mirza Khan could.[5]

History gives a lot of importance to the political exploits of Babar, the establisher of the great Mughal rule in Hindustan. But, rarely does one think about who the people were, who contributed in the making of this man, Babar, the adventurer, who became the Emperor of Hindustan, even though he had once literally lost everything he had, including his father Umar Sheikh Mirza's small principality of Farghana in Central Asia. A popular saying goes that behind every successful man there is a woman. This saying could not have been more true than in the case of Babar's life. In fact, there was not one, but quite a few women in Babar's life who contributed in shaping the life and career of Babar. But the roles played by his maternal grandmother Aisan-Daulat Begam and his mother Qutluq-Nigar Khanum were perhaps the most important in shaping his life.

Aisan Daulat Begam

Aisan-Daulat Begam, the maternal grandmother of Babar, the mother of Babar's mother Qutluq Nigar Khanum, was the wife of Yunas Khan, a descendent of Chaghatai Khan, the second son of Chingiz Khan.[6] Aisan-Daulat Begam seems to have played an important part in contemporary politics right from her young days, when she was to be married. She was the daughter of the

Sagharichi Tuman Begs, a sub-division of the Kunchi Mughals. The *Babar Nama* says that by marrying Aisan-Daulat Begam, Yunus Khan was honoured and raised to Khanship by the Sagharichi Tuman Begs who had attacked Mughulistan.[7] Born in the desert and herself used to the rigours of a wild country, Aisan-Daulat Begam was certainly the one to inculcate tenacity, self-reliance, courage to face hardships and a die-hard attitude in her grandson Babar, which together became the integral feature of Babar's character and later the key to his success. Aisan-Daulat Begam shared the many hardships of her husband's life for thirty years. Several times she fell into the hands of the enemy, but always came back from their clutches safely.[8]

The death of Umar Shaikh Mirza in 1494 A.D left Babar an insecure boy of about eleven years old. He found himself surrounded by enemies from his own family, who were keen on ousting him from his father's principality of Farghana. Right from that time, Aisan-Daulat Begam was constantly by her grandson's side, guiding him and helping him overcome many a political crisis. In her hands lay the real administrative power and control of the state affairs and Babar always took her advice in these matters. Old officers were reshuffled and new officers were put in charge of the administration of many areas like Andijan, Aush, Akhsi and Marghinan.[9]

Towards the end of 1494 A.D. Babar faced a political crisis when Hasan-i-Yaqub planned to dethrone Babar and raise his younger brother Jehangir Mirza to the throne.[10] Apart from the support of his father Yaqub, Hasan also had the support of some disaffected nobles like Muhammad Baqir Beg, Sultan Muhammad Duldai, etc.[11] But his plans were soon discovered and nobles loyal to Babar like Khwaja-i-Qazi, Qasim Quchin and Ali Dost Taghai hastened to meet Aisan-Daulat Begam to inform her about these developments.[12] Immediately Aisan-Daulat Begam took action against the conspirators. Babar was sent with some trusted people from the gate-house of the outer fort towards the citadel to seize Hasan-i-Yaqub and his supporters. On reaching the place they got to know that Hasan was out on a hawking excursion. Babar's men fell upon Hasan's supporters and made them captives. When Hasan learnt about this, he fled to Samarqand to get the help of

Sultan Mahmud Mirza. But, he changed his mind after reaching Kand-i-Badam, and decided to deliver a surprise attack on Akhsi and convert it into a base for a further attack on Andijan, where he could wait for the arrival of his ally Sultan Mahmud Mirza. Aisan-Daulat Begam got to know of this plan too and once again she took the necessary steps to deal with it. An army was sent to deal with Hasan-i-Yaqub. Hasan-i-Yaqub came forward to meet it, but in the dark of the night a chance arrow from one of his own soldiers killed him.[13] Thus, Babar was saved from the evil designs of Hasan-i-Yaqub, who had failed to understand the capabilities of Aisan-Daulat Begam, the lady who was the real power behind Babar.

Aisan-Daulat Begam continued to guide and support her grandson in his days as a wanderer. It was she who had related to him stories of the military exploits of Timur and Chengiz Khan, and these served as his preliminary lesson in the art of warfare.[14] About his grandmother Aisan-Daulat Begam, Babar in his own words say: "Few among women will have been my grandmother's equals for judgement and counsel; she was very wise and farsighted and most affairs of mine were carried through under her advice."[15]

Qutluq-Nigar Khanum

The second lady in Babar's life who also influenced him was his mother Qutluq-Nigar Khanum. She was the second daughter of Yunus Khan and Aisan-Daulat Begam.[16] Qutluq-Nigar Khanum was an educated lady and she too like her mother, was her son's constant companion in his day of difficulty when Babar was nothing but a homeless wanderer. Babar in his memoirs speaks of his mother accompanying him among great difficulties on several occasions and bearing all hardships for her son's sake.[17] In one place Babar even says that in his mother's service were 1500 to 2000 Mughals.[18] May be she had some sort of an army of her own as well. Qutluq-Nigar was with Babar even during his most difficult days of exile and great hardship due to the problem of Shaibani Khan.[19] Qutluq-Nigar Khanum proved to be a woman of great courage, patience and endurance. No wonder her son had in him the qualities and attributes that later made him the Emperor of Hindustan. Qutluq-Nigar Khanum could not see her son becoming the conqueror of Hindustan as she passed away in 1505 A.D.[20] About his mother Babar writes: "She was with me in most of my guerilla expeditions and throneless times."[21]

Matrimonial Alliances in Babar's Life

Matrimonial alliance played an important role in shaping the political career of Babar and we find three important instances when matrimonial alliances were concluded by Babar to strengthen his political position. Two of them were his own marriages, one with Maham Begam of the Shia sect, and the other with Bibi Mubarika of the Afghans. Another matrimonial alliance that Babar concluded even before these two marriages of his own, was between his elder sister Khanzada Begam and Shaibani Khan.

In May, 1501 A.D. Babar was badly defeated by Shaibeg Khan, also known as Shaibani Khan, at Sar-i-Pul. Within eight months Babar had to abandon Samarqand, and he purchased his freedom by giving his elder sister Khanzada in marriage with Shaibani Khan. Babar himself wrote that while he was leaving the town of Samarqand at midnight by Shaikh Zada's Gate, his elder sister Khanzada Begam fell into the hands of Shaibani Khan.[22] But Babar's daughter Gulbadan Begam in her *Humayun Nama* said that Shaibani Khan had asked for the hand of Babar's sister Khanzada Begam in return for peace between him and Babar.[23] Mirza Haider Doghlat too gives a similar version of the event in his *Tarikh-i-Rashidi*.[24] Through this alliance Babar thought that though he had to abandon Samarqand, this would eventually help him in his attempt to win back Farghana, his father's principality. But the future events did not turn out to be so. When Babar made attempts to get back Farghana with the help of his uncles Mahmud Khan and Ahmad Khan, it was Shaibani Khan who inflicted a crushing defeat on Babar and his allies in the battle of Archiyan in June 1503 A.D. After this incident, Babar thought of trying his fortune in the land beyond the Hindukush.[25] Khanzada Begam was later divorced by Shaibani Khan as he suspected her of having alliance with her brother Babar.

Khanzada Begam after a while was married to Sayyid Hadi and after his death in the battle of Merv, fell into the hands of the Persians. When they recognised her as Babar's sister, she was treated with great respect by Shah Ismail Safwi, who sent her back in 1511 A.D. with servants and property to her brother as a sign of goodwill and friendship.[26] She was thirty-eight years old then. Shah Ismail Beg wanted Babar's help in crushing the Uzbegs. On the other hand, Babar too was waiting for his friendship as he wanted the Shah's assistance to enable him to recover his ancestral dominions.[27] Thus, Khanzada Begam in this case acted as an ambassador of goodwill and helped in strengthening diplomatic ties between Babar and the Shah of Persia. During the time of Humayun too, Khanzada Begam continued to play an important political role, mostly that of a diplomat settling disputes.

Babar married Maham Begam in 1506 A.D. She came from Herat and belonged to the Shia sect, and was related to Sultan Husain Baiqara.[28] This marriage alliance did not have any political motive behind it but it helped Babar a lot in his political career. This marriage helped Babar to get the active support of the Shias of that time. Maham Begam stood by her husband's side during his difficult days and travelled with him to Badakshan and Transoxiana.[29] She was Babar's chief wife and the mother of Humayun, the next Mughal emperor in India.

The matrimonial alliance that Babar concluded with a political motive was when on January 30th, 1519 A.D. (Muharram 28th, 925 H),[30] he married Bibi Mubarika, an Afghan. She was the daughter of Shah Mansur Yusufzai,[31] the head of the Yusufzai tribe of Afghanistan. The reason for this marriage alliance in Babar's own words, was to establish friendly relations with the Yusufzai tribe,[32] a very troublesome Afghan tribe. With their help Babar strengthened his position in Afghanistan.[33] Bibi Mubarika was one of the most loved wives of Babar. But she bore him no children. Gulbadan Begam in her accounts lovingly refers to her as the Afghani aghacha. One of the brothers of Bibi Mubarika, Mir Jamal, accompanied Babar to Hindustan in 1525 A.D. and was in high posts under Humayun and Akbar. Bibi Mubarika died in Akbar's reign.

Women's Intervention in Politics During Babar's Time

Apart from the political effects of the above mentioned matrimonial alliances, we also find a few instances during Babar's time when Mughal women intervened in politics to seek pardon for their dear ones. Babar in his memoirs speak of the time when his younger brother Jehangir Mirza plotted against him and joined hands with Tambal. Babar and his men fought and triumphed against them. Then Babar's paternal grandmother Shah Sultan Begam arrived in Babar's camp from Andijan in order to seek pardon for Jehangir Mirza if he had been captured.[34]

At another time Babar had faced the rebellion of his relatives Mirza Khan and Mirza Muhammad Husain Gurkhan, who were holding Kabul. Mirza Muhammad Husain Gurkhan was married to Khub-Nigar, own sister of Babar's mother Qutluq-Nigar Khanum. Mirza Khan was the son of another of Babar's maternal aunts. Babar crushed their rebellion. Out of fear Mirza Khan hid in his mother's house and Mirza Muhammad Husain hid in his wife's house. Babar, in the end, forgave them their offences because of the intervention of his aunts.[35] Babar had great respect for his aunts and for their sake he forgave even such great offenders.

Thus, the women during Babar's time were quite active politically. Many of the royal Mughal ladies of Babar's time, either directly or indirectly, played important roles in political events. Moreover, these royal women along with Babar remain the link between Central Asia and India. They also foreshadow the multifarious roles the future royal Mughal ladies were to play.

Mughal Women During Humayun's Time

There weren't too many royal ladies connected to Humayun, who played an important part in politics of his time. Even then, the political roles played by his wife Hamida Banu Begam, and his aunt Khanzada Begam is worth mentioning.

Hamida Banu Begam (Humayun's Wife)

Humayun married Hamida Banu Begam in September, 1541 A.D. (948 A.H.). She was the daughter of Mir Baba Dost (alias Mir Ali Akbar Jami), a Persian Shia and a friend of Mirza Hindal. Hindal treated Hamida as his sister and was opposed to his elder brother Humayun wanting to marry her.[36] At first Hamida Banu did not like the idea of marrying an emperor. She is known to have said: "I shall marry someone; but he will be a man whose collar my hand can touch and not one whose skirt it did not reach."[37] She finally agreed to marry Humayun and the marriage was solemnized. Hamida was fourteen years old then.

This marriage alliance proved to be politically beneficial for Humayun. From then onwards the Shia powers became his staunch supporters and stood by him in his days of adversity. When Humayun was in exile, Shah Tahmasp of Persia assisted him with a powerful army. Due to this help Humayun could defeat Askari and capture the fort of Qandhar. Humayun had to hand over Qandhar to the Shah of Persia, but after the Shah's death, recovered it. From there he went to Kabul and captured it. The occupation of these two places gave Humayun a stable ground in Afghanistan and made it easy for him when he got a chance to recover his lost Empire of India.[38]

After her marriage with Humayun, Hamida Banu Begam was constantly by her husband's side in his good times and more so in his days of adversity when he lost his empire and was in exile in Sind and Persia. During these difficult days, Hamida Banu gave birth to her son Akbar on 15th of October 1542 A.D. (949 A.H.),[39] at Umarkot, a place in Sind. In 1543 A.D. she undertook the most difficult and perilous journey from Sind in order to reach Qandhar and finally join her husband. She even left her infant son behind to be by her husband's side. Hamida Banu was with Humayun in Persia where she and her husband got a kind treatment from Shah Tahmasp of Persia. In 1544 A.D. she gave birth to a daughter in Camp at Sabz-Awar. She returned from Persia with the army given to Humayun by Shah Tahmasp. It was on November 15, 1545 A.D. that she saw her son Akbar once again. In 1548 A.D. Hamida Banu and her son Akbar accompanied Humayun on his way to Kabul. She did not accompany her husband when he set out for Hindustan in November, 1554 A.D. She finally rejoined her son Akbar in 1557 A.D. (964 A.H.) during the second year of his reign. From then onwards she remained with her son and continued to intervene in the contemporary politics from time to time. She passed away in the autumn of 1604 A.D. (19th Shahriyar, 1013 A.H.), sixty-three years after her wedding, and almost fifty years of widowhood, probably at the age of seventy-seven.[40] Hamida Banu's greatness certainly lay in the sacrifices she made for the sake of her husband and also in being the mother of Akbar, the Great, one of the greatest rulers in the history of India and also of the world.

Khanzada Begam (Humayun's Aunt)

Now we come to the role played in politics by Humayun's aunt, Babar's elder sister, Khanzada Begam. We have already seen how she in her own way played a role in the politics of Babar's time. After the death of Babar's principle wife Maham Begam in 1532-33 A.D., Khanzada Begam was given the title of Padshah Begam.[41] During Humayun's time she occupied the esteemed position of the first lady in the royal harem. Humayun had great regard for her and consulted her in many matters. The political role that Khanzada Begam played during Humayun's time was that of a goodwill ambassador and peace-maker, trying to settle disputes between Humayun and his brothers, Hindal, Kamran and Askari.

In 1541 A.D., Hindal occupied Qandhar at the instance of the governor of Qandhar, Qaracha Khan. Kamran marched against him to recover Qandhar. Humayun heard about this when he was moving towards Thatta. Humayun asked Khanzada Begam to go to Qandhar and tried to bring a reconciliation between his two brothers, as the Uzbegs and the Turkmans could bring an attack upon them any time, and under such circumstances, the best thing for them was to remain as friends. Khanzada Begam went to Qandhar, but she was not successful in her mission.[42]

Once again in 1545 A.D. Humayun on his way from Iran laid siege to the fort of Qandhar. Kamran, who fell into difficulty due to this sent Khanzada Begam to his brother Askari, who was then in charge of the fort, with the secret instruction of somehow holding out the fort till the arrival of Kamran there. But the forces of Humayun could not be resisted by Askari and the fort came to the hands of Humayun. Then Askari, as per the instructions of Kamran, sent Khanzada Begam to negotiate peace terms with Humayun. Khanzada Begam requested Humayun to treat Kamran and Askari mildly, but Humayun was too angry with them. This matter was not yet solved when Khanzada Begam died in September, 1545 A.D. after a serious illness.[43]

Though the efforts of Khanzada Begam were not very successful in settling political disputes between Humayun and his brothers, yet she tried her best in her own way to establish amity and peace where her own people of the illustrious Mughal family she belonged to, were concerned. And this she did till the very last day of her life.

Akbar's Ladies, Famous and Infamous

During Akbar's reign there were quite a few royal ladies who from time to time played important parts in the politics of the time. Akbar ascended the Mughal throne in 1556 A.D. at the tender age of fourteen. Right from the time of his accession, Akbar seems to have been surrounded by some politically ambitious women. Then, there were some women who helped Akbar politically through their marriage with him, especially his Rajput wives. Akbar's mother Hamida Banu Begam too continued to play her part in the politics of Akbar's time. But the foremost name in the list of politically active women that we come across during Akbar's time is that of his Turkish nurse, Maham Anaga.

Maham Anaga (Turkish Nurse)

Maham Anaga was the wife of Nadim Khan Kuka, and had two sons by the names of Baqi and Adham Kuka,[44] or Adham Khan, as he is known in history. Nadim Khan Kuka had served Humayun faithfully. Maham Anaga was the chief nurse of Akbar, in charge of looking after his needs since he was a small child. Maham cared for him like his own mother and Akbar too loved Maham deeply and trusted her a lot. Moreover, she was connected to his mother Hamida Banu Begam and also to Haji Begam, another of Humayun's widows.[45]

In 1556 A.D. Humayun passed away and Akbar became the next emperor of the Mughal dynasty in India. Bairam Khan, who had devotedly served under Babar and Humayun, and was the man behind Akbar's coming to the Mughal throne, became the regent of the boy-king and administered the empire on behalf of adolescent Akbar. In his initial days, Akbar depended a lot on Bairam Khan, whom he respected and trusted a lot. But gradually, as he began growing up, Akbar found the extra care that Bairam

Khan showered on him and the influence he exercised in the administration, a bit too suffocating. He soon grew tired of Bairam Khan's assertive ways. Akbar now wanted a life of freedom where he could act on his own and make his own decisions.

Maham Anaga from the very beginning was politically ambitious and power crazy. She wanted to exercise her power in the administration of the empire from behind Akbar, making him some sort of a puppet in her hands. Maham always detested Bairam Khan, a Shia, for his excessive influence over the administration. Akbar's discontentment over Bairam Khan's high handed ways gave an opportunity for Maham Anaga to rise politically. Now was her chance to take revenge against Bairam Khan and throw him out of power. This became not too difficult a task for Maham Anaga. Many of her close relatives already occupied responsible and important posts under Akbar. Her son Baqi Kuka was the governor of Aligarh. Adham Khan too occupied a high post. Abul Fazl writes:

> Maham Anaga in her great loyalty and wisdom took charge of affairs and made Shihabu-d-Din Ahmad Khan and Khwaja Jahan her tools, and exerted herself to soothe those who came, and to hearten everyone.[46]

Maham also, "devised the appointment of Bahadur Khan, the brother of 'Ali Quli Khan, to the lofty office of Vakil..."[47] Abul Fazl also says that "though Bahadur Khan had the name of Vakil, yet in reality the business was transacted by Maham Anaga."[48]

In 1560 A.D. Akbar went on a hunting expedition from Agra. Maham Anaga carried on negotiations with Shihabuddin, the governor of Delhi. She urged Akbar to visit his ailing mother in Delhi. Taking advantage of Akbar's visit to Delhi where Akbar was free from Bairam's domination, Maham Anaga along with Shihabuddin poisoned the Emperor's mind against Bairam Khan. They also told the Emperor about their intention to go on pilgrimage to Mecca as they were tired of Bairam's lofty ways. Akbar did not like the idea of parting with Maham. He was already tired of Bairam Khan and wanted to break away from his control. Now Akbar publicly announced that he had taken the administration into his own hands and sent orders to Bairam Khan to go on pilgrimages to Mecca. Meanwhile, Maham Anaga and Shihabuddin spread this news about Akbar and gave hopes of jagirs and titles to all who came to visit the Emperor. Bairam Khan sent some messengers to Akbar, but Maham encouraged Akbar to arrest them saying that they might have evil motives for meeting him. The gulf between Akbar and Bairam Khan widened. Bairam, disheartened and depressed left for Gujarat, from where he intended to proceed to Arabia. But he fell among evil counsellors who tempted him to revolt. Bairam Khan was aware of Maham's hand in his downfall. Akbar crushed this rebellion but pardoned him out of his old feelings for Bairam Khan, who got the permission to go to Mecca. But Bairam Khan was murdered on his way to Mecca in 1561 A.D.[49]

Now came the day of Maham Anaga when she became free to exercise her political influence in the administration. Though formally Akbar had the reins of the government in his hands, but it was Maham Anaga who became the de facto ruler. She was intelligent and devoted to Akbar. But her triumph did not last long as she became quite pushy in matters concerning her second son, Adham Khan. Maham Anaga wanted Akbar to install Adham Khan as the prime minister. But the post that Bairam Khan had once occupied was given to Munim Khan, who celebrated the event among great festivities. Maham Anaga, in order to compete with him, soon arranged the marriage feast of her elder son, Baqi Muhammad Khan with the sister of Adham Khan's wife.[50] The celebrations were just like that put up by Munim Khan. Munim Khan was aware of the rising power of Maham and tried to complain quite a few times against this female interference in administration, but Akbar paid no heed to it. He was too occupied with the pleasures of life.

Soon Akbar's attention fell on Malwa which was ruled by Baz Bahadur. Baz Bahadur was a pleasure loving person and spent most of his time in the pursuit of music and other pleasures of life. In 1561 A.D. Akbar sent Adham Khan to Malwa. Baz Bahadur was defeated and forced to fled from Sarangpur. Adham Khan took into his possession all the property of Baz Bahadur including the women of his seraglio, and the dancing and singing girls.[51] Among Baz Bahadur's women was the beautiful and talented Rupmati, whose praises had spread far and wide. Adham Khan's soldiers tortured Baz Bahadur's people. Many of the women of his harem tried to end up their lives, Rupmati too was seriously injured and she wished to die. Adham Khan falsely promised her that if she would take care of herself and become totally cured, then she would be sent back to Baz Bahadur.

Meanwhile, Adham Khan, full of vanity and conceit, disregarded the usual rules and did not send much of the booty to the Emperor, and in stead kept it for himself.[52] Akbar sent a warning to his nurse Anaga and himself hurried off to Sarangpur and took Adham Khan by surprise. She came the next day and advised Adham Khan to surrender the booty. The Emperor went back to the capital after settling all matters. But Adham Khan continued his wicked ways. As soon as Akbar went back, Adham Khan regained possession of Rupmati and another female slaves of Baz Bahadur. This news reached Akbar, who ordered these two women to be returned to the royal camp. But in stead of returning them, Maham had them murdered, so that they would not be able to tell the tale of their abduction to the Emperor.[53]

Akbar was very angry and horrified at the misdeeds of Adham Khan, but he did not directly say anything to Maham. Maham once again tried to bring Akbar under the spell of her flattering tongue. Now Akbar started taking indirect steps to turn away from the clutches of Maham. He posted Pir Muhammad as the governor of Malwa and called back Adham Khan. Instead of Munim Khan, the post of prime minister was now given to Shams-ud-Din Ahamad Ghaznavi, the husband of Jiji Anaga, who had nursed Akbar as an infant. But the power crazy and villainous Adham Khan did not spare Shams-ud-Din and killed him on May 16, 1562 A.D. The Emperor rushed to the spot, caught Adham Khan red handed and felled the assassin with a blow of his fist. Adham Khan was thrown over the battlements of the palace and killed by Akbar's order. The Emperor himself informed Maham about her son's death saying "Mama! we have just killed Adham." Maham was totally shattered by grief and anger. She died about forty days after this incident. Akbar showed his last respect for Maham Anaga by placing his shoulder under the nurse's bier.[54] With this Akbar freed himself from the clutches of the 'Petticoat Government' of his nurse Maham Anaga. Now Akbar was totally free to administer his Empire in whatever way he pleased.

Mahchuchak Begam (Humayun's Widow)

Another Mughal lady who gave a lot of trouble to Akbar in the initial days of his reign was Mahchuchak Begam, one of Humayun's widows, and a step-mother of Akbar. Humayun married Mahchuchak Begam in 1546 A.D.[55] Her son was Mirza Muhammad Hakim. In 1554 A.D. Humayun nominated this boy, then three years old, as the governor of Kabul under the charge of Munim Khan. In 1556 A.D. Akbar confirmed the appointment. Munim Khan came to the court in 1561 A.D. and his son Ghani took his place. Mahchuchak was politically ambitious. One fine day she threw Ghani out from Kabul and took upon herself the task of directly ruling Kabul.[56] Ghani Khan came back to India. When Akbar heard of all this, he sent Munim Khan with an army against Mahchuchak.[57] Mahchuchak met him and defeated Munim Khan at Jalalabad.[58] Mahchuchak ruled Kabul with the help of three advisers, two of whom were killed earlier. Now, even the third one was killed. In their place came Haidar Qasim Kohbur.

Around this time a certain Shah Abul Maali, who belonged to the family of the great Sayyids of Tirmiz and, who had escaped from the prison at Lahore, arrived in Kabul and approached Mahchuchak Begam for refuge. The Begam welcomed him, was generous to him and gave her daughter Fakhru-n-Nisa in marriage with him. Shah Abul Maali soon grew tired of the dominating and interfering ways of Mahchuchak Begam. He wanted Kabul for himself. So he killed the Begam and Haider Qasim in 1564 A.D.[59] Akbar's half-brother and Mahchuchak's son Mirza Hakim was luckily rescued by Mirza Sulaiman of Badakshan, who defeated Abul Maali and helped Mirza Hakim to keep his hold over Kabul. The activities of Mahchuchak Begam and her political ambitions certainly proved to be a headache for Akbar and troubled him like a sore thumb, just when he was trying to consolidate his father's inherited, lost and finally gained empire in India. But he was soon freed of Mahchuchak Begam and her ambitious ways.

Bakhtunnisa Begam (Akbar's Half-sister)

Another Mughal princess who played an important part in politics of Akbar's time was Bakhtunnisa Begam (or Fakhrunnisa Begam). She was the daughter of Humayun and Mahchuchak

Begam and born in 1550 A.D. (957 A.H.).[60] Therefore she was Akbar's half-sister. Bakhtunnisa Begam was married to Khwaja Hasan Naqshbandi of Badakshan.[61] Bakhtunnisa's brother Mirza Muhammad Hakim was the governor of Kabul. In 1581 A.D. he rebelled in Kabul. He advanced to Lahore invading Punjab on the way. Here he was checked by Man Singh, the governor of that province. Akbar declared war on Mirza Hakim and himself went to Kabul. Mirza Hakim ran away to the hills.[62] Akbar pardoned him. But the governorship of Kabul was now given to his sister Bakhtunnisa Begam.[63] Akbar also promised not to show any kindness to Mirza Hakim if he misbehaved in future.[64] After Akbar came away from Kabul, Mirza Hakim got back his old position, but all the official orders were issued in Bakhtunnisa's name.[65] Thus, Bakhtunnisa Begam helped Akbar to solve the problem of Kabul region.

Matrimonial Alliances of Akbar

Akbar was a farsighted man and he knew very well that to make his foothold strong in India, he had to take the help of the powerful Rajput rulers of that time. The Rajputs were chivalrous, dauntless and very good at war and the use of arms.Therefore, their help and support were sought by Akbar for the stability and expansion of his Empire. Akbar tried many measures to win over the support of the Rajput chiefs. The foremost among those was establishing matrimonial alliances with them. Apart from the diplomatic factor, these alliances reveal Akbar's broad minded nature and the feeling of universal tolerance that pervaded his heart. The Rajput princesses who came into Akbar's harem were not converted into Islam by force. Even if some of them took up Islam, they were all given freedom of faith and belief. In the royal harem they could practise any religion they pleased. The relatives of these Rajput ladies were given high posts in the Mughal administration. Hindu festivals were celebrated in the Mughal court side by side with Muslim festivities.

Hindu/Rajput Wives

The first Rajput lady whom Akbar married in 1562 A.D. was Jodha Bai, the eldest daughter of Raja Bihari Mal of Amber.[66]

Jodha Bai occupied a very important place in Akbar's harem. She had the good fortune of becoming the mother of Salim, the future emperor. Soon after her marriage with Akbar, her father, Raja Bihari Mal, was given the highest rank of the official aristocracy, as a mansabadar of 5000 horses.[67] Later, her brother, Raja Bhagwan Das was given the title of Amir-ul-Ulema and her nephew, Raja Man Singh, was appointed a mansabdar of the rank of 7000. This status during Akbar's time was enjoyed only by his sons Salim and Daniyal.

Akbar married the niece of Raja Maldeo of Jodhpur in November 1570 A.D.[68] He also married the daughter of Rawal Hari Rai of Jaisalmer.[69] The relatives of these Rajput princesses were also given high ranks like mansabs above 1000, but none of them could achieve the status that the house of Amber held under Akbar. Akbar's policy of concluding matrimonial alliances with Rajput princesses did not limit itself to his own marriages alone. They extended to his eldest son and successor Salim as well.

The first Hindu wife of Salim was Man Bai, daughter of Raja Bhagwan Das of Amber, who was then the governor of Punjab.[70] This marriage took place on February 13, 1585 A.D. and was conducted in both the Hindu and Muslim styles. This marriage brought great wealth to Akbar in the form of dowry. Man Bai was a very beautiful lady and her fidelity and sincere devotion to Salim won for her a special place in Salim's heart.[71] She was given the title of Shah Begam after the birth of her first son Khusrau.

The second Rajput wife of Prince Salim was Jodh Bai, better known as Jagat Gossain, daughter of Udai Singh or Mota Raja and Rani Manrang De of Gwalior. The marriage took place at Mota Raja's palace on January 11, 1586 A.D.[72] Salim, it seems, fell in love with Jagat Gossain at a function which he attended with his mother. Though his parents were a bit reluctant, yet this marriage was finalised by Hamida Banu. The dowry was fixed at seventy five lakh *tankas*.[73] Jagat Gossain is famous in history as the mother of prince Khurram who later became the next Mughal Emperor Shahjahan. This marriage also proved of benefit to both the sides. After the marriage, Udai Singh was given the title of 'Raja' and a mansab of 1000 'zat'.[74] The brothers and nephews of Jagat Gossain were also given royal favours. With the Mughal help, Udai Singh crushed the vassals of Marwar into submission and got much wealth in the form of tribute. Akbar too received the full co-operation of Udai Singh in his political endeavours. Udai Singh was appointed to manage the affairs of Lahore in 1592 A.D.[75]

The third Hindu wife of Salim was a Bikaneri princess, the sixteen year old daughter of Rai Singh of Bikaner. The marriage was performed at Fatehpur Sikri on May 28, 1586 A.D. The dowry was Rs. 2,50,000.[76] The fourth Rajput wife of Salim was the daughter of Rai Kalyan Mal of Jaisalmir whom Jehangir married in 1587 A.D. She had the title of Malika-i-Jahan.[77] In 1591 A.D. Salim married Rajkumari Karamsi (Karamnasi), the daughter of Raja Keshava Das Rathor. She was Salim's fifth Hindu wife.[78] The sixth Hindu wife of Jehangir was Kanwal Rani, daughter of the ruler of little Tibet. This marriage was a total diplomatic affair. The Tibetan chief offered his youngest daughter in marriage to Salim in order to avert Akbar's attack on Tibet.[79]

The seventh and eighth Hindu wives of Salim came into his harem after the death of Akbar and when Salim became the next Mughal Emperor Jehangir. In 1608 A.D. Jehangir married the daughter of Jagat Singh, who was the eldest son of Raja Man Singh of Amber. This marriage was the outcome of Jehangir's interest and initiative. He gave Jagat Singh 80,000 rupees as marriage present. From the port of Cambay, a European tapestry of unparalleled beauty was also sent to Jagat Singh. The marriage took place in the house of Mariam Zamani (Jodha Bai). Among the other articles of dowry, Man Singh, the bride's grandfather, gave sixty elephants.[80] The eighth and last Hindu wife of Jehangir was the daughter of Ram Chand Bundela, whom he married in 1609 A.D.[81]

These matrimonial alliances with the daughters of Hindu rulers, especially the Rajput chief went a long way in strengthening the roots of the Mughal Empire in India. The Mughal administration got efficient officials and generals. Many battles were successfully won and many important and fruitful measures were introduced in the Mughal administration. Moreover, the dowry that these princesses brought with them, enriched the royal treasuries. These Rajput and Hindu Chiefs also benefited through these marriages. With the Mughal help they could conquer new lands and stabilise their political positions. Their prestige and dignity were enhanced.

Part Played by Some Mughal Ladies During Salim's Revolt

During the reign of Akbar too we find instances when the royal ladies intervened to secure pardon against the wrong doer. Akbar did not believe in women interfering in his decisions. Once his mother Hamida Banu Begam and his wife Ruqaiya Begam (Turkish Sultana Begam), by their joint effort could not secure pardon for a Sunni Muslim who had murdered a Shia in Lahore purely out of religious fanatism.[82] But, when it came to be the case of his son Salim, Akbar seems to have softened when his royal ladies tried to secure his forgiveness for his son's misdeeds.

Towards the end of the 16th century, Prince Salim had not been granted audience with the Emperor for quite some time due to his habit of excessive drinking. In 1599 A.D. when Akbar was leaving for the Deccan, due to the pleadings of Mariam Makani Hamida Banu, Salim was allowed to make Qurnish to the Emperor.[83] Prince Salim's misconduct did not stop with that. He was soon tired of his father Akbar's long reign and revolted in 1601 A.D. and assumed the royal title at Allahabad. When peaceful measures failed to put good sense into Salim. Akbar decided to deal with him very sternly.

Salim was much loved by many of the senior ladies of the royal harem. They were scared of Akbar taking stern action against him. Akbar's mother Hamida Banu Begam and his aunt Gulbadan Begam,[84] Salim's mother Jodha Bai, and another wife of Akbar and a senior lady of the harem, Salima Sultan Begam, all pleaded with the Emperor to pardon their favourite child, Salim. Some other senior ladies like Bakhtunnisa Begam,[85] Akbar's half sister and the governor of Kabul, now staying with Akbar, was also concerned in this reconciliation effort of the royal ladies to make peace between Emperor Akbar and his son Salim. Salima Sultan Begam constantly reminded Akbar of his prayers and efforts to get a son. Akbar's heart softened a bit and he asked Salima Sultan Begam to go to Allahabad and persuade Salim to give up his rebellious ways and come back to Agra,[86] where Salim could ask for his father's forgiveness. Salima Sultan Begam was successful in bringing back Salim to Agra and everybody was jubilant at her success. Hamida Banu Begam travelled two stages to welcome her grandson. Salim was lodged in her apartments. He wanted to meet Akbar at an auspicious hour but Akbar wanted to see him sooner.[87] Akbar received his son cordially and asked him no question. No explanations were given either and Salim meet his family among smiles and tears. Salim presented to his father 1000 gold mohars and about 354 elephants. This amounted to a partial disarmament. The Emperor placed his turban on his son's head. This was in early 1603 A.D.[88]

Every thing went on fine till May 1603 A.D. Akbar now wanted Salim to undertake a military expedition in order to humble Rana Amar Singh, son of Maharana Pratap of Mewar. Rana Amar Singh was trying to occupy Mughal territories in Rajasthan. But Salim was suspicious of his father's motives. Under some pretext or the other, he refused to go on this expedition. The senior ladies of the Mughal harem once again pleaded with the emperor to keep his son at the Court. Salim wanted to go back to Allahabad and Akbar, after much thought let him do so. As soon as Salim reached Allahabad, he went back to his evil ways and there came into existence a situation of reign of terror.

Akbar was distressed at his son's brutalities. He wanted to save his Empire and save his son for the Empire's future. Peaceful persuasion failed. Then Akbar left Agra with a huge army, but on the way got the news of his mother Hamida Banu's serious illness. At first Akbar could not believe it as he thought it to be put up by Hamida Banu to stop him as she loved Salim very much. To confirm it Akbar sent Prince Khurram and Hakim Ali to Agra. Khurram came back and clarified the news of Hamida Banu's illness and Akbar immediately rushed back to Agra just in time. Hamida Banu passed away soon, on 29th August, 1604 A.D.[89]

Salim was informed of his grandmother's death. He came back to Agra and Akbar accepted him and his gifts. But at the same time he wanted to teach him a lesson for his misdeeds. So Salim was imprisoned in the female apartments.[90] Opium and alcohol were stopped for him. His sisters pleaded with Akbar for his release. Akbar freed Salim after ten days and he came to live in his own palace.[91]

With this ended Salim's rebellion. This rebellion did not bring success for Salim because it could not fructify Salim's motives in overthrowing Akbar. But the rebellion of Salim did not bring success to Akbar either, who tried to crush it by all means. Every time, when he thought of dealing strictly with his rebel son, the senior ladies of the harem, his mother, sister, aunt and his wives and daughters were also more than prepared to compel him in not dealing with his son sternly. In fact, Salim owed his freedom and well-being to these special ladies of the Mughal harem. Without their intervention he could never have escaped his father's wrath.

Nur Jahan — The Light of Jehangir's World

The royal ladies of the Mughal harem like Salima Sultan Begam continued to interfere in politics even during Jehangir's time. Jehangir came to the Mughal throne in 1605 A.D. In 1606 A.D. Khusrau, the eldest son of Jehangir and his Rajput wife Man Bai, revolted his father, at the instigation of Mirza Aziz Koka, also known as Khan Azam, the son of Shamshuddin Atka. Jehangir as per the decision of his nobles thought of punishing Mirza Aziz Koka. But Salima Sultan Begam and some other leading ladies of the harem intervened in this matter and compelled Jehangir to pardon Mirza Aziz Koka. Once again Prince Khusrau revolted in 1613 A.D. and once again the royal ladies, i.e. the mothers and sisters of Jehangir compelled the Emperor to forgive Khusrau who was permitted audience with the Emperor.[92] That Khusrau was not spared by Prince Khurram and Nur Jahan is another story to be dealt with later on.

But the most prominent female personality of Jehangir's time and of the Mughal age as a whole was Nur Jahan Begam, the last wife of Emperor Jehangir. Nur Jahan originally named as Mehr-un-Nisa, was the daughter of a Persian noble, Ghiyas Beg, who came from Persia to Akbar's court in search of fortune. Ghiyas Beg and the other members of his family gradually came to occupy responsible posts in the Mughal administration. But it was from the time of Mehr-un-Nisa's marriage with Emperor Jehangir, and then onwards, that the family of Ghiyas Beg, titled Etimad-ud-Daula, saw the steady rise of their power and position.

Legend goes that, with Jehangir it was a case of love at first sight, when he as the young Prince Salim, saw Mehr-un-Nisa, the adolescent and unmarried daughter of Ghiyas Beg, for the first time in a garden. Mehr-un-Nisa's unparalleled beauty, innocent charm and youthfulness left Salim totally smitten. But Salim could not marry her then as Mehr-un-Nisa's marriage had been fixed by Ghiyas Beg with Emperor Akbar's consent, to Ali Quli Istalju, another upcoming Persian soldier at the Mughal Court, who later became the Jagirdar of Burdwan in Bengal.

After the accidental death of Ali Quli Sher Afghan, Mehr-un-Nisa returned to Agra and took up a job in the royal harem at the household of Akbar's widow Ruqaiya Begam. Jehangir once again got to see Mehr-un-Nisa during the Nauroz celebrations in 1611 A.D. The old flame is said to have ignited in Jehangir's heart and he left no stones unturned to get Mehr-un-Nisa this time. Mehr-un-Nisa seems to have kept the condition that she was to become his chief queen after the marriage. This is certainly the first great achievement in Mehr-un-Nisa's life. During the Mughal times, women were supposed to have been aged at thirty. But at the age of thirty four and already a mother of a child, Mehr-un-Nisa's beauty and charm was such that it could captivate the heart of Emperor Jehangir, who not only made her his Empress but gradually let her rule his heart as well as his empire. After the marriage, Mehr-un-Nisa was given the title of Nur Mahal (Light of the Palace), then Nur Jahan (Light of the World) and later that of Padshah Begam (the first lady of the realm) in 1613 A.D.

Nur Jahan Begam was a lady of varied interests and many talents. In her days there was hardly any field where she did not take an active interest. But, she was not contented with her contributions towards the artistic field alone, and her activities extended towards the political field as well. Nur Jahan Begam was a learned, talented, artistic, courageous, philanthropic and extremely beautiful woman. But more than anything else, she was politically ambitious and power crazy to a very great extent.

Nur Jahan's rise to power is generally divided into two periods of unequal length. The first was from 1611 A.D. to 1622 A.D. and the second was 1622 A.D. to1627 A.D. During the first period, Jehangir was active and so was Nur Jahan's *junta* which comprised of herself, her father Etimad-ud-Daula, brother Asaf

Khan and step-son Prince Khurram. The second period saw the break-up of the *junta*, the death of Etimad-ud-Daula and his wife Asmat Banu, the illness of Jehangir and his deteriorating health and Asaf Khan joining hands with his son-in-law Prince Khurram.

Nur Jahan's influence over Jehangir was so great that she became the 'de facto' ruler of the Empire and the Emperor was only too happy to leave the tedious job of running the Empire in her capable hands. Several foreign travellers who visited India during the Mughal times, speak of Nur Jahan's influence in the royal harem and in the political matters of Jehangir's times. Says Pietro Della Valle: "He (Jehangir) hath one wife, or Queen, whom he esteems and favours above all other women; and his whole empire is governed at this day by her counsel".[94] Pietro Della Valle further remarks:

> ...she commands and governs at this day in the King's Haram with supreme authority; having cunningly removed out of the Haram, either by marriage, or other handsome wages, all the other women who might give her any jealousy; and having also in the Court made many alterations by deposing, and displacing almost all the old Captains, and Officers, and by advancing to dignities other new ones of her own creatures and particularly those of her blood and alliance.[95]

Francisco Pelsaert also gives a similar opinion when he says that:

> ...Jehangir, disregarding his own person and position, has surrendered himself to a crafty wife of humble lineage, as the result either of her arts or of her persuasive tongue. She has taken and still continues increasingly to take, such advantage of this opportunity, that she had gradually enriched herself with superabundant treasures, and has secured a more than royal position. Her former and present supporters have been well rewarded, so that now most of the men who are near the king owe their promotion to her...[96]

In the later times Bernier and Manucci too spoke of Nur Jahan's power and political activities. Sir Thomas Roe, the English ambassador, who visited the Mughal Court during Jehangir's time spoke elaborately of Nur Jahan's power and the influence that she and her family members exercised in the politics and administration of that time. So did the other Englishmen like William Hawkins and Edward Terry.Terry in his accounts said about Nur Jahan: "she hath much advanced her friends, before mean, and in manner commands the commander of that empire by engrossing his affection."[97] Jehangir, who himself was charmed by Nur Jahan Begam, writes in his memoirs about her love for him. He says about her: "I did not think anyone was fonder of me."[98]

Thus, from the time Jehangir fell in love with her, Nur Jahan Begam had the biggest advantage of having the unshaken love and confidence of the Emperor, who knew or saw nothing beyond her. This situation was very intelligently exploited by the ambitious Nur Jahan. It became quite easy for her to climb the shoulders of her Emperor husband and reach the top of the administrative network from where she tried to control all that happened in the Empire. Dr. Pant even says that "...his (Jahangir's) reign after 1611 A.D. was the reign of his consort Nur Jahan..."[99]

Soon after her marriage with Emperor Jehangir, the family members of Nur Jahan Begam, who had previously fallen out of favour with Jehangir, now regained a position of respect, power and influence. Apart from keeping the condition of becoming Jehangir's chief queen, Nur Jahan, it seems, kept two other marriage conditions—first, "that her father should have the post of Etmadoulet, or first minister," and second, "that her brothers, as well as her other relations, should fill the first places at Court."[100] If these were the marriage conditions, then Jehangir certainly kept his words. Nur Jahan's father Ghiyas Beg, now Etimad-ud-Daula became the Prime Minister and given a rank of commander of 5000 horses.[101] The brothers of Nur Jahan too came to occupy high posts in the administration, especially Abul Hassan, now styled Itiqad Khan and three years later as Asaf Khan, who in 1611 A.D. was appointed master of the household.[102]

All these things were not enough to satisfy Nur Jahan. She continued to adopt various means to strengthen her position politically. The first and the most important marriage that took place between Etimad-ud-Daula's family and the royal Mughal family was that between Nur Jahan's niece and Asaf Khan's daughter Arjumand Banu Begam with Prince Khurram, son of Emperor Jehangir. The marriage took place on 1612 A.D. This marriage certainly strengthened the political position of Nur Jahan's family, but Nur Jahan could not have been the real force behind this marriage. It is said that Prince Khurram fell in love with Arjumand Banu and their betrothal had taken place some five years and three months before the wedding took place, i.e. sometime in 1607 A.D.[103] This marriage, though contributed in strengthening Nur Jahan's political position, could not have given her much happiness as some sources say that she was keen on getting her daughter Ladli Begam married to Prince Khurram, as he was the most eligible heir to Jehangir's throne. But Khurram's love for Arjumand Banu was too great for him to accept Nur Jahan's proposal.[104]

Nur Jahan then aimed at getting her daughter married to Jehangir's eldest son, Prince Khusrau. This rebellious son of Jehangir was the most popular with all classes of people, the ladies of the royal harem and the older nobility as the heir to the Mughal throne. Even Emperor Akbar is said to have had Prince Khusrau in mind as the heir to his throne. Soon after his coming to the throne, Jehangir in 1606 A.D. had to face the rebellion of his eldest son Khusrau. From that time onwards Khusrau was kept in imprisonment. Nur Jahan thought that Prince Khusrau might succeed Jehangir as the next emperor. So she tried to get her daughter married to him in order to strengthen her own position. She told Khusrau that if he agreed to marry her daughter Ladli Begam, then he would be freed from imprisonment and the miserable life he then led.[105] Khusrau's imprisonment was shared by his very devoted wife who left the life of luxury in the palace, to share her husband's difficult times. Khusrau loved his wife very much and could not think of taking another wife. So he refused Nur Jahan's offer which came to him quite a number of times.[106] Even his wife pressed him to accept it as it would free him. But Khusrau was adamant and he preferred his life of imprisonment to Nur Jahan's proposal. Della Valle says that — "For these things, Sultan Chosrou remained always much in the hatred of Nurmahal..."[107] No wonder, Khusrau always remained in captivity. Under Nur Jahan's influence, Khusrau was forbidden in 1614 A.D. to come to Court and pay his respect to the Emperor.[108] In 1616 A.D. Khusrau was handed over to Asaf Khan for safe-keeping. Now Khusrau was totally under the grip of Nur Jahan's *junta*. Roe gives a detailed description of the Khusrau problem and says that Nur Jahan used all methods of feminine persuasion to convince Jehangir that Khusrau could be still dangerous. When this failed, Etimad-ud-Daula, Asaf Khan and Shahjahan persuaded the King on the same grounds.[109] Finally Khusrau fell in Asaf Khan's hand. Effort continued to make peace between Khusrau and the *junta*. In 1619 A.D. freedom came at last for Khusrau. This was probably a publicity stunt on the part of the *junta*. But Khusrau did not live long after this and passed away in 1621 A.D. Even after his release, Khusrau was not spared from the scheming hands of the junta members who still feared him, and it seems his death finally came from slow poisoning. Says Roe:

> The prince Sultan Coronne (Khurram), Normahall the deare queene, aunt to his wife, Asaph Chan his father-in-law, brother to the Queene, and Etiman Dowlett, father of them both, being they that now govern all and dare attempt anything, resolved it was not possible for them to stand if the Prince Sultan Coronne lived, whom the nobilitye loved ... therefore practised how to bring him into their power, that poyson might end him.[110]

Having failed to get Khusrau on her side and to marry off her daughter to him, Nur Jahan finally settled with Shahriyar, the youngest surviving son of Jehangir. The other prince Parvez was a drunkard and lacked ambition and strength of mind. Shahriyar too was not a right choice as future heir to the Mughal throne. He had a feeble mind and lacked all qualities that made an emperor. But Nur Jahan settled for him as the husband of her daughter and took up the cause of pushing his candidature to the throne. Prince Shahriyar was betrothed to Ladli Begam in December, 1620 A.D. and the marriage was celebrated in April next year, amidst grandeur and pomp.[111] Shahriyar was raised to the rank of 8000 zat 4000 sawar.

Quite early in her political career, Nur Jahan Begam realised that to exercise her full control over the affairs of the empire, she needed to have able and trustworthy people around her on whom she could rely and who could form some sort of a structure that would channelise power naturally and immediately to her. Thus, the *junta* or the faction that grew around her was the result of the needs and circumstances that surrounded her. The members of this junta apart from Nur Jahan, happened to be her father Etimad-ud-Daula, her brother Asaf Khan and Prince Khurram, Asaf Khan's son-in-law and the junta's candidate as the heir to the Mughal throne. The other sons of Jehangir, as has been already discussed, were less capable than the ambitious and iron-willed Khurram, who had all the capabilities of becoming an emperor. The eldest, prince Khusrau was in imprisonment and constantly thought of as a threat by the junta members. The second, Prince Parvez was a dull and incompetent man heavily into drinking. The fourth son of Jehangir, Prince Shahriyar too lacked a strong mind and was too young at the time of the junta's rise. Therefore, Jehangir's third son, Prince Khurram, who was a man of ability, intelligence, strong will power and self-control, was the natural choice of the junta which could build up their power structure around him.

Another important man of Nur Jahan's junta was her father Etimad-ud-Daula. He was the man on whom Nur Jahan chiefly relied. He was the Prime Minister of the empire and always looked into the interests of his daughter. Beni Prasad calls him "the strongest pillar of the Nur Jahan ascendancy."[112] Next in the line came Nur Jahan's brother, Asaf Khan. He was an educated, intelligent, talented and level-headed man and an efficient administrator. He was fond of grandeur and magnificence, but was courteous and amiable in social dealings. In 1611 A.D. Asaf Khan was appointed master of the household. His importance at the royal Court increased greatly when in 1612 A.D. his daughter Arjumand Banu Begam was married to the twenty years old Prince Khurram, the third son of emperor Jehangir.

Thus came into existence the faction popularly known as Nur Jahan's junta. The real power did not lie in Emperor Jehangir's hands, but in the hands of his beautiful queen Nur Jahan and her junta. Pelsaert observed that, "he (Jehangir) is king in name only while she (Nur Jahan) and her brother Asaf Khan hold the kingdom firmly in their hands."[113] About Nur Jahan's role in the junta, Roe says that, "... Normahall fullfill(s) the observation that in all actions of consequence in a court, especially in a faction, a woman is not only always an ingredient, but commonly a principal drugg and of most vertue; and shee showes that they are not incapable of conducting business, nor herself voyd of wit and subtiltye."[114]

Nur Jahan Begam certainly lived upto Roe's description. Says Dow:

> Her abilities were uncommon, for she rendered herself absolute, in a government in which women are thought incapable of bearing any part. Their power, it is true, is sometimes exerted in the harem; but, like the virtues of the magnet, it is silent and unperceived. Noor-Jehan stood forth in public; she broke through all restraint and custom, and acquired power by her own address, more than by the weakness of Jehangir.[115]

Nur Jahan had endless power in her hands. Nothing happened in the empire without her consent. Jehangir had no objection to her decisions. Pelsaert talks of a strange method adopted by the empress to get her ways with Jehangir. According to him Nur Jahan used to get Jehangir's permission for all things when the emperor used to retire to his bed chamber at night, quite in a drunken state. At this time, Nur Jahan, who knew very well how to manage Jehangir, got her work done by getting the emperor's permission wherever it was needed.[116] We cannot say how far this particular story is true, but the truth is that Jehangir hardly ever refused anything that Nur Jahan wished for and therefore the empress had almost absolute powers in her hands. The Emperor's orders or grants of appointments and removals had no value until and unless they were approved by Nur Jahan.[117] If anyone came with a plea or an appeal to the Emperor, the case was referred to Asaf Khan who in turn took Nur Jahan's opinions regarding the particular matter.[118] If anyone, therefore, was a recipient of royal favour or a high appointment, he had the Empress to thank for and not the Emperor. All the chief offices in the administration went to her favourites. Elder statesmen and nobles like Mirza Aziz Koka reproached Jehangir for placing so much power and authority in Nur Jahan's hands.[119]

Nur Jahan's influence became so great that coins were struck in her name. This was something never known before in Muhammaden history. These coins were made of gold and bore the twelve signs of the Zodiac, one sign on each coin.[120] Opinions differ as to whether these coins were used in daily transactions or not. Pelsaert says they were not,[121] but to Manucci, they were "Current money".[122] According to Dr. Pant, "the other prerogative of having prayers read in her name was denied to her on the ground of her sex..."[123] Nur Jahan is also known to have sat for the 'jharokha darshan'[124] or conducting administrative business with the common people and hearing their pleas from a high window of the palace. The custom of `jharokha darshan' was an exclusive duty of the Emperor, but Nur Jahan replaced Jehangir even in this. Even `Farmans' were occasionally issued with her name and under her initiative. Many of these *farmans* deal with grants of land, etc., made by Begam Nur Jahan to various people, and reveal the significant part she played in Jehangir's administration.[125] Some of these farmans are dated 1027 A.H./1617 A.D., 1027 A.H./1618 A.D., 1028 A.H./1618 A.D., etc.[126] Usually these farmans have Nur Jahan Begam's name mentioned as "Nawab Mahd Uliya" or "Mahd Uliya".[127]

Along with her control over the administration, Nur Jahan also accumulated and enriched herself with a lot of wealth[128] and at the same time spent it lavishly not only on herself but also to increase the grandeur of the Empire as well. It was during her time that the widespread custom of 'nazrs' or offerings to the emperor and high officials had started.[129] Anybody who wished to gain favours with Nur Jahan and her close associates had to present themselves with costly gifts and valuable presents. Roe tells about many such occasions when he gave costly and rare presents to Jehangir, Nur Jahan, Shahjahan, Etimad-ud-Daula and Asaf Khan to gain their favours and get his work done.[130] Nur Jahan owned vast jagirs too. Beni Prasad writes that "If she could have been admitted to the order of *mansabdars*, her jagirs would have entitled her to the rank of 30,000."[131]

All these things are proof enough to show the power and might of Nur Jahan Begam. But, it must also be mentioned that Nur Jahan Begam was not just power crazy. She was an able and efficient administrator as well. She was a fine judge of men and matters and had a practical approach to all things. Never did she leave any matter to its periphery, but went right to its core to find out its real nature. Even her enemies admitted that difficulties simply melted at her touch. She was wise, tactful, bold and dauntless even at the face of grave adversities. The strict rules of *purdah* could not keep her behind the veils. To go with these qualities of the head and mind she had great qualities of the heart too. Much of her personal funds was used in charity towards helping widows, orphans and in getting poor girls married. Any poor and needy person asking for her help and charity were seldom or never returned unsatisfied. Moreover, she was a lady of taste, refinement and learning. All these things added up to make Nur Jahan Begam a worthy and capable ruler and administrator, and to criticise her alone for her unbound ambition and power loving nature will be wrong and biased on our part. Ambition and an eye for power to rise to the top are qualities that surely take one to the zenith in any field. But the fault with Nur Jahan was that these traits were present in her to such a great extent that they came to be considered the negative shades of her character. The famous quote goes — "Power corrupts and absolute power corrupts absolutely". That is what that exactly happened in Nur Jahan's case, and that which led to her downfall, and the chaos and confusion that marked Jehangir's reign from 1622 to 1627 A.D. and some time after that, till Shahjahan became the next Mughal emperor and Nur Jahan had to bring herself always from the life of active politics and settle down in Lahore for a life of self-imposed obscurity.

It has already been discussed how Nur Jahan tried her best to get her daughter married to Prince Khurram and then to Prince Khusrau, and having failed in both the cases, settled for the less capable Prince Shahrayar. Despite the differences between Nur Jahan and Khurram regarding this marriage proposal and finally Khurram's setting for his beloved Arjumand Banu Begam as his wife in 1612 A.D., relationship between Nur Jahan and Khurram were quite amicable for sometime. Over the years Khurram proved himself to be a fine general. He led successful expeditions in 1613 A.D. against Rajputana[132] and in 1616-17 A.D. in the Deccan. By then he already had the title of 'Shah'. Nur Jahan arranged a grand feast to celebrate his victory. Khurram was raised to the rank of 30,000 Zat and Sawar.[133] But the problematic Malik Amber once again tried to raise his head in the Deccan. Nur Jahan successfully solved the crisis and Malik Amber was forced to pay a sum of 50 lacs.[134] Khurram was also successful in his campaign against Kangra.

These military victories of Shahjahan were initially welcomed by Nur Jahan. But, she soon realised that Shahjahan was too proud and ambitious to let her continue with her interference in politics when he became the next Emperor. Nur Jahan wanted the position of authority desperately. She now used the youngest son of Jehangir, Prince Shahryar as a pawn for the fulfilment of her unending ambitions. She got her daughter married to him and Shahryar now was raised to very high rank. Nur Jahan's aim was to push Shahryar's candidature to the Mughal throne against that of Khurram. She was sure that if Shahryar came to the throne, she would once again be the 'de facto' ruler of the empire.

At this time came up the Central Asian crisis. The ruler of Persia, Shah Abbas, annexed Qandhar in 1622 A.D. Nur Jahan decided to send Khurram to drive out the Shah of Persia from Qandhar. Khurram was no fool and he knew that probably this was the chance that Nur Jahan wanted when she could force Jehangir to declare Shahryar as the heir to the throne. Khurram refused to go. He was also aware that the Qandhar expedition which was an almost hopeless affair, might ruin his image and prestige if he was unsuccessful.[135] This was the period of the break-up of the famous Nur Jahan junta. Etimad-ud-Daula and his wife Asmat Banu were already dead. Asaf Khan was almost turning to Khurram's side, though not yet directly. Jahangir's health was deteriorating day by day, Jehangir, it seems, was slowly turning towards his son Parvez, who according to Lane Poole, "could drink level with himself."[136] Nur Jahan was desperately hoping for power to remain in her hands, and therefore was openly supportive of Shahryar. These circumstances finally forced Shahjahan to revolt against his father who was totally under the control of his Persian wife.

Khurram started with seizing some of the jagirs of Nur Jahan and Shahryar. Jehangir sent him a *farman* directing him to mend his ways. But Khurram refused to obey him and decided to march to

Agra. Jehangir decided to march against him to punish this son of his whom he preferred to call a 'wretch' (*bidaulat*). Khurram reached Fatehpur. He was assisted by Khan-Khanan Mirza Abdur Rahim Khan, son of Bairam Khan and many other amirs who held high office in Gujarat and the Deccan. Nur Jahan's superb war strategy inflicted defeat on Khurram (Shahjahan) and drove his men to the south of Delhi in 1623 A.D. Khurram fled away to Malwa and then to the Deccan and tried to get the help of Malik Amber, but failed. From the Deccan, Khurram came to Bengal and Bihar where he captured the forts of Rohtas and Asirgarh in 1624 A.D. Nur Jahan sent an army led by Mahabat Khan to deal with Khurram. Then Khurram ran away to the Deccan in 1625 A.D. when he once again tried to form an alliance with Ahmadnagar, as Mahabat Khan sided with Bijapur. Mahabat Khan and Price Parvez were sent to the Deccan against him. They were successful. By this time, Khurram tired and losing hope, decided to surrender to his father and wrote a letter asking for his father's pardon. Jehangir, at Nur Jahan's insistence replied in March, 1626 A.D. that Khurram was to surrender the forts of Rohtas and Asirgarh and also sent his two sons, Dara and Aurangzeb as hostages to the royal court at Lahore. These terms and conditions had to be accepted by Khurram as they secured royal pardon for him. Afterwards, he with his wife and his other children stayed in Nasik for some time to normalise the situation.[137] Thus Khurram's rebellion ended after a futile period of three years when there was much bloodshed and wastage of men and money. The credit of crushing Khurram's rebellion was Nur Jahan's, though in many ways she was herself responsible for the prevailing discontentment in the Empire.

Soon after Khurram's rebellion, Nur Jahan faced another political crisis in the form of Mahabat Khan's rebellion, and this too was firmly dealt with by her. Mahabat Khan was an ambitious, able and reputed commander of the army. He was sent by Nur Jahan Begam to suppress Khurram's rebellion in the Deccan and he did so quite successfully in 1625 A.D. After this, while he was encamping near Sarangpur, Imperial orders reached him informing him that he was transferred to Bengal.[138] Nur Jahan probably in her heart of hearts feared Mahabat Khan who had earlier expressed his discontentment towards on all powerful queen.[139] Khan-i-Jahan

Lodi succeeded Mahabat Khan as Vakil to Parvez.[140] Prince Parvez refused to part with Mahabat Khan and the imperial messenger returned and conveyed this to Jehangir and Nur Jahan. A second farman with a stricter tone was sent to Prince Parvez, who this time agreed to the imperial command.[141] Next, Mahabat Khan was ordered to send to the Court the elephants he was alleged to have obtained in Bengal and Bihar at the time of Khurram's rebellion. Mahabat Khan was also required to furnish the accounts of the large sums forfeited to the state for the dismissal of disloyal jagirdars.[142] To top it all, Mahabat Khan was ordered to present himself before the royal court as he was charged with breach of royal conduct and etiquette as he had betrothed and got his daughter married without the permission of the Emperor. Mahabat Khan was furious with Nur Jahan for this harsh treatment given to him. He was convinced that Nur Jahan was behind all this. He was deeply humiliated and extremely angry at the way he was ruined.

Mahabat Khan's Revolt

All these things led to Mahabat Khan's revolt and he marched towards the Imperial Court with about 500 Rajput soldiers. Meanwhile, Jehangir had set out for Kabul in March, 1626 A.D. He was encamped on the bank of river Jhelum, when Mahabat Khan and his army approached the vicinity of the royal camp.[143] For Mahabat Khan this served as an opportunity to avenge his humiliation. He took Jehangir by surprise and through proper planning and strategy, imprisoned him.[144] Mahabat Khan here made a mistake in neglecting to take Nur Jahan too into custody. When he came back to the royal camp, he found that Nur Jahan had already cleverly managed to escape to the other side of the river in disguise. Nur Jahan alongwith Asaf Khan and some other nobles gathered an army to deal with Mahabat Khan.[145] Jehangir sent repeated messages to her asking her not to take up arms against such a powerful man.[146] But Nur Jahan did not pay heed to his advice. The bridge connecting the opposite river banks had been destroyed by Mahabat Khan. In spite of that, Nur Jahan boldly plunged into the river with her men and animals to fight Mahabat Khan. The operation was personally supervised by Nur Jahan, who, it is said, led the army herself. Along with her was her infant grand-daughter, the daughter of Shahryar, who was struck by an arrow in the arm. Nur Jahan too was injured. Her men failed badly against Mahabat Khan's army. Many men even deserted the imperialist forces and joined Mahabat Khan.[147] Nur Jahan exhibited great courage in dealing with such a grave crisis. But fate was not on her side.

It now became very hard for Nur Jahan to bear the separation of her husband whom she loved very much. She did not give up the idea of freeing her husband. But now she tried a different method which would need the power of her mind and not her might. She surrendered herself to Mahabat Khan and joined her husband in captivity. Gradually things started becoming favourable to Nur Jahan. Mahabat Khan became unpopular with many of the nobles who had come over to his side previously. His Rajput soldiers were also discontented. Nur Jahan took full advantage of these developments. Very carefully and intelligently, and without arousing the suspicion of Mahabat Khan, Nur Jahan won over many of the nobles to her side. After some time, Jehangir as per Nur Jahan's advice, tried his best to convince Mahabat Khan that he felt completely satisfied with Mahabat Khan's arrangements which had freed him from Nur Jahan's clutches. He also informed Mahabat Khan of Nur Jahan's secret arrangements to kill him by poisoning him through Abu Talib's wife, the grand daughter of the Khan-i-Khanan.[148] Nur Jahan's plot worked well and Mahabat Khan failed to realise the fact that Jehangir was siding with Nur Jahan. He decreased the Rajput guards that he had earlier placed around Jehangir. Mutamid Khan says that Jehangir, "... set Mahabat's heart at rest, and removed that doubt and suspicion with which Mahabat Khan had at first regarded him."[149]

Mahabat Khan along with the imprisoned Emperor and Empress and the rest of the Imperial cortege left Kabul for Lahore on Monday, the 1st Shahryar, 1626 A.D. In the meantime Nur Jahan continued in her efforts and got her eunuch Hushiyar Khan to collect about 200 men in Lahore and proceed towards the Imperial camp. A few miles away from Rohtas, Jehangir reviewed the troops collected by Nur Jahan and Mahabat Khan was informed about it. Now he know that his game and power possession of hundred days was over.[150] So Mahabat Khan having no other way, fled. He took along with him Asaf Khan, his son Abu Talib, and the sons of Daniyal, Tahmuras, Hoshang and Lashkari.[151] A regular Darbar was held at Rohtas. Mahabat Khan was sent an urgent mandate by Nur Jahan through Afzal Khan, commanding him to release Asaf Khan, his son and the sons of Daniyal immediately. It also said that if he failed to release Asaf Khan soon, an army would be sent after him. Mahabat Khan released the sons of Daniyal but kept back Asaf Khan and his son Abu Talib till he was reasonably safe. Nur Jahan again sent a letter of warning to Mahabat Khan. He released Asaf Khan after getting a promise of fidelity from him, but Abu Talib was still in his custody, who was later released.

The Imperial Court arrived at Lahore. Nur Jahan set about reorganising the administration. Asaf Khan became the Vakil.[152] Other important posts were given by her to people she trusted. Mahabat Khan in the meantime joined hands with Shahjahan and this made Nur Jahan afraid. She appointed Khan Jahan as the Commander-in-Chief of the Imperial army and sent him to suppress them. At this juncture Jehangir died in October, 1627 AD. near Rajauri, on his return journey from Kashmir to Lahore. This was the full stop to Nur Jahan's political ambition and career. Though she tried to place Shahryar on the throne as the next Emperor, Asaf Khan who now openly supported his son-in-law Shahjahan, defeated and captured Shahryar. Nur Jahan was also kept in confinement. Shahjahan finally reached Agra, and the Khutba was read in his name on January 19, 1628 A.D. by Asaf Khan. Shahjahan ascended the Mughal throne on Monday, February 10, 1628 A.D.

After this, Nur Jahan passed the last years of her life in Lahore, where she led a life of simplicity and obscurity. Ladli Begam too lived with her. In this manner ended the very colourful political career of the most ambitious and powerful royal Mughal lady. Whatever might have been her achievements or failures in this field, Nur Jahan's name will always be written in bold letters in Mughal history. Her courage, intelligence, sagacity and mental equilibrium at the time of danger and difficulties are certainly praiseworthy. Women of the future ages have much to learn and be inspired from the remarkable qualities exhibited by this beautiful Persian lady and Mughal Empress in war and peace.

Mumtaz Mahal

During the times of Shahjahan we come across his most beloved wife Mumtaz Mahal, the lady of the Taj, who, though not directly, is said to have played her own little part in the contemporary politics. Mumtaz Mahal or Arjumand Banu Begam, as she was originally called, was the daughter of Asaf Khan, the son of Etimad-ud-Daula, and brother of Nur Jahan Begam. Arjumand Banu was married to Shahjahan in 1612 A.D. Arjumand Banu's marriage to Prince Khurram (Shahjahan) was of great consequences. It led to the formation of the great Nur Jahan's Junta or clique. It also helped Shahjahan in his political career. She bore him fourteen children. Mumtaz Mahal died quite young when she was about 38-39 years of age, and her fourteenth child was born at Burhanpur in the Deccan. After her death in 1631 A.D. Shahjahan made her memory eternal by building her mausoleum, the famous Taj Mahal in Agra.

It is said that Shahjahan loved and trusted Mumtaz Mahal greatly. Her early death had left him completely shattered. Mumtaz Mahal too, on her part bore great love and devotion towards her husband. Her entire life revolved around her husband. She was always by his side in pleasure and in pain. Boldly and courageously she shared her husband's misfortunes and difficult days. In the process she herself had to make sacrifices like sending away two of her sons as hostages after husband's unsuccessful rebellion. Mumtaz never complained and always stood as a source of constant courage and encouragement to her husband, on whom she had complete faith and trust.

It is quite natural that when Shahjahan became the Mughal Emperor, his beloved queen Mumtaz Mahal also came to occupy a very special place and a unique position in the harem and Court. She got the title of Malika-i-Zaman and was given the foremost position amongst the ladies of the harem. Her jagirs also increased. Shahjahan very often consulted her in both private matters and state affairs.[153] She acted as his anchor, where he found love, solace and contentment. The Emperor trusted her to such an extent that the Uzuk, or the Royal seal bearing the Emperor's name was kept in her charge.[154] All important documents and *farmans* (Imperial letters) were brought to her and she affixed the seal to them.

Mumtaz Mahal was a benevolent and kind hearted lady. She undertook humanitarian activities on a large scale.[155] Widows, orphans, destitutes and other troubled and poor people came to her from all parts of the country. She listened patiently to all their pleas and brought these matters to the Emperor's attention when he retired to the Harem in the afternoons. The Emperor generously gave his permission and large sums of money and Mumtaz Mahal went ahead with her humanitarian works. In these activities she was assisted by an efficient and educated Persian lady named Sati-un-Nisa,[156] who was also the tutoress of Princess Jahanara. Through their efforts, money, land grants, pensions, and even jewellery were given to the poor and needy people.

Shahjahan, under the influence and pleas of Mumtaz, sometimes even went to the extent of forgiving serious offenders.[157] One such offender was Saif Khan, the governor of Gujarat and a relative of Mumtaz Mahal. Around 1627-28 A.D. when Shahjahan was travelling towards the North to occupy the throne, he came to know of Saif Khan's doubtful and uncooperative attitude. Shahjahan thought of imprisoning Saif Khan, but Mumtaz Mahal intervened in the matter and Saif Khan was spared of any sort of torture or trouble.[158]

Though Mumtaz Mahal was known for her soft and calm nature, some history writers like Manucci say that she was responsible for the large scale massacre of the Portuguese at Hugli.[159] It seems that these Portuguese men had captured two of her slave girls. This had infuriated her and she made Shahjahan undertake the task of their massacre. This was a great blow to the Portuguese and their settlement at Hugli. Dr. Pant even goes on to say that Mumtaz Mahal had "urged upon him (Shahjahan) a large scale persecution of the Hindus."[160] However this was not done as Shahjahan knew from earlier experiences the dangers of female intervention in politics.[161] This particular fact about Mumtaz Mahal cannot be said for sure because other sources do not mention her as anti-Hindu. Mumtaz Mahal did not live long enough to enjoy this position of power, authority and eminence bestowed on her by her loving husband. She died in 1631 A.D. at Burhanpur after the birth of her fourteenth child.

Jahanara and Roshanara Begams (Shahjahan's Daughters)

During the later years of Shahjahan's reign and during the war of succession between his four sons, his daughters Jahanara and Roshanara played very important roles in the political scenario.

Jahanara Begam, the eldest daughter of Shahjahan, was the apple of her father's eye. She was fourteen years old at the time of her mother's death. She was well educated and accomplished and very beautiful like her mother, whom she resembled greatly. Shahjahan's fondness of her is well known. Once on the night of 26th March, 1644 A.D. Jahanara met with an accident and got severely burnt[162]. Shahjahan was in great anguish and he neglected even the urgent state affairs to be by her bed-side. The best doctors were brought for her treatment. At last her burns got cured through an ointment prepared by a slave named Arif.

Among her brothers, Jahanara was particularly fond of Dara, the eldest son of Shahjahan. Jahanara and Dara shared the same wavelength of mind and attitude, and therefore had similar views regarding many things including secular ideas about religious beliefs. To her, Dara was the best suited among the sons of Shahjahan to succeed him as the future emperor of Mughal India.

Jahanara among the daughters of Shahjahan, was the favourite of the people too. Even foreign travellers like Manucci and Bernier have expressed their liking for her in their accounts. Roshanara, the younger one was not much liked by them. Says Bernier, "Rauchenara Begam, the Mogol's younger daughter was less beautiful than her sister, neither was she so remarkable for understanding;...[163]

After her mother's death in 1631 A.D. Jahanara, as she was the most loved daughter of Shahjahan, came to occupy the position of the leading lady of the harem and she remained so for the next twenty seven years, till Shahjahan became a captive at the hands of Aurangzeb. Jahanara did full justice to her new role as the leading lady of the harem and the Court. She enjoyed the title of Begam Sahib. The Royal Seal was kept with her.[164] Her wealth increased day by day with all the valuable gifts bestowed on her by the amirs whose affairs were confined to her charge. She had great powers in her hands and the Emperor had full trust in her and her advice.

Jahanara was not politically inclined like her sister Roshanara, who resented every bit of the power and influence that the elder one enjoyed. But the turn of events during Shahjahan's reign forced Jahanara to involve herself in politics as she was concerned about the well being and happiness of her father and peace of her family as a whole. She loved and cared for her father deeply. Therefore, it is quite natural that things and events that troubled her father troubled her too. In her own special way she tried as a peacemaker, to settle differences between her father and her brothers. Jadunath Sarkar writes— "...her loving kindness healed all discords in the imperial family ..."[165]

Among Jahanara's brothers, it was Aurangzeb who got into trouble with Shahjahan often. Power loving that he was, Aurangzeb resented the loving treatment that Dara, his eldest brother got from their father Shahjahan. In 1644 A.D. Aurangzeb got into trouble with Shahjahan because of some foolishness on his part as a result of which his rank and *jagirs* were confiscated. It was Jahanara who succeeded in pacifying Shahjahan who forgave Aurangzeb and gave back his former rank, office and position.[166]

In 1654 A.D. Shahjahan sent an expedition against Raja Prithvichand of Srinagar. After two years of war, in 1656 A.D. Raja Prithvichand was tired and lost all hope. He then corresponded with Jahanara, assuring her of his loyalty and expressing his willingness to submit if Dara Shukoh would intercede. With the help of Jahanara matters settled down peacefully. Prithvichand's son Medini Singh was sent to Dara, who introduced him to the Court and secured pardon for Prithvichand.[167]

Once again Aurangzeb had differences of opinion with Shahjahan regarding the Deccan state of Golconda in 1656 A.D. Aurangzeb wanted his sway over this rich Deccan kingdom. He was also angry with its ruler Abdullah Qutb Shah for arrears in paying tribute timely and also for imprisoning Aurangzeb's Wazir Mir Jumla. Aurangzeb urged Shahjahan to annex Golconda. But Abdullah Qutb Shah appealed to Jahanara and Dara for help. They were convinced by Abdullah's agent at Delhi of Aurangzeb's unjust and unwarranted attack on Golconda.[168] They intervened and Qutb Shah was pardoned after paying indemnity.[169] Aurangzeb was angry at not getting his way out of this matter. He felt that

Jahanara and Dara had influenced Shahjahan in this regard because they were sure that if Aurangzeb was permitted to "pursue his designs against the king of Golconda, he would become too powerful.[170]

The War of Succession

The events which brought out in totality the political activities of Shahjahan's daughters, Jahanara and Roshanara, was the war of succession between the four sons of Shahjahan, which followed Shahjahan's illness in 1658 A.D. During this war of succession Jahanara supported her favourite brother Dara, and Roshanara, anti as she was against Jahanara and Dara, took up the task of passing out secret information of the harem and Court to Aurangzeb,[171] and this ultimately helped him a lot in being able to come to the throne.

From December 1657 A.D. onwards Shahjahan started remaining ill. His ambitious sons who were waiting to capture power found this as a good opportunity to try their luck. Shahjahan was aware of his sons' aspirations. Jahanara tried her best to wipe out his fears. She sent separate letters to all her brothers confirming the fact that Shahjahan's health condition was all right and that he was still in full command of the affairs of the state.[172] Shahjahan, in reality, was not yet fit to run the administration. This was now done by Jahanara and Dara. The other three brothers, meanwhile, kept themselves informed about these happenings through their respective supporters at the Court. They also got together to discuss these matters themselves. Their sisters were also active. Gauharara Begam sent information to Murad and Roshanara Begam acted as a valuable supporter of Aurangzeb.

In May 1662 A.D. Aurangzeb fell very ill. Roshanara was in charge of his chamber. Shahjahan too was ill. Roshanara kept Aurangzeb's illness a secret. She had no hopes of his recovery. She took away the royal seal and wrote to various Rajas, Chiefs and nobles in favour of Aurangzeb's third son Prince Azam, then nine years old. His another son, Muazzam, did not like this. Roshanara behaved badly towards him and towards many more. Aurangzeb recovered soon and was offended with Roshanara for all this and she fell in his regard.[173]

Jahanara's Emphasis on Dara as the Successor

Aurangzeb mentally was the strongest among his brothers. He was a staunch and devout Sunni Muslim. The liberal and broadminded views of Dara made him a heretic in the eyes of Aurangzeb. Roshanara was well aware of Aurangzeb's religious orthodoxy. She took full advantage of this and wrote a letter to him informing him about the Court events and also how Dara was to be soon formally announced as the legal heir. She also wrote that the orthodox section of the nobility were waiting to stage a revolt in case the crown passed to his non believer Dara. They were looking forward to Aurangzeb and that she was sure he would not let them down.[174]

Aurangzeb made up his mind to get the throne for himself. He sent urgent communication to Shuja and Murad to join hands with him against their common enemy Dara. In fact Aurangzeb had been preparing himself against Dara for quite sometime. In December 1652 A.D. he joined hands with his brother Shuja for forming an informal dual alliance against Dara, and sealed it by engaging his son Mohammad Sultan to Shuja's daughter Gulrukh Banu.[175]This marriage however never took place because of the outbreak of the war of succession. The three brothers, Shuja Aurangzeb and Murad decided to march towards the capital.

Defeat of Dara on Aurangzeb's Hands

First of all an army was sent under Dara's son Sulaiman Shukoh and Raja Jai Singh to check the advance of Shuja. In the battle fought at Bahadurgarh in February 1658 A.D. Shuja was defeated. Aurangzeb joined hands with Murad, and Raja Jaswant Singh and Kasim Khan were sent to deal with Aurangzeb and Murad's combined forces. But Aurangzeb defeated them in the Battle of Dharmat in April 1658 A.D. In May 1658 A.D. Aurangzeb reached Gwalior via Ujjain from where he had set out on 30 April, 1658 A.D.[176] Jahanara continued her efforts to bring back Aurangzeb in the right path. She sent a letter to him which was evident of her master stroke in diplomacy, because through the sweet words of sisterly love she tried to make Aurangzeb change his mind and policy so that it will give a chance to her favourite brother Dara to become the next emperor. She also urged him to meet their father and solve all differences between him and Dara. Aurangzeb sent brief reply in which he refused this offer and listed out the sins of Dara, which included his usurping power.[177] Shahjahan was now sure that Aurangzeb would not give up. The next defeat of Dara in Aurangzeb's hands came in the Battle of Samugarh, 10 miles east of Agra, on May 28, 1658 A.D. Dara ran away.

In early June, Shahjahan surrendered to Aurangzeb who kept him in captivity in the Agra Fort. Shahjahan felt dejected, but Jahanara did not give up easily. She made Shahjahan continue to send help to Dara in the form of gold and elephants.[178] Jahanara also decided to visit Aurangzeb personally and make him an offer by which the Empire was to be divided among the four princes — Dara to be sent to Punjab, Shuja to Bengal, Murad to Gujarat, Aurangzeb's eldest son, Prince Muhammad Sultan be made governor of the Deccan, with Aurangzeb receiving control over the rest of the Mughal domain. He was also to be given the rank of heir apparent to the throne and the title of Buland Iqbal (which was to be taken away from Dara).[179]

Failure of Diplomatic Tactics

Aurangzeb was informed by Roshanara that Dara was being sent help from Shahjahan and Jahanara. She also informed him about the presence of some Tartar women kept by Shahjahan to kill Aurangzeb when he entered the castle.[180] In spite of all this, Aurangzeb welcomed Jahanara and heard her offer. At first he refused to see the Emperor saying that Dara was an infidel. But after a long discussion his mind changed and the next day he started his trip to visit Shahjahan. But on his way Shaista Khan and Shaikh Mir informed him that the result of his trip would lead to his murder in the hands of Tartar slave women which had been planned by Shahjahan. A letter of Shahjahan to Dara also fell into Aurangzeb's hand which confirmed this. Aurangzeb, very much displeased at all this, made Shahjahan's captivity even stricter and his communication with the outside world was stopped.[181] After this there was no further communication between Jahanara and Aurangzeb. Thus, Jahanara's efforts and diplomatic tactics failed to bring about a political reconciliation between her father Shahjahan and her brother Aurangzeb. After this Jahanara's life was spent in serving her old and heartbroken father imprisoned inside the Agra Fort till his death on 31st January, 1666 A.D. at the age of 76.[182]

Rise and Fall of Roshanara Vs. Jahanara Begam

Shahjahan's second daughter Roshanara Begam rose into prominence during Aurangzeb's time because of her constant support of Aurangzeb in his deeds or if we can say misdeeds against his father and eldest brother Dara, which eventually led him to the Mughal crown. Hamilton mistakenly called Roshanara as Nur Mahal but says about her that, "...she was a woman of great Genius and vivacity, she fish out all the Designs of her father and brothers, and acquainted Aurangzeb with them by letters, and promised her assistance to set him on the throne."[183] She is said to have been the one who excited Aurangzeb to undertake the bloody and heartless killing of Dara Shukoh.[184] But soon, because of her illicit love affairs, she started falling in Aurangzeb's esteem and regard. This once again brought Jahanara in the forefront as the reinstated first lady of the realm. Roshanara Begam mysteriously died soon. Jahanara Begam continued to exercise her influence in the harem and the court. Dara's daughter Jani Begam was married to Aurangzeb's third son Azam. It was only Jahanara who could have the courage and authority to criticise Aurangzeb's actions and religious bigotry. When Aurangzeb imposed the Jazia, she repeatedly pleaded with the Emperor to reconsider it. But Aurangzeb refused to listen. Later, she refused to accompany Aurangzeb to the Deccan as she was old. She wanted him to stop his hostilities towards these states as it was difficult and she also told him that if he went there then they might not meet again. True to her words, Jahanara passed away on 7th September, 1681 A.D. in her mid 60s.

Thus ended the life and career of a remarkable Mughal princess, Jahanara Begam, popularly known as Begam Sahib, the beloved daughter of Shahjahan. In her lifetime she did much, but politically her achievements were few. Even then, her efforts to bring peace in her family cannot be underestimated. In comparison to her younger sister Roshanara Begam, she certainly stands apart as the more nobler, saintly and virtuous one. Her devotion to her father is also praiseworthy. She was so worthy of respect that in spite of her support to Dara in the war of succession, Aurangzeb's regard for her never diminised and he always held her in great esteem. A believer in righteousness and virtue, this courageous lady braved many difficult times and even had courage to point out the mistakes of someone like Aurangzeb. Truth and virtue always win and the upholder of these is not only worthy of her people's respect, but also those of the later times who read about her.

Zeb-un-Nisa and Zinat-un-Nisa (Daughters of Aurangzeb)

Aurangzeb's reign was not totally devoid of politically ambitious and influential royal ladies. His sisters Roshanara and Jahanara continued to exert their respective influences in various matters as long as they lived. Aurangzeb in his old age was much under the spell of the beauty and youthful charm of his most loved concubine Udipuri Mahal, the mother of his son Kam Bakhsh. Kam Bakhsh was not a man of lofty character and was at fault quite often. But his mother's influences over Aurangzeb secured the Emperor's pardon for him.[185]

A lot cannot be said about the political ambitions of Aurangzeb's daughters. His eldest daughter Zeb-un-Nisa, a poetess and a mystic, did play her own part in political field too. She was her father's favourite child and probably because of this she could compel Aurangzeb to pardon people who had offended him. One such person was Zeb-un-Nisa's maternal grandfather and Aurangzeb's father-in-law Shah Nawaz Khan, who had not extended any help to Aurangzeb during the war of succession and was therefore imprisoned. It was Zeb-un-Nisa who secured pardon for her grandfather from her father and Shah Nawaz Khan was finally released.[186] Many years later Aurangzeb's son Prince Azam got into trouble for quarrelling with the harem superintendent. He sent his petition of pardon through Zeb-un-Nisa[187] as he was sure of being pardoned by his father if Zeb-un-Nisa appealed for him.

Prince Muhammad Akbar's Rebellion

Though Aurangzeb loved Zeb-un-Nisa very much, yet he was not kind to her when she supported her younger brother Prince Muhammad Akbar when he revolted against their father

Aurangzeb in 1681 A.D. Prince Muhammad Akbar had accompanied Aurangzeb in his wars against the Rajput States in 1679 AD. Soon he had the full army corps under his command. But he fell under the influence of evil advisers. He rebelled against his father, proclaimed himself emperor and even marched against his father in 1681 A.D. Zeb-un-Nisa actively lent her support to this brother of hers during his rebellion. She was secretly in correspondence with her brother. After the suppression of Prince Akbar's rebellion, her letters were discovered and then she became the recipient of her father's wrath, as her letters clearly revealed how closely attached she was to her brother's interests. Her entire property was seized and pension of four lakhs a year stopped. She was imprisoned in the Salimgarh Fort where she spent the rest of her life till her death in 1702 A.D.[188]

Shivaji's Escapade

In some places we come across an interesting story of how Zeb-un-Nisa's love for the Maratha Chieftain Shivaji made her plan Shivaji's escape in fruit basket from the imprisonment imposed on him by Aurangzeb.[189] It seems that this was also one of the reasons for her imprisonment as Aurangzeb was greatly enraged at this,[190] because the Princess had succeeded in outwitting her father and saving the life of her hero.

Aurangzeb's second daughter Zinat-un-Nisa Begam, afterwards surnamed Padshah Begam, was known for her piety and extensive charity. She was in charge of her father's household in the Deccan for many years till his death in 1707 A.D. and after that continued to enjoy the respect as the senior lady of the harem. Aurangzeb had entrusted her with the task of taking care of the Maratha captives, Yesu Bai, the widow of Shambhaji, and her son Sahu.[191] Zinat-un-Nisa also loved her brother Akbar very much and therefore was sympathetic with the Marathas as they had been friendly with Akbar. She protected Yesu Bai and Sahu from her father's wrath. In 1707 A.D. when Sahu crossed the Narmada and started for the Deccan, Zinat-un-Nisa helped him a lot to facilitate his journey. In 1718 A.D. when Balaji Vishwanath led an expedition against the Mughals for the release of Sahu and his mother, Zinat-un-Nisa helped in the process of their release.[192]

Therefore we can conclude that whatever part the Mughal ladies played in contemporary polities right from the times of Babar to Aurangzeb, had been very significant, and they sometimes even went to the extent of changing the complete political scenario. They solved differences of opinions, settled disputes, secured pardon for their loved ones, acted as an instrument to conclude peace with the enemy, and sometimes even went out themselves to face the enemy. To a certain extent all this was all right. But when they tried to interfere too much with politics, chaotic situations arose which generally went out of their control. This is quite evident in Nur Jahan's case. Even then, the strength of mind, determination and courage that some of the Mughal ladies exhibited is indeed praiseworthy.

REFERENCES

1. J.H. Sanders, tr., *Tamerlane or Taimur—The Great Amir* (London : 1936), p. 324.
2. Ralph Winston Fox, *Genghis Khan* (Essex: 1962), p. 45.
3. *Ibid.*, p. 44.
4. Kiran Pawar, "Role of Some Royal Women in the Career of Babur", *Proceedings of the Indian History Congress*, 52nd Session (New Delhi: 1991-92), p. 349.
5. *Babur Nama*, tr. A.S. Beveridge (New Delhi: 1979), Vol. I, p. 341 n.
6. *Babur Nama*, (tr.), Vol. I, p. 19.
7. *Ibid.*, pp. 20-21.
8. A.S. Beveridge in Gulbadan Begam's *Humayun Nama* (tr.), p. 244 n.
9. Radhey Shyam, *Babur* (Patna: 1978), p. 35.
10. *Babur Nama* (tr.), Vol. I, pp. 43-44.
11. Radhey Shyam, *Babur*, pp. 38-39.
12. *Babur Nama* (tr.), Vol. I, p. 43.
13. *Ibid.*, p. 44.
14. Radhey Shyam, *Babur*, p. 52.
15. *Babur Nama* (tr.), Vol. I, p. 43.
16. *Babur Nama* (tr.), Vol. I, p. 21.
17. *Ibid.*, pp. 88, 91, 135-36, 147, 187.
18. *Ibid.*, p. 105.
19. *Ibid.*, p. 184 (Translator's note).
20. *Ibid.*, p. 21.
21. *Ibid.*, p. 21.
22. *Babur Nama* (tr.), Vol. I, p. 147.
23. Gulbadan Begam, *Humayun Nama* (tr.), p. 85.
24. Mirza Haider Doghlat, *Tarikh-i-Rashidi*, tr. E. Denison Ross (London: 1895), p. 175.

25. R.C. Mazumdar, ed., *The Mughal Empire,* Bharatiya Vidya Bhavan Series (Bombay: 1974), p. 26.
26. *Tarikh-i-Rashidi* (tr.), p. 239.
27. *Babur Nama* (tr.), Vol. I, p. 352.
28. A.L. Srivastava, *History of India,* p. 346.
29. *Babur Nama* (tr.), Vol. I, p. 358.
30. *Humayun Nama* (tr.), p. 266 n.
31. *Ibid.*, p. 266.
32. *Babur Nama* (tr.), Vol. I, p. 375.
33. S.K. Banerji, *Humayun Badshah,* Vol. II (Calcutta: 1983), p. 322.
34. *Babur Nama* (tr.), Vol. I, p. 113.
35. *Humayun Nama* (tr.), pp. 88-89.
36. *Humayun Nama* (tr.), p. 150.
37. *Ibid.*, p. 151.
38. A.L. Srivastava, *History of India,* pp. 367-68.
39. *Humayun Nama* (tr.), pp. 157 and 240 (notes).
40. A.S. Beveridge in *Humayun Nama,* pp. 240-41 (notes).
41. *Babur Nama* (tr.), Vol. I, pp. 314-15.
42. *Humayun Nama* (tr.), pp. 160-61.
43. R. Misra, *Women in Mughal India,* pp. 19-20.
44. *Humayun Nama* (tr.), p. 255 (notes).
45. *Ibid.*, pp. 59-60 (Introduction).
46. *Akbar Nama* (tr.), Vol. II, p. 149.
47. *Ibid.*, p. 150.
48. *Ibid.*, p. 151.
49. Badauni, *Muntakhab-ut-Tawarikh,* Vol. II, tr. Lowe, pp. 31-32; Nizamuddin Ahmed, *Tabqat-i-Akbari* tr. B. De, Vol. II, pp. 237-50; *Akbar Nama* (tr.), Vol. II, pp. 152-60, 168-76; Stanley Lane Poole, *Medieval India Under Mohammaden Rule* (Delhi: 1990), pp. 242-44.
50. *Akbar Nama* (tr.), Vol. II, pp. 204-205.
51. *Akbar Nama* (tr.), Vol. II.
52. *Akbar Nama* (tr.), Vol. II, p. 214.
53. *Ibid.*, pp. 219-21.
54. *Akbar Nama* (tr.), Vol. II, pp. 269-72; A.S. Beveridge in *Humayun Nama,* pp. 60-62 (Introduction); Lane Poole, *Medieval India Under Mohammedan Rule,* pp. 244-45.
55. *Humayun Nama* (tr.), p. 62.
56. *Akbar Nama* (tr.), Vol. II, p. 289.
57. *Ibid.*, p. 289.
58. *Ibid.*, p. 290-93.
59. *Akbar Nama* (tr.), Vol. II, p. 317-19; Badauni, *Muntakhab-ut-Tawarikh,* Vol. II, tr. Lowe, pp. 54-57; Bayazid Biyat, *Tarikh-i-Humayun Wa Akbar,* ed. Hidayat Hussain (Calcutta: 1941), p. 284; *Humayun Nama* (tr.), p. 62-63; Nizamuddin Ahmad, *Tabaqat-i-Akbari,* tr. B. De, Vol. II, pp. 277-78; V.A. Smith, *Akbar the Great Mughal,* pp. 46-47.
60. *Humayun Nama* (tr.), p. 214 (notes).
61. *Ibid.*, p. 214.

62. *Akbar Nama* (tr.), Vol. II, p. 536.
63. Antonio Monserrate, *Mongolica Legationis Commentarius or the Commentary,* tr. J.S. Hoyland (London: 1922), p. 153.
64. R.P. Tripathi, *Rise and Fall of the Mughal Empire* (Allahabad: 1960), p. 271.
65. V.A. Smith, *Akbar the Great Mughal,* p. 143; Sir Richard Burn ed., *The Cambridge History of India,* Vol. IV (*The Mughal Period*), (Cambridge: 1937), p. 128.
66. *Akbar Nama* (tr.), Vol. II, pp. 242-43.
67. Lane Poole, *Medieval India Under Mohammaden Rule,* p. 251.
68. R.C. Muzumdar ed., *The Mughal Empire,* p. 124.
69. *Akbar Nama* (tr.), Vol. II, pp. 518-19.
70. *Akbar Nama* (tr.), Vol. II, pp. 677-78; *Tuzuk-i-Jahangiri* (tr.), Vol. I, p. 15.
71. *Tuzuk-i-Jahangiri* (tr.), Vol. I, pp. 55-56.
72. Beni Prasad, *History of Jahangir,* p. 26.
73. C.M. Agrawal, *Studies in Medieval Indian History* (Jalandhar: 1988), pp. 48-49.
74. Ibid., p. 49.
75. Ibid., p. 49.
76. *Akbar Nama* (tr.), Vol. II, p. 364.
77. *Tuzuk-i-Jahangiri* (tr.), Vol. II, pp. 325-26.
78. *Ibid.*, pp. 18-19.
79. *Akbar Nama* (tr.), Vol. III, pp. 117, 647 and 921.
80. *Tuzuk-i-Jahangiri* (tr.), Vol. I, pp. 144-45.
81. *Ibid.*, p. 160.
82. Md. Yasin, *A Social History of Islamic India* (Lucknow: 1958), p. 128.
83. *Akbar Nama* (tr.), Vol. III, p. 1140.
84. *Ibid.*, p. 1223.
85. *Humayun Nama* (tr.), p. 214 (notes).
86. *Akbar Nama* (tr.), Vol. III, p. 1223.
87. Beni Prasad, *History of Jahangir,* p. 55.
88. *Akbar Nama* (tr.), Vol. III, pp. 1140-1230.
89. *Ibid.*, pp. 1243-45.
90. *Akbar Nama* (tr.), Vol. III, pp. 1247-48.
91. *Akbar Nama* (tr.), Vol. III, p. 1248.
92. *Tuzuk-i-Jahangiri* (tr.), Vol. II. p. 107.
93. Beni Prasad, *History of Jahangir,* p.195.
94. Edward Grey ed., *The Travels of Pietro Della Valle in India,* (London: 1891), p. 53.
95. *Ibid.*, p. 54.
96. Pelsaert, p. 50.
97. *Edward Terry in Early Travels in India,* p. 329.
98. *Tuzuk-i-Jahangiri* (tr.), Vol. I, p. 266.
99. C. Pant, *Economic History of India Under the Mughals* (Delhi: 1990), p. 255.
100. C. Pant, *Economic History of India Under the Mughals,* p. 255.
101. De Laet, *The Empire of Great Mogol,* tr. J.S. Hoyland, p. 182.
102. Beni Prasad, *History of Jahangir,* p.189.
103. *Tuzuk-i-Jahangiri* (tr.), Vol. I, p. 224 n to 225 n.
104. Findly, *Noorjahan..,* p. 51.
105. Della Valle, pp. 56-57.

106. *Ibid.*, pp. 56-57.
107. *Ibid.*, p. 57.
108. Findly, *Noorjahan...*, p. 55.
109. Thomas Roe, *The Embassy of Sir Thomas Roe to India*, ed. William Foster (London: 1926), Vol. II, pp. 281-82.
110. Foster ed., *The Embassy of Sir Thomas Roe to India*, Vol. II, p. 245.
111. *Tuzuk-i-Jahangiri* (tr.), Vol. II, pp. 183, 187-88, 199, 202-3.
112. Beni Prasad, *History of Jahangir*, p.188.
113. Moreland and Geyl tr., Jahangir's India, The Remonstrantic of Francisco Pelsaert, p. 50.
114. Foster ed., *The Embassy of Sir Thomas Roe to India*, Vol. II, p. 325.
115. A. Dow tr., *The History of Hindostan* (New Delhi : 1973), Vol. III, p. 184.
116. Pelsaert, p. 53.
117. *Ibid.*, p. 50.
118. *Ibid.*, p. 51.
119. Aziz Ahmed, *Studies in Islamic Culture in the India Environment*, (Oxford : 1964), p. 46.
120. Pelsaert, p. 29.
121. *Ibid.*, p. 29.
122. Manucci, *Storia...*, Vol. I, p. 157.
123. Pant, *Economic History of India Under the Mughals*, p. 255.
124. Beni Prasad, *History of Jahangir*, p.193.
125. K.P. Srivastava ed., *Mughal Farmans*, (Lucknow : 1974), Vol. I, pp. 24-26.
126. *Ibid.*, pp. 24-30.
127. *Ibid.*, pp. 24, 26, 29-30.
128. Pelsaert, p. 50.
129. B.P. Saksena, *History of Shahjahan of Dihli*, p. 298.
130. Foster ed, *The Embassy of Sir Thomas Roe to India*, Vol. I, pp. 99, 108 n, Vol. II, pp. 396, 426.
131. Beni Prasad, *History of Jahangir*, p.194.
132. *Tuzuk-i-Jahangir* (tr.) Vol. I, pp. 277-78.
133. Sugam Anand, *History of Begum Nurjahan*, p. 91.
134. *Waqiat-i-Jahangiri* tr. in Elliot & Dowson, Vol. 6, p. 380.
135. Beni Prasad, *History of Jahangir*, p. 342.
136. Stanley Lane-Poole, *Medieval India UnderMohammedan Rule*, p. 322.
137. *Tatimma-i-Waqiat-i-Jahangiri* tr. in Elliot and Dowson, Vol. 6, pp. 385-96.
138. Beni Prasad, *History of Jahangir*, p. 399.
139. *Intikhab-i-Jehangir Shahi* tr. in Elliot & Downson, Vol. 6, pp. 450-452.
140. Iqbal Nama-i-Jahangiri, E & D, Vol. 6, p. 418.
141. Beni Prasad, *History of Jehangir*, p.399.
142. *Ibid.*, p. 400.
143. Mutamid Khan, *Iqbal Nama-i-Jahangiri*, (text), p. 276.
144. Iqbal Nama-i-Jahangiri, E & D, Vol. 6, p. 422.
145. *Ibid.*, pp. 422-24.
146. *Ibid.*, p. 424.
147. *Ibid.*, pp. 424-26.
148. Beni Prasad, *History of Jahangir*, pp. 354-55.

149. *Iqbal Nama-i-Jahangiri*, Elliot and Dowson, Vol. 6, p. 426.
150. *Ibid.*, pp. 426-27.
151. *Ibid.*, p. 427.
152. *Iqbal Nama-i-Jahangiri*, E & D, Vol. 6, p. 308.
153. W. Hansen, *The Peacock Throne*, p. 93; Maharani Sunity Devee, *The Beautiful Mogul Princesses* (London : 1918), p. 25.
154. Ishwari Prasad, *A Short History of Muslim Rule in India*, p. 342; Maharani Sunity Devee, *The Beautiful Mogul Princesses*, p. 25; Jadunath Sarkar, *Studies in Mughal India*, p. 22.
155. Jadunath Sarkar, *Studies in Mughal India*, p. 22.
156. *Ibid.*, p. 94.
157. W. Hansen, *The Peacock Throne*, p. 93.
158. B.P. Saxena, *History of Shahjahan of Dihli*, p. 61.
159. Manucci, *Storia...*, Vol. I, p. 182; B.P. Saksena, *History of Shahjahan of Dihli*, pp. 106-107; H.N. Varma and Amrit Varma, *Eminent Indian women* (New Delhi : 1978), p. 126.
160. Pant, *Economic History of India Under the Mughal*, p. 175.
161. *Ibid.*, p. 175.
162. Lahori, *Padshah Nama*, Vol. II, pp. 363-369.
163. Bernier, *Travels* (Constable & Smith), p. 14.
164. Jadunath Sarkar, *Studies in Mughal India*, p. 24.
165. Jadunath Sarkar, *History of Aurangzib*, Vol. I & II, p. 39 (Vol. I).
166. J. Sarkar, *History of Aurangzib*, Vol. I, p. 76.
167. K.R. Qanungo, *Dara Shukoh* (Calcutta : 1935), Vol. I, pp. 136-37.
168. R.C. Majumdar ed., *The Mughal Empire* (Bombay : 1974), p. 477.
169. K.R. Qanungo, *Dara Shukoh*, Vol. I, pp. 136-38; J. Sarkar, *History of Aurangzib*, Vol. I, pp. 212-39.
170. Bernier, *Travels*, p. 21.
171. N.L. Mathur, *Red Fort and Mughal Life*, New Delhi, 1964, p. 2.
172. B.P. Saxena, *History of Shahjahan of Dihli*, p. 329.
173. J. Sarkar, *History of Aurangzib*, Vol. III, p. 59; N.L. Mathur, *Red Fort and Mughal Life*, p. 49.
174. Muni Lal, *Shah Jahan*, pp. 307-308.
175. W. Hasen, *The Peacock Throne*, p. 318.
176. Inayat Khan, *The Shah Jahan Nama*, ed. by Begley and Desai, p. 551.
177. Inayat Khan, *The Shah Jahan Nama* (tr.), p. 551.
178. Bernier, *Travels*, p. 65.
179. Inayat Khan, *The Shah Jahan Nama*, (tr.), p. 553; J. Sarkar, *History of Aurangzib*, Vol. I & II, p. 264 (Vol. II).
180. Bernier, p. 65.
181. Inayat Khan, *The Shah Jahan Nama*, (tr.), p. 553. J. Sarkar, *History of Aurangzib*, Vol. I & II, pp. 264-65 (Vol. II).
182. *The Shah Jahan Nama* (Tr.), p. 565.
183. Alexander Hamilton, *A New Account of the East Indies*, ed. W. Foster (London: 1930), p. 101.
184. W. Hansen,*The Peacock Throne*, pp. 448-52.
185. J. Sarkar, *History of Aurangzib*, Vol. I, p. 64.

186. Rekha Misra, *Women in Mughal India*, p. 50.
187. *Ibid.*, p. 50.
188. *Maasir-i-Alamgiri*, tr., Jadunath Sarkar, p. 126; Jadunath Sarkar, *Studies in Mughal India*, p. 20; N.L. Mathur, *Red Fort and Mughal Life*, p. 49.
189. Maharani Sunity Devee, *The Beautiful Mogol Princesses*, pp. 77-78.
190. Magan Lal., tr. *The Diwan of Zeb-un-Nissa*, p. 17 (Introduction).
191. G.S. Sardesai, *New History of the Marathas* (Bombay : 1946), Vol. I, p. 350.
192. *Ibid.*, p. 350.

Five

Literary Contributions

Establishments of Madrasas and Colleges

The Mughal Emperors were cultured and educated, they knew the value of education and took interest for the encouragement and spread of education. They established madrasas, maktabs and centres of higher education in large numbers and founded libraries. Almost all the Mughal emperors except Akbar was learned. Babar and Jehangir even wrote their autobiographies. Humayun, a great bibliophile and scholar, established a madrasah in Delhi, where special arrangements were made for teaching mathematics, astronomy and geography.[1] Though Akbar received no formal education, he patronised men of learning. He even introduced certain educational reforms in the existing curriculum of learning, especially at the primary level.[2] Certain important subjects like arithmetic, logic, mensuration, geometry, astronomy, physiognomy, accountancy, public administration and agriculture were included in the course of study at his command.[3] Thus, under Akbar, secular touch was given to the educational system which had a strong religious basis so far. Akbar built colleges at Fatehpur Sikri, Agra and some other places.[4] These colleges were not always residential institutions, and students could attend these without having to live in them as well.[5]

Education continued to flourish under Jehangir who made a rule that if a noble died without an heir, his property was to be utilised for the maintenance of madrasas.[6] Shahjahan founded a madrash near the Jama Masjid in Delhi and provided sufficient funds for its maintenance.[7] Aurangzeb too like his predecessors was a patron of learning, but his educational system was more religious than secular. He established a number of Madrasas at many places and gave stipends to teachers and students. One of the madrasas of his time was the Madrasai Rahimiyya.[8] He issued orders to his Provincial Diwans that all students who studied the Mizan and Kashahaf be given financial help from the provincial treasury.[9]

Maintenance of Libraries

Since the Mughal Emperor were extremely fond of learning and education, it is quite natural that they maintained well-equipped libararies with a collection of large number of books including many rare books and translation works. These libraries served as great centres of knowledge and learning. Humayun had such a library and died by falling from the staircase of this library.

Akbar was very fond of books and he had a grand library which had about 24,000 manuscripts and books on various subjects, such as history, philosophy, theology and sciences. There were in addition Persian translations of many Sanskrit,Arabic and Greek works.[10] Akbar enriched his library by adding many valuable books which in the course of his conquests, he procured from the libraries of Gujarat, Kashmir, Jaunpur, Bihar, Bengal and Deccan. The books that he brought from Gujarat seems to have belonged to Itimad Khan Guvarati.[11] The Imperial Library was located on the side of an octagonal tower in Agra Fort. Talking about Akbar's library, Abul Fazl says:

> His Majesty's library is divided into several parts; some of the books are kept within, and some without the Harem. Each part of the library is sub-divided, according to the value of the books and the estimation in which the sciences are held of which the books treat. Prose books, poetical works, Hindi, Persian, Greek, Kashmirian, Arabic, are all separately placed. In this order they are also inspected. Experienced people bring them daily and read them before His Majesty, who hears every book from the beginning to the end.[12]

Jehangir inherited this grand library from his father. Since he too was very fond of book, he had his personal collections also. Whenever he went on a journey or an expedition he always carried with himself certain selected books.[13] Shahjahan had a very big library which is said to have contained nearly 24,000 well-bound books.[14] This library was enlarged largely under Aurangzeb.

Library officials

The libraries belonging to the members of the royal family were set up in separate buildings which had sufficient light and air and whose floors were kept free from worms and dampness so that the books might not be damaged.[15] There were several officers who looked into the organisation and administration of the library. The highest official was the 'Nazim', also known as 'Mutamid', who was in charge of the appointment and dismissal of the subordinate employees and the income and expenditure of the library.[16] Next to him came the 'Muhtamin' or 'Darogha',[17] who looked after the internal administration of the library. He had to be a man of experience and ability and was in charge of selecting, purchasing and classifying the books subject-wise. There were a number of officers, clerks and other employees under him. Some of these officials arranged the books in serial numbers. Some had the duty to take out the books at regular intervals and clean them free of dust, and separate the pages if they had stuck together.[18] There were book-binders (Jild-Saaj) attached to the libraries, calligraphists (khusnavis) employed to copy rare books, and painters, who painted beautiful pictures on the margins of the pages.[19] Thus, the Imperial library of the Mughals was a well organised department, well looked after and well-equipped and a great place for the quest of knowledge.

Female Education

In an absolutely male dominated medieval society, female education was not given importance. We have already discussed how female education in medieval India was not encouraged and it was a privilege confined to the ladies of aristocratic and royal families alone. Even then very few women got higher education and in most cases the education was limited to the primary level alone. Several social factors like the purdah system, child marriage and the low position that women generally occupied, played a great role in the low level of education among women.

As we have already seen, the Mughal emperors were men of

letters and great patrons of learning and education and had contributed a lot towards the cause of education. But, their greatest contribution towards this field was educating their daughters and other women of their harem by making suitable arrangements for female education in their palaces. Suitable aged tutors and tutoresses were appointed to teach various subjects and languages to the princesses. Some chambers in the royal palaces were set aside for the purpose of female education. The well-equipped Imperial Library could provide the necessary books to the royal ladies who certainly had access to the Emperor's library and sometimes had their own libraries as well. Right from Babar to Aurangzeb, during the period of all the Mughal emperors, we come across highly educated and accomplished Mughal ladies who were not just satisfied with getting higher education, but also contributed a great deal towards the cause of learning and education and also sometimes left behind them literary works of great value which have made them immortal.

Learned Mughal Women in Babar's Time

The Mughal women have been busy in their literary pursuits right from the days of Babar. Both Babar's mother Qutluq-Nigar Khanum, and his maternal grandmother Aisan-daulat were educated ladies and they both acted as great influences in shaping Babar's life, who is said to have inherited his artistic and intellectual faculties from them. One of Babar's daughters, Gulrukh Begam, seems to have composed a number of verses.[20] Some of Babar's many wives were also educated and cultured ladies. But, the first Mughal lady who left behind her a work of literary and historical importance was Babar's daughter Gulbadan Begam, well known for her famous *Humayun Nama*, the biography of her brother Humayun.

Gulbadan Begam

Gulbadan Begam (Princess Rose-body) was the daughter of Babar by his wife Dildar Begam. She was born somewhere about 1523 A.D. when her father was the lord of Kabul, and she was the child of a man with strength of mind and will power, in whom was united the blood of Timur, the Turk, through his son Miran

Shah, and Chingiz, the Mongol, through his son Chaghatai.[21] Gulbadan spent her childhood under her father's rule in Kabul and Hindustan, her girlhood and young wifehood saw the fall and exile of Humayun, and her ageing years were spent under the protection of her nephew Akbar.

Neither Babar in his memoirs, nor Gulbadan Begam in her *Humayun Nama,* say anything much about Gulbadan's mother Dildar Begam. When Gulbadan was about two years old, she was adopted by Maham Begam, the chief wife of Babar, and the mother of Humayun. Maham had lost four children after her eldest son Humayun. Probably because of this reason and also may be because of her importance as the principal wife of Babar, Maham Begam adopted two of Dildar's children. Hindal and Gulbadan. Gulbadan was brought up and educated under the loving care of Maham Begam[22] of whom she fondly speaks in her Humayun Nama and mentions her as 'My Dearest Lady'. After the death of Babar, when Dildar Begam lived with Hindal, she got back Gulbadan, who was still an unmarried girl then.[23] After Babar's conquest of Hindustan, Gulbadan came to this new land with Maham Begam and her father.[24] Later, during the reign of Humayun, she was given in marriage to Khizr Khan Khwaja.[25]

Gulbadan inherited her father's literary taste and intellect. She was an educated woman and had good knowledge of both the Persian and Turkish languages, though no source speaks of the method by which she received education. But sources do speak of her interest and achievements in the literary field which are proof enough of her being highly educated. Gulbadan Begam was a woman of considerable poetic talent and is said to have composed many beautiful verses.[26] But her verses no longer exist as they have not been preserved. Just two lines of hers have been preserved by Mir Mahdi Shirazi in his Tazkirat-ul-Khwatin -

(Tr.) A beauty that is unfaithful to the lover
Believe me, she will find life untrue to her.[27]

Gulbadan Begam was also fond of collecting books and owned a library of her own which had many valuable and rare collection of books gathered from various places.[28] Out of the nine copies that were made of Bayazid's *Humayun-Nama,* written according to Akbar's command, one was given to Gulbadan

Begam,[29] probably because of her keenness and interest in collecting books and preserving them in her library.

Humayun Nama

But, the best expression of Gulbadan's literary accomplishment is found in her *Humayun Nama*, the memoirs of her brother Humayun. When as an old lady Gulbadan stayed under the protection of her nephew Akbar, the then Mughal Emperor in India, around 1587 A.D., as per the wishes and command of Akbar, she wrote the *Humayun Nama*, in order to provide information for the composition of the *Akbar Nama* of Abul Fazl.[30] This book is of great historical value and is a first-rate authority on the domestic relations of the first two Mughal rulers, Babar and Humayun, with their wives, sons, daughters, and other members of their family, and on their social and political life. The book is written in Persian with a lot of Turki words and phrases. Turki was Gulbadan's native language and Persian was an accomplishment. The only available Persian manuscript of Gulbadan's *Humayun Nama* (preserved in the British Museum) is incomplete and ends with the blinding of Mirza Kamran.[31]

No other source speaks of Gulbadan Begam's *Humayun Nama* and therefore, the book is its sole witness. A.S. Beveridge says that the *Humayun Nama* "... is not literature, but a simple setting down of what she knew or had heard for the help of the *Akbar Nama*."[32] Even if the book has more historical value then literary value, yet it speaks a lot about the lady who wrote it, a lady who had intelligence, wit and humour. On this aspect Mrs. Beveridge remarks - "It is not only her book that lets us know she had a lively mind, but the fact of its composition at an age when wits are apt to be rested by domestic peace. Only a light that was strong in childhood would have burned so long to guide her unaccustomed pen after half a century of life and only a youth of happy thoughts and quick perceptions have buoyed her, still gay and vivacious, across the worries and troubles of Humayun's times."[33]

Gulbadan gives a brief account of Babar and a detailed account of Humayun's life and career. Also we get a vivid picture of the life of the loyal ladies in the harem and many important events related to them. From Gulbadan Begam's account we come to know of many interesting events of Babar's, Humayun's and Akbar's times. We are informed of how Khanzada Begam married Shahi Beg Khan or Shaibani to save her brother Babar from Shaibani's enmity;[34] about Babar's invasion of Hindustan and his sending valuable presents to his ladies in Kabul, after the "treasures of five kings fell into his hands",[35] coming of Gulbadan to Hindustan;[36] the strange way of passing away of Babar after Humayun's recovery from serious illness;[37] Humayun's accession;[38] Humayun's marriage with Hamida Banu Begam, who was at first opposed to the idea of marrying Humayun;[39] the birth of Akbar and ceremonies attached to it;[40] etc.

Thus, the *Humayun Nama* of Gulbadan makes interesting reading and provides us with an ample information about the events of her times, mostly those connected to her father Babar and her brother Humayun and the royal ladies of their household, the wars, campaigns, births, deaths, marriages, special occasions of feasts and festivities and on the whole the various moments of joy and sorrow, victory and defeat.

Learned Mughal Women of Akbar's Time

During the time of Akbar too we come across educated ladies in the royal Mughal harem. Akbar's mother Hamida Banu Begam was an educated women. Akbar's nurse Maham Anaga was also educationally inclined and was a patron of education. Maham Anaga built a college (madrasah) at Delhi known as 'Khair-ul-Manzil', which had a mosque attached to it.[41] Akbar had educated wives too. The most outstanding royal lady during Akbar's time, who engaged herself actively in literary pursuits was one of his wives Salima Sultan Begam.

Salima Sultan Begam

Salima Sultan Begam was the daughter of Mirza Nuru-d-din Muhammad Chanqaniani[42]. Her mother was one of Babar's daughters, probably Gul-rukh Begam, or as some sources call her Gul-barg Begam.[43] Therefore, she was Humayun's niece and Akbar's cousin. In 1557 A.D. (965 H) she was married to Bairam Khan-i-Khanan. After the murder of Bairam in 1560 A.D. (968 H.) Salima Sultan was married by Akbar. She was probably older to

Akbar. After that she occupied a place of respect and importance in Akbar's harem and played an important role in many future events. She was a charming and highly cultured lady. Salima Sultan passed away in 1612 A.D. (1021 H).[44]

Salima Sultan Begam was a woman of intelligence and literary accomplishments. She had good knowledge of the Persian language and came to be known as a poetess.[45] Her verses were of a high standard and she ranked among the eminent verse composers of her times. Salima Begam wrote her verses in Persian under the pen name of 'Makhfi'[46] (the concealed or hidden one). One of her popular verses ran thus -

(Tr.) "In my passion I called Thy, lock the 'thread of life'.
I was wild and so uttered such an expression'[47].

Salima Sultan Begam not only composed verses, but was also known to have been a collector of books.[48] She even maintained a library of her own.[49] Certain important manuscripts like the one of Duval Rani Khizr Khan, by the poet Amir Khusrau Dihlavi in the library of Shahjahan and Aurangzeb, once belonged to Salima Sultan Begam.[50]

Thus, Salima Sultan Begam, with her literary talents, accomplishment and intelligence, without doubt enriched art and culture of the Mughal times and carved a place for herself among the prominent ladies of the Mughal household.

Nur Jahan Learned Mughal Women of Jehangir's Time

As in most other fields, Nur Jahan Begam, the highly cultured, educated, accomplished and exceedingly beautiful wife of Jehangir, was a lady of literary excellence. Mehr-un-Nisa, as Nur Jahan Begam was previously called, was the daughter of Mirza Ghiyas Beg, a Persian noble who came to India in search of fortune during the time of Emperor Akbar. On way to Hindustan, his wife Asmat Banu Begam, amidst trying situation, gave birth to a daughter who brought them good fortune later. Ghiyas Beg and his family were cordially received at the Royal Court of Akbar, and Ghiyas Beg was given good rank in the administration. The royal favours granted to him made his family life happy and comfortable.

Mehr-un-Nisa spent her happy childhood at her father's

home. She grew up to be a beautiful, intelligent, educated and accomplished girl. At the age of seventeen, in 1595 A.D. she was married to a Persian youth Ali Quli Istalju at the Court of Akbar. Ali Quli or Sher Afghan, as he was known as, was later given an independent Jagir at Burdwan in Bengal. He started living there with his wife Mehr-un-Nisa and their daughter Ladli Begam, who was born in 1597 A.D. In 1607 A.D. Sher Afghan was killed in an encounter with Qutub-ud-Din Khan, the new Governor of Bengal and a very close friend of Jehangir. Some historians have alleged Jehangir of planning Sher Afghan's murder, as he had an eye for Mehr-un-Nisa, whom he had known and loved before her marriage, but could not marry her himself. Many other historians do not accept this view. Whatever may be the case, after the death of Sher Afghan, Mehr-un-Nisa along with her little daughter came back to Agra. After that she became the lady-in-writing to Akbar's widow Ruqaiya Begam, who was very kind and affectionate to her.

On occasion of Nauroz in 1611 A.D. Jehangir saw Mehr-un-Nisa and fell head over heels in love with her.[51] Two months after this meeting, the two of them got married on 25th May, 1611 A.D. Mehr-un-Nisa was now called Nur Mahal (Light of the Palace). In 1616 A.D. Jehangir gave her the title of Nur Jahan (Light of the World).[52] In 1622 A.D. she won the title of Padshah Begam (The First Lady of the Realm).[53]

Nur Jahan's marriage with Emperor Jehangir brought her family into prominence, and her father Etimad-ud-Daula (Ghiyas Beg), and brother Asaf Khan, came to occupy important posts in the administration of the Empire. Very soon through her intelligence, beauty and accomplishments, Nur Jahan not only became the ruling lady of Jehangir's heart, but of his Empire as well, and the real power came to be vested in her hands. Jehangir was only too happy for this new arrangement as he was blinded by his love for Nur Jahan, and he also greatly appreciated the many qualities of head and heart in his Persian wife, like determination, courage, sagacity, capabilities, to name a few. After the death of Jehangir in 1627 A.D. Nur Jahan tried to put her son-in-law and Jehangir's youngest son Shahriyar on the throne but failed in her attempt. Thereafter she retired from politics totally and led a quiet life in Lahore till her death in 1645 A.D.

History will always remember the charismatic and talented Nur Jahan Begam for her many-sided achievements which we have been discussing, and will continue to discuss chapter wise. In this chapter we shall deal with her literary achievements and contributions towards the field of learning and education.

Since her very childhood, Nur Jahan Begam, or Mehr-un-Nisa, as she was then called, received good education. Her father employed educated tutors to teach her various subjects, and Maulvis to give her religious education. By the age of fifteen she was proficient in History and Persian classics.[54] She had knowledged of Arabic as well.[55] It is not a strange factor that Nur Jahan Begam was highly educated and literally inclined since young days. She belonged to a line of literary and scholarly achievements and many of her relatives had engaged themselves in poetic activities. Her grandfather, Muhammad Sharif "Hijri"; her great-uncle Khwajagi Razi and his son Mirza Ahmad named Shapur; her father's brother Muhammad Tahir "Wasli" and her father himself were all poets and much of their works have survived.[56] Her sister Manija Begam's husband Qasim Khan was a poet of very high order and a master of extempore verses. He was an active participant in the poetry contests or Mushairas at the Mughal Court and was often the best of the lot.[57]

Poetry was a passion with Nur Jahan and she composed verses in the Persian language which carried spontaneous outflow of her emotions. Her verses echo with the feelings of intense love, despondency, suffering, and Sufi sentiments. Khafi Khan has quoted some of her verses in his work which bear testimony to this.[58]

Wit and humour happen to be very evident in Nur Jahan's verses, especially in her extempore verses, most of which were composed as replies to Jehangir's queries, and the exchange of verses between them. Here are a few examples:

Said Jehangir:

(Tr.) *I am not the nightingale to fill the air with my plaintive cries.*
I am the moth that dies without uttering a single moan.

Nur Jahan replied:

(Tr.) *I am not the moth that dies an instantaneous death. I suffer a lingering dath like the candle which burns through the night without uttering a single moan.*[59]

(Tr.) *Why do old men go about with their backs bent?* asked Jehangir.

(Tr.) *They are searching in dust for the days of their youth,* replied Nur Jahan.[60] Once Emperor Jehangir wore a Qaba (long gown) which had ruby buttons.

Said Jehangir:

(Tr.) *Thy collar my love, has not been dyed with saffron, engrained therein is the pallor of my face.*

Nur Jahan commented:

(Tr.) *And it is the ruby-drops of my heart which have lent their hue to those ruby-buttons on thy silken coat.*[61]

Jehangir sighting the Id moon, marking the end of Ramzan fasting said:

(Tr.) *The crescent of the feast is apparent at the apex of the celestial sphere.*

Nur Jahan responded:

(Tr.) *The crescent of the Id has at last appeared in the face of the heaven. The key of the wine-shop (tavern) has been lost, and at last it has been found.*[62]

Jehangir seeing tears of reunion in Nur Jahan's eyes—

(Tr.) *A pearly tear from your eye is rolling (down your cheek).*

Nur Jahan replied:

(Tr.) *The water I drank (the tears I kept back) without you comes forth from my eyes.*[63]

Talib Amli was a poet who fell out of favour with Jehangir. He said to Nur Jahan:

(Tr.) *I was so embarrassed I turned into water, and water cannot be broken; so I am perplexed why my honour ("face-water") has been broken.*

Nur Jahan said to him:

(Tr.) *It (your honour) turned into ice and was shattered.*[64]

Once seeing a meteor in the sky, Nur Jahan remarked:

(Tr.) *No star has ever raised its head so far; it is the celestial sphere, loins girded in service to the King.*[65]

Nature seems to have formed an integral part of Nur Jahan's poetry, whether they expressed love, joy, separation, sorrow or any other emotions. Especially appealing are her love poems and verses. To quote a few—

The love has melted my body and it has become water. Any antimony that might have remained became the antimony of the bubble's eyes.

The bud may open by the morning breeze which blows in the garden, but the key to the lock of my heart is the smile of my beloved.[66]

I do not give my heart to form until the course of action is known;
I am a slave to love, and the seventy-two sects are known.
Ascetic, do not cast fear of doomsday into our hearts; we have suffered the terrors of separation, so doomsday is already known.[67]

When I lift the veil from my face, a cry rises from the rose;
if I put the comb to my tress, a moan comes forth from the hyacinth.
When I pass through the garden in such beauty and perfection,
a cry of "blessed" arises from the nightingale's souls.[68]

The heart of one held prisoner by beauty and affection knows not roses, colour, aroma, face or trees.[69]

We have purchased Lahore with our soul; we have given our life and bought another paradise.[70]

Nur Jahan's verses, also called poetry of high order, are proof enough for her talent in that field. She too, like Salima Sultan Begam, wrote under the pen-name of 'Makhfi'.[71] Through her charm, intelligence and accomplishments, she succeeded in casting a spell over her husband, Emperor Jehangir.[72]

Nur Jahan Begam was not just content with composing limpid and soulful verses. She had a keen interest in collecting books and had her own library as well.[73] She continued to add books to it by making purchases from time to time. She is known to have purchased the *Diwan-i-Kamran* for three Mohars (gold coins). The first page of this book has three lines - "Three Muhars the price of this treasure, Nawab Nur-un-Nisa Begam."[74]

Nur Jahan Begam was a patron of learning and the learned. Under her patronisation, eminent poets, scholars and writers flocked to the Mughal Court. She lent her support to them and gave them financial assistance. Under her influence, Jehangir too extended more than generous patronage to many poets and scholars many of whom came from Persia. Some of them were Naziri, Talib, Isfahani, Shaida, Munir Lahauri, Nishani, Saida-i-Gilani-Naqib Khan, Niyamat-Ullah and Abdul Haq Dehlvi.[75] Nur Jahan was extremely generous in her patronage towards female poetesses of her time. One of her ladies in waiting, Mehr Harwi, was a poetess and her Sarapa-i-Mehri still survives.[76]

Nur Jahan was active in organising poetic competitions during her time in the royal courts at Lahore, Agra, Fatehpur Sikri and other places.[77] In these competitions, also known as 'Mushairas', many celebrated poets from far and wide participated. Qasim Khan, the brother-in-law of Nur Jahan, was one of the famous participants of these Mushairas, and Nur Jahan was proud of his achievements.[78]

Thus, Begam Nur Jahan's outstanding contributions towards the literary field, as in many other fields, certainly made her one of the, or perhaps, the leading and most remarkable royal lady of the Mughal dynasty in India. Her achievements have made her the unforgettable star in the Mughal horizon. Her epitaph is a reflection of her great mind which knew ambition side by side with humility and simplicity:

> (tr.) *On the tomb of us poor people there will be neither a light nor a flower, nor the wings of a moth, nor the voice of a nightingale.*[79]

Learned Mughal Women of Shahjahan's Time

Mumtaz Mahal

Arjumand Banu Begam was the daughter of Etimad-ud-Daula's son and Nur Jahan's brother Asaf Khan, a powerful noble at Jehangir's court. Arjumand Banu grew up to be a beautiful, educated, cultured and accomplished young lady, well versed in Persian and Arabic. She was betrothed to Jahangir's third son Prince Khurram (Shahjahan) when he was 18 years old, and married two years later. After Shahjahan ascended the Mughal throne, Arjumand Banu came to be known as Mumtaz Mahal (Crown of the Seraglio). Mumtaz Mahal bore Shahjahan fourteen children and died at childbirth in 1631 A.D., after her fourteenth child, a daughter, was born. She was only thirty-eight years old then. Shahjahan was completely shattered emotionally at the death of his queen whom he loved with all his heart, the mother of his children, and his constant companion in all joys and sorrows. He immortalised his love for her by building her mausoleum, the Taj Mahal. Mumtaz Mahal was known for her charity and her patronisation of many scholars, poets and learned men.

Mumtaz Mahal was a woman of literary tastes and composed verses. Her verses, like her aunt Nur Jahan's, were mostly witty remarks said in reply to Shahjahan's comments, in between conversations. Here are a few examples:

Once Shahjahan (The King of the World), with Mumtaz by his side, was watching from his palace, the river Jamuna leap and foam over the stones below. As a compliment to his wife, the Emperor remarked:

(Tr.) *To see the lustre of thy face the river cometh all this way.*

Replied Mumtaz

(Tr.) *And because of the awe of the 'King of the World' (Shahjahan) it dasheth its head against the stones.*[80]

A maid-servant of Mumtaz Mahal was entrusted with the duty of waking up Shahjahan every morning. Once by mistake she woke up the Emperor before dawn. Shahjahan in extreme anger came to Mumtaz Mahal and said:

(Tr.) *The head must be chopped off.*

Mumtaz immediately replied:

(Tr.) *The head must be chopped of that bird who hath sung before her time, for what does this fairy creature know of dusk or dawn.*[81]

Though much is not known about Mumtaz Mahal's literary achievements, yet her witty verses reveal her lively mind and intelligence. On the whole she was a cultured and educated lady.

Jahanara Begum

Princess Jahanara was the eldest daughter of Shahjahan and Mumtaz Mahal. At the death of Mumtaz Mahal in 1631 A.D., Jahanara was fourteen years of age. She was the dearest and most loved child of Shahjahan. After her mother's death, she took upon herself the task of looking after her bereaved father, and this she did with the utmost dedication till Shahjahan's last day. Shahjahan too loved and depended on her as he could not do on anyone else, not even his other children, except Dara to a certain extent. During the war of succession that followed the dethronement of Shahjahan and was followed by the Emperor's banishment to the Agra Fort, Jahanara Begam left the life of pleasure and luxury, took upon herself the life of exile and started living with her father within the confines of the Agra Fort. After the death of Shahjahan, Jahanara was given back her former position as the first lady of the royal court and household by Aurangzeb. In 1666 A.D. she moved to Delhi and lived there till her death on 6th September, 1681 A.D. She died a spinster. Aurangzeb mourned her death and ordered to be referred as 'Sahibat-uz-Zamani' (The Mistress of the Age) from then onwards. Princess Jahanara, like her mother Mumtaz Mahal had a heart full of kindness and compassion for the helpless, poor and the needy. She undertook works of charity to help orphans, widows and other poor people.

Jahanara from her very childhood was a charming and intelligent girl, and she received the best of education that was available for the royal princesses in the Mughal seraglio. As her tutoress Shahjahan appointed a Persian lady by the name of Sati-un-Nisa (The Lance-Head Among Women). She belonged to a family of scholars and physicians and was herself highly educated, could recite the Quran well and was knowledgeable in Persian prose and poetry. Under the able and loving guidance of Sati-un-Nisa, Princess Jahanara, within a short time learnt to read the Holy Quran and gained good knowledge of Persian. Soon Jahanara began composing verses[82] on her own. Her verses earned her appreciation from one and all for their literary merit. Her own epitaph in the form of a Persian couplet,[83] which is found on her simple marble grave near the grave of Saint Nizamuddin Aulia in Delhi goes thus—

(Tr.) *Let nothing cover my grave except the green grass*
For the green turf is covering enough for the poor.[84]

The extraordinary humility of this royal Princess, the beloved daughter of Emperor Shahjahan, is clearly evident in the lines of her epitaph.

Jahanara Begam grew up to have a spiritual and mystic bent of mind. She wrote many Risalas (pamphlets) on the subject of mysticism and spirituality.[85] The highest mark of Jahanara's literary achievements happens to be a work called *Munis-ul-Arwah*, which she wrote in 1681 A.D.[86] The work is a biography of the Sufi Saint of Ajmer, Khwaja Moin-ud-Din Chisti. It also gives biographical notes on some of his descendants and disciples.[87] This kind of Persian literature dealing with the lives and teachings of Muslim saints and Sufis is known as 'Malfuzat'.[88] Another work called *Risala-i-Sahibiya*, the life of Mulla Shah Badakshi, is also said to have been Jahanara's work.[89]

Jahanara Begam's contribution towards the literary field did not limit itself to her verse and literary works. Princess Jahanara, or Begam Sahib, as she was popularly known as, was an active patron of learning and men of letters. Many poets, scholars and literary men flocked to her and she gave them rewards and allowances.[90] As a gratitude for the generosity and patronage, Mir Muhammad Ali Mahir, also known as Murid Khan, wrote a masnavi (long poem) in praise of Jahanara Begam.[91] Jahanara Begam is known to have founded a Madrasa attached to the Jama Masjid at Agra.[92] This madrasa acquired great renown and continued to prosper even in later times.

Learned Mughal Women of Aurangzeb's Times

Zeb-un-Nisa

During the time of Aurangzeb, the literary achievements of his daughters Zeb-un-Nisa and Zinat-un-Nisa are indeed worth mentioning, especially that of Zeb-un-Nisa who was a poetess of renown.

Zeb-un-Nisa (The Ornament of Womanhood), the eldest daughter of Aurangzeb by his wife Dilras Banu Begam, was born on 15th February, 1638, at Daulatabad,[93] when her father was the Viceroy of the Deccan and her grandfather Shahjahan was still the Emperor of Mughal India. Elaborate details of the life of Zeb-un-Nisa are clearly unknown except that she was a beautiful, educated, intelligent and cultured lady with a mystic bent of mind. She was skilled in the use of arms,[94] had a beautiful and melodious voice and courteous manners. She was a deeply religious lady but not in the conventional sense of the term. In other words, she was not a religious fanatic like her father. She was rather liberal in her religious views but at the same time had deep knowledge of the principles and doctrines of Quran. Many a time she was called to settle religious disputes at the Court.[95]

Aurangzeb was extremely fond of his eldest daughter, who with her eloquence and knowledge of the Quran, gave ample reasons to her father to be proud of her. But later, due to certain grave differences of ideas and opinion with her father, she became bitter. She even incurred her father's wrath by extending her support to her brother Akbar, when the later rebelled against Aurangzeb.[96] Zeb-un-Nisa was imprisoned at the Salimgrah fortress by her father, who not only held her captive, but stopped. Zeb-un-Nisa passed away in Delhi on 26th May, 1702,[98] living all these days under restraint and obscurity with a heart filled with grief and misery.

Princess Zeb-un-Nisa inherited her father's keen intellect and literary tastes, and spent most of her time in literary pursuits. From her early childhood, like many other royal princesses, she received good education. As her tutoress she had a learned lady by the name of Hafiza Mariam, the wife of Mirza Shukrullah of Kashmir, whose family originally came from Naishabur in Khurassan.[99] She had another lady teacher by the name of Miyabai,[100] and another who was a poet named Shah Rustam Ghazi.[101] Very soon Zeb-un-Nisa gained proficiency in Arabic and Persian and learnt subjects like astronomy and arithmetic.[102] She became a 'Hafiz'[103] at the tender age of seven years, when she learnt the Quran by heart.[104] Her father, Aurangzeb, was overjoyed at her achievement and feasted the whole army, gave 30,000 gold mohurs to the poor and kept the public offices closed for two days.[105] The Princess also got a reward of 30,000 gold coins from her father.[106] Zeb-un-Nisa also started writing a commentary on the Quran, but this was not allowed by her father,[107] probably on account of her belonging to the fairer sex. She was also capable of writing different kinds of Persian hand like nastaliq, maskh and shikaste with style and neatness.[108]

Princess Zeb-un-Nisa was fond of learning. At the same time she was equally fond of the sources of learning, especially books. She collected several valuable books and manuscripts, and maintained a personal library,[109] in the Imperial palace, where her father with her choice set aside for her some spacious rooms to be utilised as her library.[110] Many skilled calligraphers were employed by her to copy rare and valuable books for her.[111] She also had a scriptorium in Kashmir, where this work went on continuously because of the excellence of Kashmir paper and scribes.[112] She took great interest in this work, and every morning she personally went through the previous day's work. She employed many translators for the purpose of translating many valuable works of other languages into Persian.[113] The Princess spent several hours in a day studying in her library, and none disturbed her then. The ladies who waited upon her in her library were specially chosen to help her in her studies.[114]

Princess Zeb-un-Nisa was a great patron of learning. We have already discussed about her library. Apart from her interest in books, Zeb-un-Nisa patronised many scholars and poets who flourished under her.[115] Her liberality and bounty compensated for the lack of literary patronage under her father. She spent much of her personal allowance of four lakhs every year in encouraging men of letters and helping the poor and needy people.[116] With her support and encouragement Mulla Safiuddin Ardheli of Kashmir translated the Arabic work *Tafsir-i-Kabir* (Great Commentary) of Imam Razi into Persian, and named it *Zeb-ut-Tafsir*, after the name of his patroness.[117]

The greatest achievement of Zeb-un-Nisa in the literary field lies in her poems. Poetry had appealed to her since her childhood days. At first she wrote verses in Arabic, but an Arabian scholar, who saw her work, found them imperfect and criticised them.[118] Thereafter her desire for perfection led her to compose verses in Persian. Shah Rustam Ghazi, a scholar and tutor of Zeb-un-Nisa, encouraged her in this field.[119] He discovered her verses which she wrote at first in secret, and found them to be of a very high standard. He requested Aurangzeb to provide a fitting literary circle for the Princess by inviting poets from Persia, Kashmir and other parts of India to come to Delhi so that the Princess could benefit in their company.[120] Some of these poets were Nasir Ali, Sayab, Shamshi Wali Ullah, Brahmin and Behraaz.[121] A poetess, Imami, was her close friend and companion.[122]

With all her poet and poetess companions, Zeb-un-Nisa often engaged in poetical tournaments known as Mushairas, a sort of war of wits.[123] In these, one person proposed a line, sometimes even a question. Another person provided the answer of it, or contradicted it, or qualified it, or expanded it by a line or lines, in the same meter and rhyming. Poet Nasir Ali, who came from Sarhind, was much admired by Zeb-un-Nisa, and he came to be regarded almost as her rival poet.[124] Zeb-un-Nisa's verses were much appreciated by her father's elder brother Dara Shukoh, a kind hearted, liberal and enlightened man. When she first began to write, she modestly attributed her verses to him, and many of her verses are found in the Diwan of Dara Shukoh.[125]

Zeb-un-Nisa wrote under the pen-name of 'Zeb'.[126] She also used the pen-name of 'Makhfi'[127] (the concealed one) like two of her predecessors. Once Nasir Ali said to her—

(Tr.) *O envy of the moon, lift up thy veil and let me enjoy the wonder of thy beauty.*

Zeb-un-Nisa answered—

(Tr.) *I will not lift my veil, -*
For, if I did, who knows?
The Bulbul might forget the rose,
The Brahman worshipper
Adoring Lakshmi's grace
Might turn, forsaking her,
To see my face;
My beauty might prevail
Think how within the flower
Hidden as in a bower
Her fragrant soul must be,
And none can look on it,
So me the world can see
Only within the verses I have writ—
I will not lift the veil.[128]

Yet at another time she says:

(Tr.) *When from my cheek I lift my veil,*
The roses turn with envy pale,
And from their pierced hearts, rich with pain,
Send forth their fragrance like a wail.
Or if perchance one perfumed tress
Be lowered to the wind's caress,
The honeyed hyacinths complain,
And languish in a sweet distress

And, when I pause, still groves among,
(Such loveliness is mine) a throng
Of nightingales awake and strain
Their souls into a quivering song.[129]

Zeb-un-Nisa's poems deal with feelings of love, beauty, pathos, and spirituality. In 1724 A.D., quite a few years after her death, her scattered writings were collected in a book named *Diwani-i-Makhfi*, or 'The Book of the Hidden One'.[130] It contained 421 ghazals and severals rubias. In 1730 A.D. some other ghazals were added to it.[131] Some historians like Sir Jadunath Sarkar are of the view that the *Diwan-i-Makhfi* could not have been written by Zeb-un-Nisa Begam, as the pseudonym `Makhfi' was used by many poets in those days.[132] May be the *Diwan-i-Makhfi* was not written by Zeb-un-Nisa's hand. Someone else might have written it according to Zeb-un-Nisa's dictations. The beautiful verses of the *Diwan-i-Makhfi* reveal great poetic talent and Sufi ideas, where God Almighty is worshipped as a form of 'Supreme Beauty', the Divine Beloved, who is loved and adored, but who is tyrannical and reduces the lover to despair, but bestows on him a ray of hope when he is at the point of death.

The path of Divine Love is a very difficult one, filled with many obstacles.

(Tr.) *Here is the path of love — how dark and long*
Its winding ways, with many snares beset!
Yet crowds of eager pilgrims onward throng
And fall like dove into the fowler's net.[133]

But, ultimately on reaching Love's path, there is solace and eternal bliss, and the mind realises the futility of life without the Divine Friend.

(Tr.) *O Foolish heart,*
Thy carelessness how can I comprehend?
Hast thou no strength, no will, to tear apart
The barrier that divides me from my Friend?
.....
Treading love's path so long,
Under such heavy burden did I bow.
At last my chastened heart has grown so strong,
No task, no pain, can bend my spirit now.
.....

I have wiped clean my heart
From actions, yea, and from desires as well,
And yearn alone for peace, to have no part
At Judgement Day, either in Heaven or Hell[134]

The love of the Beloved, which is all encompassing, binds the lover in chains, from where there is no escape. The heart then yearns for only one thing — the vision of the Beloved, His beauteous form that fills the heart with joy and longing.

(Tr.) *The love of Thee the bulbul sings.*
The moth that burns its silken wings
Thy love has drawn into the fire,
And see the wine of Thy desire -
On every goblet's lip it clings -
No case, no respite anywhere
And now for me, for in Thy snare
Blindly or willingly I fall,
No liberty have I at all,
Bound by the fetters of Thy hair.[135]
Long, long am I denied
The vision of Thy face, for o'er it flows
The musky darkness of thy waving hair,
As though a temple-curtain should enclose
The Kaaba, and our hearts, unsatisfied.
Could never see it there.

...

Night after endless night
I sat in lonely grief remembering thee;
Tears fell into my heart disconsolate
How long have I, in striving to be free,
Broken my bleeding nails, but never quite
Untied the knot of fate!

....

Stronger my love shall grow:
Bearing the bonds of sorrow for thy sake,
More patient and more proud my heart shall be,
Like the imprisoned bird who tries to make
His cage a garden, though his wild heart knows
He never shall be free[136]

Let not thy curl, whose loveliness
Maddens the world, bring new distress
Upon thy lovers, floating free,
Tossed by the wind that all may see
And fall beneath thy sorcery.
Let not the valley of thy love
A place of bitter torment prove
For dolorous souls, already worn
By all the penance they have borne
Betrayed by love and left forlorn[137]

The only joy for the distressed and tormented heart lies in the glimpse of the Divine Beloved.

(Tr.) *When thou unveil'st thy shining countenance,*
Burnt are my lashes by thy lightning glance,
And all the night I passionately weep
While o'er my heart tempests of longing sweep;
And if I see it not, desiring it,
My heart is darkened like a lamp unlit.
I have no hope, no comfort anywhere,
Caught by the fluttering of thy hair.[138]
No remedy can heal the heart's distress
Except the vision of thy loveliness.
Here, suffering souls, the solace that you need!
Tear not your wounds, no longer make them bleed.[139]

All sorrows and sufferings of the soul are wiped out once the lover has the vision of the Beloved, and the heart fills with gratitude for the Divine grace showered on the lover.

(Tr.) *From the glance Thou bestowed, O Beloved,*
flows beauty no words can express;
My life - it were little to offer in thanks
for Thy bountifulness.[140]

Some of the verses of the *Diwan-i-Makhfi* echo with the idea of oneness of God, the Omnipresent One, who is the Supreme Beloved. They also combine the Hindu and Muslim ideas. Says Makhfi:

(Tr.) *Whether it be in Mecca's holiest shrine,*
Or in the Temple pilgrim feet have trod,
Still Thou art mine,
Wherever God is worshipped is my God.[141]

O Makhfi, if the Kaaba keeper close
To thee his door,
Complain not: thou possessest even more
A holy place;
For look into the well-Beloved Face,
Over His Eyes
Arches more fair than Kaaba gates arise;
Thy heart shall bend.
Itself an archway welcoming the Friend.[142]
In the mosque I seek my idol shrine.
On the Day of Judgement we should have
had much difficulty in proving that we were
true believers, had we not brought with us
our beloved Kafir idol as a witness.[143]

Zeb-un-Nisa, unlike her father, had liberal ideas about religion and believed in the worship of one God with the name and in the form of the Divine Beloved, the Supreme Friend. Some of her verses reflect the feeling of religious harmony.

(Tr.) *No Muslim I,*
But an idolater,
I bow before the image of my Love,
And worship her:
No Brahman I,
My sacred thread
I cast away, for round my neck I wear
Her plaited hair instead.[144]

Quite a few years of Zeb-un-Nisa's later life were spent in captivity and loneliness, she being also deprived of all her property. Says Zeb-un-Nisa about this irony of the fate—

(Tr.) *I am the daughter of an emperor, yet I have set my face towards poverty. This is what adorns my beauty and my name is Zeb-un-Nisa (the adorner of women).*[145]

Talking of her misfortune she writes—

(Tr.) *Long is thine exile, Makhfi, long thy yearning,*
Long shalt thou wait, thy heart within thee burning,
Looking thus forward to thy home-returning.
But now what home hast thou, unfortunate?
The years have passed and left it desolate,

The dust of ages blows across its gate.
If on the Day of Reckoning
God say, "In due proportion I will pay
And recompense thee for thy suffering."
Lo, all the joys of heaven it would outweigh;
Were all God's blessings poured upon me, yet
He would be in my debt.[146]

During her days of confinement and grief, her friends except Nasir Ali, gradually turned away from her side.

(Tr.) *Friends had I, many friends, who shared with me*
Days glad and sad,
But mine they are no more, I am cut free
From all I had.[147]

Yet, at another place she says:

(Tr.) *So long these fetters cling to my feet! My friends have become enemies, my relations are strangers to me.*
What more have I to do with being anxious to keep my name undishonoured when friends seek to disgrace me?
Seek not relief from the prison of grief, O Makhfi; thy release is not politic.
O Makhfi, no hope of release hast thou until the Day of Judgement come. Even from the grave of Majnum the voice comes to my ears - "O Laila, there is no rest for the victim of love even in the grave."
I have spent all my life, and I have won nothing but sorrow, repentance and the tears of unfulfilled desire.[148]

Zeb-un-Nisa indicated her father's cruelty in a bleak verse couplet which runs like an epitaph:

(Tr.) *I have experienced such cruelty and harshness in this land of Hind,*
I shall go and make myself a home in some other land.[149]

Zeb-un-Nisa Begam is also known for her witty and smart poetic remarks and answers to questions.

Once, one of her attendants in the palace said to Zeb-un-Nisa—

(Tr.) *The Chinese mirror is broken and gone.*

Zeb-un-Nisa replied—

(Tr.) *All's well: an object of vanity and self-seeing is gone.*[150]

In another case, to the statement—

(Tr.) *Rarely has a piebald pearl (half black half white) been seen.*

Zeb-un-Nisa remarked:

(Tr.) *Unless it be the tear of a damsel with collyrium in her eyes.*[151]

Once Zeb-un-Nisa, dressed in green and walking on the palace-roof was noticed by Aqil Khan, who was courting her. He remarked:

(Tr.) *A form dressed in green appears under the blue vault of heaven.*

Zeb-un-Nisa quickly replied:

(Tr.) *Neither force nor gold nor guile will bring her to thee (by heaven).*

And when Aqil Khan continued to press his suit, she quoted from poet Sadi:

(Tr.) *Why should the wise man (Aqil) commit an act which brings repentance in its train?*[152]

Her grief and pain are also evident in this verse:

(Tr.) *Oh waterfall for whose sake art thou mourning? For whose sake art thou hanging thy head down in grief?*
And what manner of pain was it that like me through the lifelong night thou didst dash thy head on the ground and weep?[153]

Zeb-un-Nisa's verses more than anything else, reflected the pain and misery she underwent in life. Perhaps this grief that she experienced, turned her thoughts towards spirituality. But her liberal religious views prevented her from becoming a religious fanatic like her father. Her poems on spirituality echo with Sufi sentiments like love of the Supreme Beloved, the bliss incarnate, who can be reached through a very difficult and thorny path, whose love binds the lover (devotee) in chains from where there is no escape. Her religious views also extended to the oneness of God and unity of religions. Her verses are indeed praiseworthy and speak of her high merit as a poetess. In her own words she says—

(Tr.) *In the field of poetry, I am a concealed one, like the odour of the rose which remains hidden in the petals. Whoever looks at my poetry is inclined towards me.*[154]

Zinat-Un-Nisa

The second daughter of Aurangzeb, Zinat-un-Nisa was also educated. She too was the daughter of Dilras Banu Begam and was born at Aurangabad on 5th October, 1643 A.D.[155] She was in charge of her father's household in the Deccan for many years till Aurangzeb's death in 1707 A.D., and some years after that even. She was known for her piety and charity. At her personal expense she built a mosque called the Zinat-ul-Masjid, in Delhi. Here she was buried after her death.[156]

Zinat-un-Nisa, like her elder sister, was also a poetess, though much information about her poems are not available. Probably, like many other Mughal princesses she too engaged in this as a mere pastime. She wrote her epitaph in Persian which says—

(Tr.) *In my grave the grace of God is my only help. It is enough if the shadow of the cloud of mercy covers my tomb.*[157]

Thus, the Mughal age witnessed a considerable amount of development in the literary field, where like the Mughal men, the royal ladies and princesses too contributed in their own ways. Composing verses seems to have been the favourite pastime and hobby for many of these royal ladies who were well educated, cultured and highly accomplished. Some of them were not just satisfied with composing verses and getting good education. These ladies went a step forward and composed works of great literary, historical and cultural value. Many royal ladies had a fascination for collecting books and maintained their own libraries inside the royal palaces. Many were great patrons of learning and built schools and colleges for the spread of learning and education. They also gave land and monetary grants to scholars, poets and learned men who flocked to them in large numbers.

REFERENCES

1. Yusuf Husain, *Glimpses of Medieval Indian Culture* (Bombay: 1962), p. 79.
2. Abul Fazl, *Ain-i-Akbari*, Vol. I (tr.), pp. 288-89.
3. *Ibid.*, p. 289.
4. F.E. Keay, *Indian Education in Ancient and Later Times* (London: 1938), p. 119.
5. *Ibid.*, p. 119.
6. A.L. Srivastava, *Medieval Indian Culture* (Agra: 1964), p. 106.
7. Yusuf Husain, *Glimpses of Medieval Indian Culture*, p. 86.
8. *Ibid.*, p. 86.
9. *Ibid.*, p. 87.
10. A.L. Srivastava, *Akbar the Great*, Vol. II (Agra: 1967), p. 96.
11. Abdul Qadir Badauni, *Muntakhab-ut-Tawarikh*, Vol. II, tr. Lowe (Delhi: 1973), p. 205.

12. Abul Fazl, *Ain-i-Akbari,* Vol. I, tr. Blochmann, pp. 109-110.
13. P.N. Ojha, *Some Aspects of North Indian Social Life* (Patna: 1961), p. 131.
14. M.S. Commissariat, *Mandelslo's Travels in Western India* (London: 1931), p. 118.
15. S.A. Zafar Nadvi, "Libraries During the Muslim Rule in India", *Islamic Culture,* January 1946, p. 18.
16. P.N. Ojha, *Some Aspects of North Indian Social Life* , p. 133.
17. *Ibid.,* p. 133.
18. *Ibid.,* p. 134.
19. *Ibid.,* p. 134.
20. Rekha Misra, *Women in Mughal India,* p. 88.
21. A.S. Beveridge in *Humayun Nama* (tr.), p. 1 (Introduction).
22. *Ibid.,* p. 9.
23. *Ibid.,* p. 10.
24. A.S. Beveridge in *Humayun Nama* (tr.), p. 22.
25. *Ibid.,* p. 22.
26. A.S. Beveridge in *Humayun Nama* (tr.), p. 76.
27. *Ibid.,* p. 76 (Verse quoted from Tazkirat-ul-Khwatin, Eng. tr. in P.N. Chopra, *Life and Letters Under the Mughals,* p. 322).
28. Keay, *Indian Education in Ancient and Later Times,* p. 80; Law, *Promotion of Learning in India During Muhammaden Rule,* p. 201-202; Shelat, *Akbar,* Vol. II (Bombay: 1959), p. 341.
29. A.S. Beveridge in *Humayun Nama,* p. 76.
30. A.S. Beveridge in *Babur Nama* (tr.) Vol. I, p. 441 (Translator's Note); A.S. Beveridge in *Humayun Nama,* pp. 76, 78.
31. V.A. Smith, *Akbar, the Great Mogul* (Delhi: 1988), p. 343.
32. A.S. Beveridge in *Humayun Nama* (tr.), p. 76.
33. *Ibid.,* p. 22.
34. A.S. Beveridge in *Humayun Nama* (tr.), p. 85.
35. *Ibid.,* pp. 93-95.
36. *Ibid.,* p. 100.
37. *Ibid.,* pp. 105-9.
38. *Ibid.,* p. 110.
39. *Humayun Nama* (tr.), pp. 149-51.
40. *Ibid.,* pp. 176-79.
41. Keay, *Indian Education in Ancient and Later Times,* p. 80; Law, *Promotion of Learning in India...*p. 202; Shelat, *Akbar,* Vol. III, pp. 341-42; Banerjee, *Humayun Badshah,* Vol. II, p. 324; Yusuf Husain, *Glimpses of Medieval Indian Culture,* p. 82.
42. A.S. Beveridge in *Humayun Nama* (tr.), p. 276 (Translator's Note).
43. *Ibid.,* pp. 276-77.
44. *Tuzuk-i-Jahangiri* (tr.), Vol. I, p. 232.
45. A.S. Beveridge in *Humayun Nama* (tr.), p. 58, Keay, *Indian Education in Ancient and Later Times,* p. 80.
46. A.S. Beveridge in *Humayun Nama* (tr.), p. 279; *Maathir-ul-Umara* (tr.), Vol. I, p. 371; *Ain-i-Akbari,* Vol. I (tr.), p. 322.
47. Maathir-ul-Umara (tr.), Vol. I, p. 371.
48. A.S. Beveridge in *Humayun Nama* (tr.), p. 76.
49. R. Misra, *Women in Mughal India,* p. 89.

50. S.C. Welch, *India, Art & Culture* (New York: 1985), p. 153.
51. Mutamid Khan, *Iqbal Nama-i-Jahangiri* (text) (Calcutta: 1865), p. 56; Mutamid Khan, *Iqbal Nama*, tr. in Elliot and Dowson, Vol. 6, pp. 404-405; De Laet,p. 181.
52. *Tuzuk-i-Jahangiri* (tr.), Vol. I, p. 319.
53. R.P.Tripathi, *Rise and Fall of the Mughal Empire* (Allahabad: 1960), p. 421.
54. Mutamid Khan, *Iqbal Nama-i-Jahangiri*, tr. in Elliot & Dowson, Vol. 6, p. 405.
55. Keay, *Indian Education in Ancient and Later Times*, p. 80.
56. Findly, *Noorjahan, Empress of Mughal India*, (New York: 1993), p. 226.
57. *Ain-i-Akbari*, Vol. I (tr.), pp. 559-60.
58. Khafi Khan, *Muntakhab-ul-Lubab*, Vol. I, ed. Kabiruddin Ahmad and Woolsley Haig (Calcutta: 1860), pp. 269-271.
59. Quoted from Hadi Hasan, *A Golden Treasury of Persian Poetry* (New Delhi: 1972), pp. 368-69.
60. *Ibid.*, p. 368-69.
61. Khafi Khan, *Muntakhab-ul-Lubab*, Vol. I, p. 270; English tr. from Hadi Hasan's *Mughal Poetry* (Aligrah: 1952), p. 79.
62. Khafi Khan, Vol. I, pp. 270-271; English tr. by Barakat Ullah in Macnicol ed. *Poems by Indian Women*, p. 78.
63. English translation in Findly's *Noorjahan..*, p. 227.
64. *Ibid.*, p. 227.
65. *Ibid.*, p. 227.
66. English tr. by Barakat Ullah in Margaret Macnicol ed. *Poems by Indian Women*, (London: 1923), p. 76.
67. English translation in Findly's *Noorjahan*, p. 227.
68. *Ibid.*, p. 227.
69. *Ibid.*, p. 227.
70. *Ibid.*, p. 227.
71. Khafi Khan, Vol. I, p. 270.
72. Beni Prasad, *History of Jahangir* (Madras: 1922), p. 172.
73. P.N. Ojha, *Some Aspects of North Indian Social Life*, p. 131.
74. *Ibid.*, p. 131.
75. Sugam Anand, *History of Begum Nurjahan*, p. 67.
76. K.S. Lal, *The Mughal Harem*, p. 76.
77. Sugam Anand, *History of Begam Nurjahan*, p. 67; Findly, *Noorjahan...*, p. 226.
78. Findly, *Noorjahan...*, p. 226.
79. English tr. by Barakat Ullah in Margaret Macnicol ed., *Poems by Indian Women*, p. 79.
80. Quoted from Hadi Hasan, *Golden Treasury of Persian Poetry*, pp. 374-75.
81. *Ibid.*, pp. 374-75.
82. Law, *Promotion of Learning in India....*, p. 203; S.M. Jafar, *Education in Muslim India* (Lahore: 1936), pp. 195-96.
83. Law, *Promotion of Learning in India...*, pp. 203-4; S.M. Jafar, *Education in Muslim India*, pp. 195-96.
84. English tr. in K.S. Lal's *The Mughal Harem*, p. 98.
85. R. Misra, *Women in Mughal India*, p. 90.
86. R.C. Majumdar ed., *The Mughal Empire* (Bombay: 1974), p. 14.
87. *Ibid.*, p. 14.

88. *Ibid.*, p. 14.
89. R. Misra, *Women in Mughal India*, p. 93; Zinat Kausar, *Muslim Women in Medieval India* (New Delhi: 1992), p. 159.
90. Law, *Promotion of Learning in India...*, p. 203; S.M. Jafar, *Education in Muslim India*, p. 196.
91. M.A. Ansari, *Social Life of the Mughal Emperors* (New Delhi: 1983), p. 119.
92. Yusuf Husain, *Glimpses of Medieval Indian Culture*, p. 86.
93. Jadunath Sarkar, *History of Aurangzeb*, Vol. I, pp. 68-69; *Studies in Mughal India*, p. 79.
94. Magan Lal tr., *The Diwan of Zeb-un-Nissa* (London: 1913), p. 14.
95. *Ibid.*, p. 11.
96. Jadunath Sarkar, *Studies in Mughal India*, pp. 86-88.
97. Jadunath Sarkar, *Studies in Mughal India*, p. 87; Macnicol ed., *Poems by Indian Women*, p. 36.
98. Jadunath Sarkar, *History of Aurangzeb* , Vol. I, p. 69; *Studies in Aurangzib's Reign* (Calcutta: 1933), p. 141.
99. Jadunath Sarkar, *Studies in Mughal India*, p. 79; Maharani Sunity Devee, *The Beautiful Mogul Princesses* (London: 1918), p. 55.
100. Magan Lal tr., *The Diwan of Zeb-un-Nissa*, p. 8.
101. *Ibid.*, p. 9.
102. Jadunath Sarkar, *Studies in Mughal India.*, p. 79; Magan Lal tr., *The Diwan of Zeb-un-Nissa*, p. 8.
103. Magan Lal tr., *The Diwan of Zeb-un-Nissa*, p. 8.
104. Magan Lal tr., *The Diwan of Zeb-un-Nissa*, p. 8; Mustaid Khan's *Maasir-i-Alamgiri* tr. in Elliot and Dowson, Vol. 7, p. 196.
105. Magan Lal tr., *The Diwan of Zeb-un-Nissa*, p. 8.
106. Sunity Devee, *The Beautiful Mogul Princesses*, p. 55; Sarkar, *History of Aurangzib*, Vol. I & II, pp. 37-38 (Vol. I); Mustaid Khan's *Maasir-i-Alamgiri* tr. in Elliot and Dowson, Vol. 7, p. 196.
107. Magan Lal tr., *The Diwan of Zeb-un-Nissa*, pp. 8-9.
108. Sarkar, *Studies in Mughal India*, p. 79.
109. Sarkar, *Studies in Mughal India*, p. 79; Sarkar tr. *Maasir-i-Alamgiri*, p. 322; Magan Lal tr., *The Diwan of Zeb-un-Nissa*, p. 13; Yusuf Husain, *Glimpses of Medieval Indian Culture*, p. 93.
110. Sunity Devee, *The Beautiful Mogul Princesses*, p. 55.
111. Sarkar, *Studies in Mughal India*, p. 79.
112. Magan Lal tr., *The Dewan of Zeb-un-Nissa*, p. 13.
113. Ila Mukherjee, *Social Status of North Indian Women* (Agra: 1972), p. 106.
114. Sunity Devee, *The Beautiful Mogul Princesses*, p. 58.
115. Sarkar, *Studies in Mughal India*, p. 79.
116. Magan Lal tr., *The Dewan of Zeb-un-Nissa*, p. 13.
117. Sarkar, *Studies in Mughal India*, p. 79. Sarkar tr. *Maasir-i-Alamgiri*, p. 322.
118. Magan Lal tr., *The Dewan of Zeb-un-Nissa*, p. 9.
119. *Ibid.*, p. 9.
120. Magan Lal tr., *The Dewan of Zeb-un-Nissa*, p. 9.
121. *Ibid.*, p. 9.
122. D.S. Roy, *Warring Women of Ind.* (Bombay: 1973), p. 6.

123. Magan Lal tr., *The Dewan of Zeb-un-Nissa*, p. 9.
124. *Ibid.*, pp. 9-10.
125. Magan Lal tr., *The Dewan of Zeb-un-Nissa*, p. 11.
126. Macnicol ed., *Poems by Indian Women*, p. 36.
127. Magan Lal tr., *The Dewan of Zeb-un-Nissa*, p. 11; Sarkar, *Studies in Mughal India*, p. 80.
128. Magan Lal tr., *The Dewan of Zeb-un-Nissa*, pp. 11-12.
129. Poem tr. by Sarojini Naidu in Macnicol ed., *Poems by Indian Women*, p. 77.
130. Magan Lal tr., *The Dewan of Zeb-un-Nissa*, p. 20.
131. *Ibid.*, p. 20.
132. Sarkar, *Studies in Mughal India*, p. 80.
133. Magan Lal tr., *The Dewan of Zeb-un-Nissa*, Verses V, p. 31.
134. *Ibid.*, Verse XIV, p. 47.
135. Magan Lal tr., *The Dewan of Zeb-un-Nissa*, Verse XXXVIII, p. 86.
136. *Ibid.*, Verse XLIV, p. 95.
137. *Ibid.*, Verse XLIX, p. 105.
138. *Ibid.*, Verse XXXVII, p. 85.
139. *Ibid.*, Verse XLVII, p. 103.
140. *Ibid.*, Verse VIII, p. 37.
141. *Ibid.*, Verse II, p. 27.
142. *Ibid.*, Verse III, p. 28.
143. *Ibid.*, p. 22.
144. *Ibid.*, p. 22.
145. Verse tr. by Barakat Ullah in Macnicol's *Poems by Indian Women*, p. 78.
146. Magan Lal tr., *The Dewan of Zeb-un-Nissa*, p. 18 (Introduction).
147. *Ibid.*, Verse XII, p. 4.
148. *Ibid.*, p. 18.
149. W. Hansen, *The Peacock Throne* (Great Britain: 1973), p. 465.
150. Quoted from Hadi Hasan, *Mughal Poetry*, p. 8; *A Golden Treasury of Persian Poetry*, pp. 402-403.
151. *A Golden Treasury of Persian Poetry*, pp. 402-3.
152. Quoted from Hadi Hasan, *Mughal Poetry*, p. 80; *Golden Treasury of Persian Poetry*, pp. 404-405.
153. *Mughal poetry*, p. 79; *A Golden Treasury of Persian Poetry*, pp. 402-3.
154. Ila Mukherjee, *Social Status of North Indian Women* (Agra: 1972), p. 105.
155. Sarkar, *History of Aurangzib*, Vol. I, p. 70.
156. *Ibid.*
157. Verse translated by Barakat Ullah in Macnicol ed. *Poems by Indian Women*, p. 79.

Six

Artistic Contributions

The Mughals were men of artistic inclinations. They were great builders, literati, musicians, painters, garden layers, dress designers and patronisers of almost all forms of arts and crafts. The contribution of the Mughals in the field of Art and Architecture is without doubt remarkable. R.C. Mazumdar is of the opinion that, "the Mughal period was not entirely an age of innovation and renaissance, but of a continuation and culmination of processes that had their beginning in the later Turko-Afghan period. In fact, the art and architecture of that period after 1526, as also of the preceding period, represent a happy mingling of Muslim and Hindu art traditions and elements."[1]

ARCHITECTURE

The Mughal ladies lived in utmost luxury in fine apartments and palaces built for them by the emperors and the princes. These apartments were separately built, spacious and splendid, according to the position of the woman in the emperor's harem. Each of those had their own garden, fountains and reservoirs of running water and many other facilities that made life a pleasure. This fact is quite evident from the Mariam's Kothi, Turkish Sultana's Apartments, Jodha Bai's Mahal and the apartments of other ladies of the harem at Fatehpur Sikri, the quarters of Bilqis Makani (Jehangir's mother), Nur Jahan and the Bengali Mahal where the ladies of various nations resided, at the Agra Fort, the Imtiyaz and Rang Mahals of the ladies at the Red Fort in Delhi, and also from the women's apartments in the Lahore Fort.

The beautiful and luxurious living quarters of the Mughal women did not prevent them from plunging into construction work themselves. During the Mughal age we come across remarkable women like Haji Begam, Jodha Bai, Nur Jahan, Jahanara, Roshanara, Zeb-un-Nisa and Zinat-un-Nisa, whose remarkable buildings exist even today, sometimes in totality and sometimes partially.

Monuments Built by Mughal Women

We do not come across any building worth mentioning constructed by the Mughal women during Babar's or Humayun's times, except some gardens which will be discussed later on. The first monument built under the supervision of any Mughal lady in India was the Humayun's Tomb in Delhi, built by one of Humayun's widows named Haji Begam during the reign of Emperor Akbar. Gulbadan calls her Bega Begam.[2] She was Humayun's cousin and wife of his youth.[3]

Contribution of Haji Begum

Humayun's Tomb, Delhi

The Humayun's Tomb was built eight years after Humayun's death[4] by Humayun's widow Haji Begam in Delhi and she became its faithful attendant thereafter.[5] It is one of the first garden tombs built by the Mughals in India[6] and in some ways provided the model of the later built Taj Mahal.[7] According to Percy Brown, the Humayun's tomb "is not only one of the most arresting examples of the building art in India but it is also an outstanding landmark in the development of the Mughal style."[8] In structure and spirit, the Humayun's Tomb is an example of the synthesis of the Persian and the Indian building traditions. To Havell, it is "a Persianized version of Sher Shah's tomb."[9] The tomb is built of Tantpura red sandstone, with dressings of white Makrana marble.[10]

The construction of the tomb began in c. 1560 A.D. and was completed in 1573 A.D.[11] It stands on a large square platform, 22 ft. in height, having arches, whose piers are ornamented with white marble inlay work.[12] The main tomb is an octagonal apartment, 47 ft and 4 inches across and crowned by a dome of white marble.[13] In the corner rooms are the tombs of Haji Begam and some nine other members of the royal family. All the apartments add up to make a building square in plan and about 155 ft. each way, "with the angles slightly cut away".[14] The tomb has a beautiful garden attached to it.

The building is quite unlike any of Akbar's buildings and the plan had to be someone else's. Fergusson is of the opinion that the "most marked characteristic" feature of the Humayun's Tomb "is its purity—it might almost be called poverty of design."[15] Sir Sayyid Ahmad Khan praises the monument thus:

(Tr.) *If anyone has the desire to see paradise, tell him to come and see the garden of Humayun.*[16]

Haji Begam also built a *sarai* called 'Arban Sarai' in 1560 A.D. which had an accommodation of 300 people.[17]

Baoli of Maryam-Uz-Zamani

During the time of Emperor Jehangir, in the pargana of Jusat, 1½ *koss* from Biana, by the orders of Jahangir's mother, Maryam-uz-Zamani Jodha Bai, a *baoli (step-well)* accompanied by a garden was built.[18] Jehangir in his memoirs writes - "This baoli (step-well) was a grand building and had been built exceedingly well."[19] This *baoli* still exists. William Finch in his account speaks of a place called Menhapoore near Bayana where he had gone to buy indigo and lodged at a great saray where there was a *mahal* or summer house of the Queen Mother (Jehangir's mother), "Very curiously contrived."[20] These two places were probably one and the same.

Contributions of Nur Jahan Begam

Nur Jahan Begam, the exceedingly beautiful wife of Jehangir, the ruler of his heart as well as his Empire, and the most versatile of all Mughal ladies, left no field in fine and practical art untouched without the mark of her achievement and contribution whether it was literataure, architecture, gardening, dress designing, decoration, hunting, shooting or anything else.

The most permanent of all of Nur Jahan's artistic achievements was in the field of architecture, in the buildings and monuments she designed and patronized. Among them were the tomb of her father, Etimad-ud-Daula, at Agra, Nur Mahal sarai near Jalandhar, Pathar Masjid at Srinagar, tomb of Jehangir at Shahdara, Lahore and her own tomb in Lahore.

The Tomb of Etimad-ud-Daula, Agra

One of the most outstanding buildings constructed during the reign of Jehangir was the tomb of one of his most powerful nobles Ghiyas Beg, titled Etimad-ud-Daula (The Pillar of Government), who was also the father of his queen Nur Jahan. Constructed under the supervision of Nur Jahan, the tomb of Etimad-ud-Daula took six years to get completed, i.e. from 1622 A.D. to 1628 A.D.[21]

The tomb is situated on the left bank of the river Jamuna in Agra amidst a garden which is surrounded by a wall measuring 540 ft. on each side,[22] having red sandstone gateways on all sides. The tomb occupies the central position of the garden and stands on a raised square platform, measuring 69 ft. on each side.[23] The tomb has two storeys with an octagonal tower at each of the four sides, surmounted by an open pavilion. The upper pavilion contains a second pair of cenotaphs surrounded on each side by large latticed windows.[24] The lower storey has a central chamber in the form of a parallelogram measuring 22 ft. and 3 inches on each side.[25] This chamber contains the main cenotaphs of Etimad-ud-Daula and his wife Asmat Banu Begam. The floor is made of marble and is richly decorated with mosaic work. The walls have inscriptions from the Islamic scriptures. The four corner chambers are occupied by the brother, sister and some other members of Etimad-ud-Daula's family.[26] There are three arches opening out each side of the main portion of the building, separated from one another by latticed lancets.[27]

The design of the tomb is intensely feminine. The tomb is not very big or massive and one is drawn more towards its decoration than its form. It is built entirely of white marble and covered throughout with inlay work called "pietra dura"— the white marble surface worked with polished inlays of semi-precious stones in a technique similar to that developed in Florence in the sixteenth century.[28] This type of ornamentation of this tomb was the first of its kind in India.[29] The lower exterior of the tomb has geometrical patterns mainly, and the upper exterior and interior surfaces of the building has inlaid designs of flowers, cypress tress, creepers, grapes, vases, water jugs, etc. The surface decoration is so exquisite and remarkable that it appears "bejewelled...like a brilliant casket."[30] Construction of this beautiful tomb was a very costly affair. According to De Laet, this magnificient tomb was built at an estimated cost of more than 10 million rupees.[31] As per Pelsaert's estimates, when the tomb was not yet complete, it had "already cost fully 350,000 rupees," and was likely to cost 1,000,000 more" before it was finished.[32] A certain legend goes that Nur Jahan thought of building this tomb entirely of pure silver, but was advised to use white marble instead, as it was more suitable to the Indian weather conditions.[33] The entire expense was borne by Nur Jahan's treasuries.

The tomb of Etimad-ud-Daula was an innovation in many ways. It marked a transition between the Indianised red sandstone and marble constructions of Akbar and Jehangir, and the Persianized pure marble creations of Shahjahan.[34] In ways more than one its design was adopted in the later built Taj Mahal,[35] like the entire structure of white marble, pietra-dura inlay work, use of Persian motifs on the walls, etc. The whole structure of Etimad-ud-Daula's tomb along with the octagonal towers at the four corners provided the model for Jehangir's tomb at Shahdara, Lahore.[36] Percy Brown speaks highly of the monument when he says,

> There is no other building like it in the entire range of Mughal architecture, the delicacy of treatment and the chaste quality of its decoration placing it in a class by itself...[37]

Nur Mahal Sarai, Jalandhar

The Mughal age was an age of development in almost every field we can think of including economy. The growing importance of trade and commerce and politics too, led to the construction of a network of roads that connected places of commercial and political interests. Along the sides of these roads shady trees were planted, wells dug out and resting places for travellers called *sarais* constructed. In these activities too the Mughal ladies participated side by side with their emperors.

The Nur Mahal Sarai near Jalandhar in the Punjab is one of the best examples of such type of activities undertaken by some Mughal women. This *sarai*, as its name suggests, was built by Nur Jahan Begam around 1620 A.D., who bore the entire expenses too.[38] It is situated 16 miles south of Jalandhar, 25 miles east south-east of Sultanpur and 13 miles west of Phalor.[39] The *sarai* was built on a site measuring 551 square feet. It had octagonal towers at the corners. The western gateway, called Lahore gate is double-storied and built in red sand-stone. Its front is divided into panels ornamented in sculptured relief. There were figures of angels, lotuses, nymphs, lions, elephants, birds, peacocks, men on horseback, etc. The scenes represented by many of these had historical importance depicting the life of Mughal emperors like scenes of elephant fight or four horsemen playing Chaugan.[40] Over the entrance to the gateway is an inscription, flanked by scenes of fighting animals and sculpted lotus-mounds. The inscription written in four rhyming verses, reads as follows:

1. During the just rule of Jehangir Shah, son of Akbar Shah, whose like neither heaven nor earth remembers.
2. The Nur Saray was founded in the district of Phalor by command of that angel, Nur Jahan Begam.
3. The poet happily discovered this date of its foundation: this Saray was founded by Nur Jahan Begam in 1028.
4. Knowledge of the date of its completion was found in the words: "This Saray was erected by Nur Jahan Begam" 1030.[41]

There were plenty of rooms, Emperor's quarters, a well and a mosque inside the Sarai area. Jehangir mentions this *sarai* in his memoirs when he says:

> ...I took up my quarters at Nur-Saray. At this spot the Vakils of Nur Jahan Begam had built a lofty house, and made a royal garden. It was now completed. On this account the Begam, having begged for an entertainment, prepared a grand feast, and by way of offering, with great pains produced all kinds of delicate and rare things. In order to please her I took what I approved. I halted two days at this place.[42]

In his memoirs, Jehangir mentions this place at another time also.[43] Nur Jahan's Sarai near Jalandhar was quite famous during those times and 'Serai Noor Mahal' in local usage came to mean some spacious and important edifice.[44]

Nur Mahal Sarai, Agra

Nur Jahan Begam built another *sarai,* also called Nur Mahal Sarai, near Agra. Situated in the district of Nur Mahal,[45] Peter

Mundy speaks of this building in his accounts. Mundy halted in this place on 6th August, 1632 A.D. Talking about the *sarai* he said that it was "a very faire one, built by the old Queene Noor Mohol...for the accommodation of Travellers."[46] Mundy estimated that it could accommodate two to three thousand people and five hundred horses.[47] It was made completely "of Stone, not one piece of Timber in it, the rooms all arched each with severall Copula." It stood "between Two gardens, built also by her."[48] Sir Richard Carnac Temple says that one of these gardens was the Moti Bagh and the other, the Nawal or Nawab Ganj built during Shahjahan's time.[49]

Pathar Masjid (Stone Mosque), Srinagar

One of the mosques found in Kashmir belonging to the Mughal times the Pathar Masjid constructed by Nur Jahan Begam,[50] also known by the names of Shahi Masjid (Royal Mosque) and Nau Masjid (New Mosque). The mosque is made of grey limestone and has a front facade of nine arches, the central arch being bigger than the other eight.[51] It is said that this mosque had been deserted and never been used for the purpose of which it was built. This was because the Muslims despised the building as it was made under the supervision of a woman. It was used as a store-house.[52]

Jehangir's Tomb, Shahdara, Lahore

Nur Jahan Begam is also said to have designed and supervised the construction of Jahangir's tomb at Shahdara, Lahore.[53] It is situated 6 miles north-west of Lahore, in the Dilkusha Garden, once a pleasure ground of Nur Jahan Begam, now called Shahdara.[54] The plan of this tomb resembled that of Etimad-ud-Daula's[55] at Agra and of Akbar's[56] at Sikandra.

The layout comprised of an outer *sarai* with a series of alcoves round the walls to provide shelter for the travellers, a tall gateway leading to the inner garden and the main tomb building inside this garden.[57] There are gateways on all the four sides. The mausoleum stands on a low plinth, 256 ft. square and consists of a terraced platform with octagonal minarets of three storeys above the terraced roof, surmounted by white marble cupolas. It is surrounded by arcades, having a central arch flanked by a doorway and five other arches on each side.[58] The sarcophagus is made of white marble with pietradura inlay work and is placed in an octagonal chamber.[59] It is said that this marble parapet was carried off by Raja Ranjit Singh and later restored.[60] In fact, much of the tomb was harmed by Ranjit Singh when he carried away the marble for his own buildings.[61] The building lacks a dome and it is not known for sure whether the tomb had a central dome which was never completed or subsequently destroyed.[62] Round the base of the catafalque runs a beautiful design of cyclamen and tulips like those found in Kashmir.[63] The building is made of red sandstone with marble inlay.

Nur Jahan's Tomb, Lahore

Nur Jahan Begam's own tomb in Lahore is very simple and humble compared to the other rich and lofty buildings constructed under her supervision and with her money. After the death of Jehangir in 1627 A.D., Nur Jahan led a quiet life in Lahore till her death in 1648 A.D. Here she was buried at Shahdara, along the banks of the river Ravi, not very far away from her husband.

Nur Jahan's tomb was set on a square platform occupying the centre of a Charbagh having boundary walls. The original garden does not remain any more, but it once is said to have had canals, tanks, waterfalls, fountains, cypress trees, tulips, roses, jasmine and fruit trees, especially date palms.[64] The tomb of Nur Jahan had many similarities with that of her father Etimad-ud-Daula's and her husband Jahangir's. It was square in shape, one story, with seven arches, opening out the corridors on each of the four sides. The interior was arranged in a series of three arched and columned galleries. In the central part is a square room which has the cenotaphs of Nur Jahan and her daughter Ladli Begam, placed on a platform in the centre.[65] Much of the decorative part of the tomb was destroyed in course to time though some of it was restored later with red sandstone and marble inlay.[66] Whatever remains of the interior surface decoration reveal painted design rather than of inlaid stone.[67]

Nur Jahan's tomb will always remain a mystery to all. What it was in its original totality or what it was intended to be can never be known. But the humility of the whole structure and its occupant is quite evident from the epitaph which says:

Upon my grave when I shall die,
No lamps shall burn nor jasmine lie,
No candle, with unsteady flame,
Serve as a reminder of my fame,
No bulbul chanting overhead,
Shall tell the world that I am dead.[68]

Contributions of Jahanara Begam

Shahjahan's secondary wives Akbarabadi Mahal built the Akbarabadi Mosque (destroyed by the British in 1857), Fatehpuri Mahal built the Fatehpuri Mosque in Chandni Chowk and Sarhindi Begam built the Sarhindi Mosque at Lahori Gate, near Khari Baoli Bazar in Delhi. Akbarabadi Mahal also constructed two stepped wells (Baoli) and a *Sarai.*[69] But the real contributions in this field during that time were made by Shahjahan's daughters, Jahanara and Roshanara.

Jahanara and Roshanara like some of the royal Mughal ladies that we have discussed so far, were actively involved in construction works and have left behind them some monuments still with their touch like their own mausoleums. Jahanara's contribution in the field of architecture was not confined to building her mausoleum alone, but extended to the construction of gardens, palaces, mosques, *sarai*, monastery and even market places.

Mosques

In the Kashmir valley, Princess Jahanara, popularly known as Begam Saheb, is known to have built a mosque "in an exquisite artistic style," at the cost of rupees 40,000, the entire funds being provided by the Princess herself.[70] This mosque was built for a certain learned man called Mulla Shah Badakshani who, on this occasion was presented with a valuable diamond on behalf of Jahanara.[71] This mosque was surrounded by large buildings meant for the habitation of the poor, constructed at a further cost of rupees 20,000.[72] Khafi Khan too mentions this building and its cost.[73] Jahanara Begam also built another mosque in Agra, known as the Jami Masjid, once again out of her personal allowances and funds.[74] It stands outside the Agra fort on the north-west direction.

It was completed after five years of work in 1648 A.D., and had cost five hundred thousand rupees. It is a fine structure of bold design, excellent finish and magnificient proportions. She wished it to bring her eternal and everlasting fame and reward in life later. Shahjahan had once been interested in the construction of the same mosque, but later allowed Jahanara to build it.[75] Jahanara is said to have built a Rabat (monastery) too.[76] Taking into consideration Princess Jahanara's religious bent of mind, it is quite natural that she constructed quite a few edifices connected to religion.

Caravansarais and Market Places

Jahanara contributed towards the development of trade and commerce by constructing caravansarais and market places. Manucci, Bernier, Tavernier and Thevenot speak of the caravansarai of Jahanara Begam or Begam Saheb,[77] as she was popularly known as. This Caravansarai was built in Delhi and had a lovely garden and a reservoir. Describing the Caravansarai, Bernier writes:

> The Karuansara is in the form of a large square with arcades, like our Palace Royale, except that the arches are separated from each other by partitions, and have small chambers at their inner extremities. Above the arcades runs a gallery all round the building, into which open the same number of chambers as there are below.[78]

Provision was made for adequate safety for the travellers and merchants, the gates being closed at night. The caravansarai is said to have been meant for the rich Persian, Usbek and other foreign merchants.[79] The Begam Sarai was destroyed after the Sepoy Mutiny.[80]

Jahanara Begam planned and supervised the building of the Chowk Sarai Bazaar in Lahore.[81] She also built the famous Chandni Chowk Bazaar near the Red Fort in Delhi,[82] which is even to this day a hub of commercial activities in the Capital.

Jahanara's Tomb

Jahanara Begam's tomb at the shrine of the Sufi saint Nizam-ud-din Aulia in Delhi is simple, yet revealing her artistic sense. Her white marble grave is open to the sky and had grass grown in a hollow on top of the edifice. This was done at her special request. There are no other ornamentations on it, except a lily carved of precious jade, green in colour.[83]

Roshanara Begam's Tomb, Delhi

Roshanara Begam, another daughter of Shahjahan too designed her own tomb along with its garden, situated in the north-western parts of Delhi. The mausoleum is beautiful, built in pure white marble with exquisite ornamentation on the exterior parts. It stands on a low wide platform in the centre of the upper terrace in the gardens still bearing her name.[84]

Purhunar Banu Begam, a daughter of Shahjahan is said to have been buried in a mausoleum built under her supervision.[85] Which of his daughters exactly bore this name cannot be said for sure.

Tomb of Zeb-Un-Nisa Begam

During the time of Aurangzeb, one of his wives Nawab Bai, the mother of Muhammad Sultan, Muhammad Muazzam and Badr-un-Nisa, is said to have built a *sarai* at Fardapur and founded the place of Baijipura in this suburb of Aurangabad.[86] But the real contribution in the field of architecture during the time of Aurangzeb was made by two of his daughters: the eldest Zeb-un-Nisa and the second, Zinat-un-Nisa.

Zeb-un-Nisa Begam built a number of gardens like the Char-Burji and Nawan Kot in Lahore, where she was finally buried.[87] Her tomb was made of fine marble with a pinnacle of gold. But according to Sir Jadunath Sarkar, she was "buried in the garden of `Thirty Thousand Trees', outside the Kabuli gate."[88] Her tomb was later demolished for the construction of a railway line. Her coffin and inscribed tomb-stone are now in Akbar's mausoleum at Sikandra.[89]

Contributions of Zinat-Un-Nisa Begam

Lastly, we come to the contributions of yet another Mughal princess, Zinat-un-Nisa, the second daughter of Aurangzeb, in the field of architecture. She is known to have built around fourteen caravansarais.[90] At the age of 37, Zinat-un-Nisa undertook a project to construct a number of inns of the highway linking Oudh with Bengal. This effort of hers earned the praise of her father.[91] These were probably the caravansarais built by her.

A splendid mosque, the Zinat-ul-Masjid, was built at her expense in Delhi.[92] There she was buried after death, but her grave was later removed somewhere else by the British Military authorities when they occupied the building.[93] Tradition goes that Zinat-un-Nisa demanded the amount of her dowry from her father, and spent it in building this mosque.[94]

Mughal Monuments Inspired by Mughal Ladies

After we have finished discussing about the various construction works undertaken by the royal Mughal ladies, we will leave the account incomplete if we do not mention the monuments that were inspired by the Mughal Emperor's love for his lady. We know that Jehangir had built a lovely mausoleum for his beloved Anarkali in Lahore. He also built the garden tomb of one of his favourite queens, Shah Begam, the mother of Khusrau, in Allahabad. But the greatest monument ever built to commemorate the love of an emperor for his empress is the Taj Mahal at Agra — the finest monument of conjugal love in the world.

The Taj Mahal, Agra

The death of Mumtaz Mahal in 1631 A.D. after the birth of her fourteenth child is said to have left Shahjahan heart broken. The court festivities were stopped for days and the Emperor refused to take part in any public affair. His grief was without limits at the sad and untimely demise of the lady he loved so much, the lady, who was his constant companion in difficulty as in happiness and success. Shahjahan decided that even though Mumtaz Mahal was dead, she would live forever in the mausoleum that would be built as her final resting place. Thus, the Taj Mahal came into existence. The land on the banks of the river Jamuna towards south of Agra, that belonged to Raja Man Singh[95] and later his grandson Raja Jai Singh, was acquired at the site for the Taj Mahal.[96]

The Taj Mahal, the 'Venus de Milo' of the East, took approximately 20 years to get completed (1632 A.D. - 1652 A.D.).

20,000 workmen were employed in its construction. The expenses upto 50 lakhs of rupees, but some sources estimate it to be 9 crores and 17 lakhs of rupees.[97] The work was supervised by Mukarramat Khan and Mir Abdul Karim.[98] Ustad Isa was its chief architect. Artisans and material were brought from various places of the world like Qandhar, Ceylon, Nile, Sea of Ormuz, Basrah, Yemen, Persia, and other places.

The whole mausoleum is placed within a rectangular area 1900 ft. by 1000 ft.,[99] enclosed on all sides, except the river front by a high wall with octagonal turrets. On three sides there are gateways similar to each other, but only one of them, the southern gateway is functional. The entrance portal, like all the other gateways is made of red sandstone with marble inlay. Along the frame of the central alcove are found Quranic inscriptions in black letters against white marble background. The main gateway descends down to a square garden measuring 1000 feet on each side and approximately 42 acres in area.[100] On the western side of the mausoleum is a mosque. The main tomb stands on a marble platform at the northern end of the garden and not at the centre as the usual Mughal garden tombs were designed. The tomb building occupies the centre of this platform.

The aesthetic beauty, grace, delicacy and serenity of the Taj Mahal can never be described in words, how much ever we might try. It is to be felt and experienced personally. This entire huge structure built of pure white marble is not disproportionate in any way. Every single aspect of it matches with the others in perfect harmony making it an out of the world beauty. It is made of very costly material and yet it has a marked simplicity about it. The final result of it is certainly what it was intended to be. For no one, who has seen and experienced the beauty and serenity of the Taj Mahal, can ever forget it.

MUGHAL GARDENS

The Mughal rulers and their ladies were just not satisfied with building beautiful monuments, but were also fond of laying exotic gardens which accompanied these buildings or were accompanied by beautiful constructions. Since ancient times India has always been a land of large variety of flora and fauna. Flowers have always been a necessity in social and religious life of the people of this country. Long before the Mughals came to India, certainly gardens had existed in this country, but they were not geometrically designed and laid out.[101] It was from Central Asia and Persia that the splendid garden traditions came into India. It were the Mughals who carried the art of gardening in Hindustan to its zenith.[102]

The Mughals brought with them their own ideas of gardening. This new style developed in Persia and Turkistan was characterised by "artificial irrigation in the form of channels and tanks and dwarf waterfalls ... and the plan involved a series of terraces on slopping ground, usually numbering eight to correspond with the eight divisions of the Quranic paradise; but sometimes seven to symbolise the seven planets. The main pavilion was built on the topmost terrace and sometimes of the lowest terrace in order to enable the occupant to have an uninterrupted view of foliage and the water-fall."[103] After coming to India the new Mughal style of gardening developed quickly. The water became the central motive and quite a few new flowering shrubs, fruits and vegetables were introduced.[104] The Hindu influence in gardening came with Akbar's marriage to Jodha Bai (Mariam uz Zamani), the Rajput princess of Amber.[105]

Famous Flowers and Trees

Some of the famous flowers of those days were: Banafsha, Yasaman, and Nasarin, which were of foreign origin, being introduced to India from Persia; and Baila, Kevra, Champa, Molsiri, Sevtri, Damra, Karma and Laung, which were of Indian origin.[106] Some Indian flowers given Persian names were Gul-i-Kuza, Gul-i-Sadbarg and Qaranful or Laung.[107] The Mughal gardens were filled with a variety of fruit trees as well. Among the most famous fruits found in these gardens were mangoes, apples, bananas, grapes, oranges, pomegranates, apricots, almonds and many others.[108] Some trees, even though they bore no fruits were planted for the purpose of ornamentation like the Sarv,[109] Cypress and Chinar[110] trees. These trees are found in some of these gardens even today.

The Mughal gardens were symmetrically laid, geometric in

pattern, accompanied by beautiful buildings, artificial lakes, fountain, wells, reservoirs, aqueducts, bathhouses provided with hot water, and many such things which enhanced the beauty of these gardens. Edward Terry writes:

> For places of pleasure they have curious gardens, planted with fruitful trees and delightful flowers, to which Nature daily lends such a supply as that they seeme never to fade. In these places they have pleasant fountaynes to bathe in and other delights by sundrie conveyances of water, whose silent murmure helps to lay their senses with the bonds of sleeps in the hot seasons of the day.[111]

These gardens usually had three large enclosures, one leading to the other — the semi-public garden of the Diwani-i-Am, the Emperor's garden with its Diwan-i-Khas where he received his chiefs and special people, and the purdah garden of the empress and her ladies.[112]

The Mughals were quite particular in choosing the sites for laying the gardens. Most of their gardens are found in Kashmir, Lahore, Kabul, Agra and Delhi. Kashmir became a favourite spot for gardens during the time of Jehangir. Jehangir and his Empress Nur Jahan's love for Kashmir is well-known. In his memoirs Jehangir writes:

> Kashmir is a garden of eternal spring, or an iron fort to a palace of kings — a delightful flower-bed, and a heart-expanding heritage for dervishes.[113]

Famous Mughal Gardens

Some of the famous Mughal gardens in Kashmir are the Shalamar Bagh, Nishat Bagh, Achabal, Vernag, Darogha Bagh (Lalla Rookh's garden), Bagh-i-Bahar Ara and the Nur Afza Garden near the Dal Lake. In Agra we have the Ram Bagh, Dehra Bagh, Zahara Bagh (Nur-Manzil Garden), the Taj Mahal Garden, Garden of Etimad-ud-Daula's tomb, and the Moti Bagh. The famous Mughal gardens of Lahore were the Shalamar Bagh, Shahadara, the Badshahi mosque garden, the Chau-Burji Bagh, and the Nawan Kot Bagh. Then there are the Wah Bagh, Hassan Abdal in Rawalpindi, Khusrau Bagh in Allahabad, Lake Palaces' Gardens in Udaipur, Humayun's Tomb Garden and Shalamar Bagh in Delhi.

These beautiful gardens were used for many purposes. They served as pleasure grounds for emperors and their ladies, places of rest and relaxation and holidaying. Feasts were organised here and guests entertained. Jehangir in his memoirs speaks of the royal feast given by Nur Jahan Begam in the Nur-Afshan garden on the occasion of Jehangir's visit there[114] and the grand feast given by Nur Jahan in the Nur Sarai garden.[115] Gardens also accompanied the tombs of the Mughals like the garden tomb of Etimad-ud-Daula and the Taj Mahal gardens in Agra, the Shahdara gardens of Lahore and the Humayun's tomb's garden and Roshanara gardens of Delhi. Gardens served other purposes too. It was in the Shalamar garden of Delhi that Aurangzeb was hurriedly crowned after he had deposed his father Shahjahan, and the formal coronation took place later in the Red Fort of Delhi.[116]

The royal Mughal ladies, right from the time of Babar have been actively taking part in laying gardens in different places and amidst beautiful surroundings. They themselves supervised these constructions and employed suitable men for the same. Sometimes the emperors gifted beautiful gardens to their ladies and their daughters, the royal princesses.

The Gardens of Kabul

During the Mughal times, in Kabul, we find quite a few gardens belonging to the royal ladies. Both Gulbadan Begam in her *Humayun Nama* and Jehangir in his memoirs talk about these gardens of Kabul. Among the royal Mughal ladies who had their gardens in Kabul was Bega Begam or Bika Begam, who is said to be a grandmother of Akbar, but it is not known for certain which wife of Babar had that title. A.S. Beveridge is of the opinion that, of Babar's wives, Bibi Mubarika (Afghani Aghacha) is probably this Bega Begam[117], who is said to have carried Babar's bones to Kabul.[118] Other royal ladies who had their gardens in Kabul were Shahr-Banu Begam, daughter of Mirza Abu Sa'id and Babar's own-aunt, and Hamida Banu Begam, Jahangir's grandmother and Akbar's mother. Gulbadan Begam speaks of Bega Begam's garden where the royal ladies celebrated the feast of the circumcision of Akbar in Kabul when Akbar was five years old.[119]

Giving an account of the Gardens of Kabul, Jehangir writes:

> First of all I walked round the Shahrara (city-adoring), then the Mahtab (moonlight) garden, then the garden that Bika Begam (Bega Begam), grandmother of my father had made...then a garden that Maryam-Makani, my own grandmother had prepared.... The Shahr-Ara garden was made by Shahr-Banu Begam, daughter of Mirza Abu Said, who was own aunt to the late King Babar. From time to time, it has been added to, and there is not a garden like it for sweetness in Kabul.... While I was at Kabul I had several entertainments in the Shahr-Ara garden, sometimes with my intimates and courtiers and sometimes with the ladies of the harem.[120]

Dehra Bagh and Zahara Bagh, Agra

Dehra Bagh and Zahara Bagh in Agra are said to have belonged to Babar's daughters.[121] The Zahara Bagh, built for Babar's daughter Zahara (we are not sure which one of Babar's daughters was called so), "was one of the largest garden-palaces in Agra, lying between the Ram Bagh and the site of the Chini-ka-Roza."[122] It had a great octagonal well which apparently survived until about 1912.[123]

Garden Tomb of Humayun, Delhi

Humayun's tomb in Delhi was one of the first garden tombs built by the Mughals. It was built by Haji Begam, one of Humayun's widows. According to the Tartar and Mongol traditions, garden tombs, during their owner's lifetime, were places of resort and pleasure. At death, the central pavilion became the mausoleum and the site was handed over to the care of holy men.[124] The surroundings layout of the tomb was probably begun during Humayun's lifetime. It is the earliest Mughal garden plan known to survive without alteration.[125] It is in the Charbagh pattern. Minute differences of level in the channels and tanks are created to exploit the ripple of water. The supply of water came from great wells outside the garden.[126] The flowers, most of the trees and the water are no longer found. Even then, from whatever exists, we can undoubtedly guess what it once might have been.

The Garden of Maryam-Uz-Zamani Jodha Bai's Baoli

In the pargana of Jusat, 1½ koss from Biana, by the orders of Jehangir's mother Maryam-uz-Zamani, a garden and a baoli (step-well) was built at the cost of Rs. 20,000.[127] Jehangir writes - "The baooli (step-well) was a grand building, and had been built exceedingly well."[128] The garden is seen no more but the *baoli* still exists.[129] William Finch in his account speaks of a place called Menhapoore near Bayana where he had gone to buy indigo. There he lodged at a great saray where there was a garden and a mahal or summer house of the Queen Mother (Jehangir's mother), "very curiously contrived."[130] These two places were probably one and the same.

Nur Jahan's Gardens

During the time of Emperor Jehangir, his last wife Empress Nur Jahan took an active interest in garden laying as in other arts, and she contributed a lot in this field. Nur Jahan has been ranked with Babar as the best and the most prolific of all those who inspired and designed Mughal gardens.[131] Villiers Stuart calls Nur Jahan "the greatest garden lovers of them all."[132]

The Kashmir valley was a perfect setting for gardens and it was a favourite one for Jehangir and Nur Jahan. There were an abundance of fruits, flowers and water in Kashmir. Moreover, gardens here could be layered and terraced in a number of ways unlike the usual flat ones in the plains. Kashmir on the whole was famed for its natural beauty with its snow-capped mountains, deep valleys, lakes, waterfalls and beautiful flowers like roses, tulips, jasmines, lilies, violets, narcissus, irises and many others.[133] It has been rightly called paradise on earth. The Mughal emperors and their ladies, especially from Jehangir's time onwards, were extremely fond of visiting Kashmir on holidays, and no wonder some of their most beautiful gardens with pleasure resorts were built here. Holidays here also meant escaping the heat of the plains in the scorching summer and improving health conditions.

Shalamar Bagh, Dal Lake, Kashmir

Of all Jehangir and Nur Jahan's gardens in Kashmir, the most remarkable and famous one is the Shalamar Bagh, built on the old Hindu grounds of Pravarasena II.[134] Jehangir reports:

> In these two or three days I frequently embarked in a boat, and was delighted to go round and look at the flowers of Phak and Shalamar... Shalamar is near the lake. It has a pleasant stream, which comes down from the hills, and flows into the Dal Lake. I bade my son Khurram dam it up and make a waterfall, which it would be a pleasure to behold. This place is one of the sights of Kashmir.[135]

Though Shahjahan's contribution towards the Shalamar Bagh of Kashmir is quite evident in the famous black marble work done in the pavilions,[136] the Shalamar Bagh when laid out by Jehangir, was certainly much influenced by Nur Jahan,[137] and the overall design of it bears the mark of Nur Jahan in taste and innovation.[138] Bernier gives a detailed description of the Shalamar Bagh which he calls the most admirable of the King's Gardens.[139]

The Shalamar Bagh is divided into three main areas: an outer or public garden containing the grand canal extending from the lake to the first large pavilion, the Diwan-i-Am to the Diwan-i-Khas and the royal bath houses (*hammam*) to an upper wall with small guardrooms at each end; and lastly, the *zenana* garden for the ladies of the harem which had the large black marble pavilion and the elaborate water works set in and across it.[140] This *zenana* gardens was in Charbagh style. It was the central point from where the four vistas opened. The Garden on the whole is simple in design with all the trees, canals and buildings matched with each other giving an unerring sense of proportion. The mountains behind form an apt background for the Shalamar.[141]

Ellison Banks Findly is of the opinion that Nur Jahan's contribution towards the design of Shalamar is seen more clearly in the functional division of the individual terraces, which made it a place not just for private pleasure, but for the discharge of imperial duties as well.[142] The Zenana garden stood as the greatest symbol of women's transformation, where "women were no longer veiled bearers of morality by visible paradigms of the affirmation of the body and its sensual attributes."[143] The Shalamar Bagh with all its beautiful features was called Farah-Baksh (the Bestower of Joy) in the Mughal days.[144] The name Shalamar dates back to the 6th century A.D. when Pravarsena II built a house there calling it Shalamar, the Abode of Love.[145]

Achabal, Kashmir

About 8 km towards south of Srinagar, close to the old direct road from Jammu to Srinagar, where the valley of Kashmir abruptly ends and the great hills begin to descend, is Achabal, which was a beautiful spot with springs and flowers and plants and it was developed into a beautiful garden by Nur Jahan and Jehangir. Being a creation of Nur Jahan, Achabal was called Begamabad after her once upon a time.[146] Villiars Stuart calls it "an ideal site," and adds, "If I were asked where the most perfect modern garden on a medium scale could be devised, I should answer without hesitation, Achibal."[147] Achabal was built around a powerful waterfall that rises out of the Sosanwar hill.[148] The water fall is flanked by two small summer-houses. Below it are wide pools enlived by fountains with a pleasant island pavilion set within them. Below that the water again passes under a larger pavilion and down the length of the garden to fall with great force over the final change of level.[149] Achabal had earlier been an ancient Hindu site of worship named Akshavala.[150] Describing Achabal, Peter Mundy writes:

> The garden is very handsome, laid out in regular walks and full of fruit trees—apple, pear, plum, apricot and cherry. The waterfall produced the finest effect imaginable, specially at night, when innumerable lamps fixed in parts of the wall adapted for that purpose, are lighted under the sheet of water.[151]

Akbar in his days had visited Achabal often, which to him was a source of delight and of religious refuge.[152] Jehangir and Nur Jahan were very fond of Achabal and went there often.[153] To Jehangir, "it was a piece of Paradise."[154] Bernier gives description of the fountain and says that the water is so abundant that it ought rather to be called a river than a fountain.[155]

Vernag, Kashmir

Jehangir and Nur Jahan are said to be fond of Vernag above all other places. It is situated further south-east of Srinagar (Shahabad) on the approach to the Banihal Pass. Prior to the Mughals it was a religious place for the Hindus. The rare beauty, seclusion and remoteness of Vernag made it a very special place for Jehangir and Nur Jahan. The name Vernag is derived from snake-worship, an ancient religion of Kashmir, and Jehangir writes, "The source of the Bihat is a spring in Kashmir called the Vir-nag; in the language of India a snake is vir-nag. Clearly there had been a large snake at that place."[156]

Talking about the flora and fauna at Vernag, Jehangir observes,

> ...of the trimness of the canal and the verdure of the grass that grew below the fountain, what can one write? Various sorts of plants and sweet-smelling herbs grew there in profusion, and among them was seen a stem (buta), which had exactly the appearance of the variegated tail of a peacock. It waved about in the ripple, and bore flowers here and there.[157]

The unique thing about Vernag that appealed to Bernier most were the fishes in the pond. He says,

> ...in one of its Ponds there are Fishes that come when they are called, and when you cast bread to them; the biggest whereof have golden rings in their Noses, with inscriptions about them, which say that renowned Nour-Mehalle, the wife of Jehan-Guire, the Grandfather of Aureng-Zebe, caused to be fastened in them.[158]

On the whole Vernag was certainly a very fascinating place. Jehangir felt that, "in the whole of Kashmir there is no sight of such beauty and enchanting character."[159]

The Nur Afza Garden, Hari Prabat Fort, Dal Lake, Kashmir

Inside the palace fort, on the Hari Prabat hill to the west of Dal Lake, which was built by Akbar, there is a small garden with a small building in it. During Jehangir and Nur Jahan's first visit to Kashmir, they found it to be in ruins. Seeing this state of it, Jehangir along with Mutamid Khan made "every effort to put the little garden in order and repair the buildings"[160] and it soon became very beautiful. A terrace 32 yards square in three divisions was added where paintings could be hung.[161] There were very productive cherry trees in Nur Afza garden. Jehangir also built a canal to bring in extra water to irrigate the plants there.[162] The garden, after its restoration, had a new name, Nur Afza[163] (Light

Increasing) and this might have been because Nur Jahan Begam had a great share in its restoration and from that time became its patron.[164]

Bagh-i-Bahar Ara, Dal Lake, Kashmir

The Bagh-i-Bahar Ara is situated on the western side of the Dal Lake at Sadurkhun. It is said to have been laid out by Nur Jahan in 1623 A.D. but no longer exists in totality. It had two terraces with excellent views of the water, one approaching the lake and the other on a higher level.[165] There was a stone pavilion in between the terraces.[166] These terraces were prepared in the chahar chenar pattern[167] which had four chenar trees planted evenly over a square plot to provide shade the whole day long.[168] The water to feed the plants came from the Suid Canal,[169] a canal dug from the river Indus.[170]

Darogha Bagh (Lalla Rookh's Garden), Manasbal Lake, Kashmir

Among the many mountain gardens of the Mughals, this place has a palace that according to some, was built for Nur Jahan. It is set on terraced walls and planted with popular trees.[171] It juts out into the calm water "like some great high-decked galleons,"[172] a sort of protection against the ravaging floods of the reign.[173]

Shahadara, Lahore

Lahore, the capital city of Jehangir and Nur Jahan, was another favourite place of the royal couple. Here too Nur Jahan laid several gardens along the river Ravi. Towards the north-west of Lahore, along the right bank of river Ravi, at a distance of approx. 5 miles from Lahore, is found Nur Jahan's famous pleasure garden, called Dilkusha garden (Garden of Delight). It was in this Dilkusha Bagh, later named as Shahdara, that Jehangir was buried after his death, in spite of his dying request to take him back to Vernag in Kashmir.[174] Nur Jahan designed Jehangir's garden tomb after the model of the garden tomb of her father Etimad-ud-Daula (and her mother Asmat Banu) at Agra.[175]

The Shahdara gardens are entered through a serai courtyard.[176] A tall gateway gave access to the inner garden with the tomb.[177] The garden is very large one, about 540 yards square, extending to 60 acres.[178] "with fine interlocking patterns of raised causeways, canals and tanks, in which bricks, traditional in Lahore, has been beautifully used."[179] Eight large chabutras are formed from a series of raised fountain tanks encircling the mausoleum.[180] The canals are bordered by cypress trees and flowers. A narrow channel running along the edge of the terrace watered the fruit trees in the plots.[181] Customary barrages regulated the flow of water, and it simply fell to the garden about four feet below.[182]

Not far away from Jahangir's tomb lies Nur Jahan in a bare and simple grave amidst open fields. It was set on a square plinth. The charbagh was 400 yards square and contained the small palace where she lived.[183] Hardly anything remains of her mausoleum and garden today, whose limits cannot even be traced.

The Nur Sarai Garden, Jalandhar

It is situated 16 miles south of Jalandhar city. Here Nur Jahan built a *sarai* and a garden in 1620 A.D. About it Jehangir wrote, "...I took up my quarter at Nur Saray. At this spot the vakils of Nur Jahan Begam had built a lofty house, and made a royal garden."[184]

The Garden-Tomb of Etimad-ud-Daula, Agra

In Agra we find quite a few beautiful gardens laid by Nur Jahan as the Empress of India, or those which were given to her by Jehangir. Some of them were the garden tomb of her father Etimad-ud-Daula, Moti Bagh, Zahara Bagh (Nur Manzil Garden), Ram Bagh (Nur Afshan Garden), etc. These gardens were set along the banks of river Jamuna, most of the sites extending along the river's eastern curve.

The garden-tomb of Etimad-ud-Daula was constructed next to the edge of the river Jamuna in Agra by Nur Jahan. Villiers Stuart calls it "one of the most beautiful of all the Mughal garden-tombs."[185] The garden has gateways in the middle of three sides of the surrounding wall with a waterfront pavilion to the outside of the structure on the river side. The garden is in the traditional charbagh from, which has water channels dividing the square into four equal quadrants with the mausoleum in the centre, at the confluence of the streams. On each side of the central platform there are four small tanks on each side, each having a fountain. Angular channels carry water to all four corners of the small enclosure.[186] The main gate house is approached by a straight drive with orchards on both sides planted at regular intervals.[187] On the whole it is one of the most sophisticated of all the Mughal gardens.

Moti Bagh, Agra

Some foreign travellers who visited India during the Mughal days have attributed the Moti Bagh (Moti Mahal) in Agra to have belonged to Nur Jahan Begam. They were Pelsaert and Peter Mundy. Mundy in his accounts speaks of Darree ca baug (Dehra Bagh) and King Ecbars (Akbar's) garden on the side of the river Jamuna and Mootee ca baag on the other side of the river which was "built by Noore Mohol."[188] Pelsaert also speaks of two gardens which he calls Charbagh and Moti Mahal, this being the Moti Bagh.[189]

Peter Mundy also speaks of two gardens which had a *sarai* in between them, situated on the eastern banks of the Jamuna and according to him they belonged to Nur Jahan. Says Mundy:

> I departed from ... Agra ... and crossing over the river, I came to Noore Mohol ca Sara ... built by the old Queene Noore Mohol for the accommodation of Travellers ... It stands between Two gardens built also by her.[190]

One of these gardens is said to have been the Moti Bagh.[191]

Ram Bagh, (Nur Afshan or Gul Afshan Garden) Agra

The Ram Bagh or Aram Bagh (garden of Repose) was originally laid out by Babar and was called Gul-Afshan (flower scattering) Garden. It is situated on the left bank of the Jamuna river. In it Babar built a large well to supply water for his hot bath, tanks and houses for his own use and the use of his other people.[192] During Jahangir's time this garden belonged to his queen Nur Jahan.[193] The garden now came to be known as Nur Afshan (Light Scattering) garden. Nur Jahan is said to have changed Babar's design to some extent.[194] Nur Jahan got new buildings constructed here.[195] The garden was especially known for its excellent fruit trees and some of the fruits found there were grapes, melons, mangoes, pineapples and tamarinds.[196] The Nur Afshan garden was frequently visited by Jehangir and his ladies. Here guests were entertained and feasts organised. Jehangir mentions one such occasion in his memoirs where he says:

> On Wednesday, together with the ladies seated in a boat, I went to the Nur-afshan garden and rested there at night. As the garden belongs to the establishment of Nur Jahan Begum, on Thursday the 4th, she held the royal entertainment and presented great offerings.[197]

This feast was in celebration of the commencement of the 16th year of Jahangir's reign.[198]

The Ram Bagh or Nur Afshan garden is supposed to be one of the oldest recognisable Mughal gardens in India. The original geometric pattern and much of its constructions do not exist in totality any more.

Zahara Bagh, (Nur Manzil Garden) Agra

In the memoirs of Jehangir we also come across a garden called the Nur Manzil located south of the Ram Bagh, on the eastern bank of the Jamuna. H. Beveridge says that this Nur Manzil was the same garden as the Dahra Bagh,[199] where Jehangir often stayed when he left Agra to go on hunting expeditions or diplomatic missions as he did in 1613 and 1614 A.D.[200] This Dahra Bagh is the same as the Zahara Bagh which is said to have belonged to a daughter of Babar.[201] It is not known from any source if this garden belonged to Nur Jahan. But Elison Findly is of the opinion that from the new name of this garden and "from the time of its ascendance" it was certainly "one of the main projects of the queen."[202]

The Nur Manzil garden was beautifully laid with its newly erected buildings, highly decorated residence, reservoirs, tanks, fountains, cascades, and a large well just outside the gate from where thirty-two pairs of bullocks continuously drew water to irrigate the plants and trees.[203] Jehangir had spent many happy days there. On one such visit he writes, "I passed the time in enjoyment in that rose-garden of delight."[204]

Gardens of Royal Ladies, During Shahjahan's Times

The Taj Mahal Garden

Taj Mahal, the unforgettable mausoleum built by Shahjahan for his favourite queen Mumtaz Mahal was inspired by Shahjahan's love for his queen. Situated on the banks of the river Jamuna in Agra, and inside a beautiful garden, it is set on a river front terrace above the end of a Charbagh. This placement is a departure from the usual tradition where the monument is placed in the centre of a Charbagh. The tomb complex with the garden is well planned. To insure even distribution and equal water pressure in the fountains, copper pots were inserted between the underground water pipes and the fountains in the watercourse.[205] The fountains did not rise until water filled all the pots. The fountains of marble shaped like lotus buds were placed in the main water channel and not in the cross channel. The raised, square, foliated pool in the centre of the garden has five fountains. The water supply for the garden came from the Jamuna and stored in a huge tank outside the western gate of the Taj enclosure. Purs, which were a rope and buckets pulled by bullocks treading a huge ramp, raised the water from the river into a high aqueduct which fed the storage tank.[206] There are an abundance of trees and flowers.

The Shalamar Bagh, Delhi

It was built in imitation of the Shalamar Bagh in Kashmir and Lahore by one of Shahjahan's wives, A'azzu-n-Nissa, known as Bibi Akbarabadi.[207] This garden, according to Inayat Khan was given to Akbarabadi Mahal by Shahjahan.[208] After her the place was known as Azzabad.[209] It is situated 6 miles north-west of Shahjahanabad (Delhi), close by the Grand Trunk Road near Badli Sarai, at a distance of 2½ koss from the precincts of the palace.[210] According to Muhammad Saleh's estimates, it was completed in four years at a cost of 2 lakhs of rupees,[211] but according to Inayat Khan 20 lakhs of rupees were spent for it.[212] A'azzu-n-Nissa Begam or Bibi Akbarabadi in her garden had combined all the various architectural beauties of the Kashmir gardens. The garden was formally opened in September 1650 A.D. on occasion of some festival.[213] Bernier found the garden regal and beautiful, but according to him it was a mere shadow of Fontainebleau or

Versailles.[214] The garden hardly exists now, much of its valuable thing being plundered by the end of the 18th century.

Gardens of Jahanara and Roshanara

Both Jahanara and Roshanara, the daughters of Shahjahan, laid quite a few gardens in Delhi, Kashmir and some other places. Though Jahanara Begam's tomb at the shrine of saint Nizam-ud-din Aulia in Delhi is a very simple one made of white marble with no beautiful garden to accompany it, she built many beautiful gardens such as the Bagh-i-Jahan Ara,[215] Bagh-i-Safa,[216] Bagh-i-Nur or Bagh-i-Nur Afshan and Bagh-i-Aishabad[217] in Kashmir, which were laid out under the supervision of Jawahar Khan Khwajasara.[218] Another Kashmir garden, the Bagh-i-Shahara was given by Shahjahan to Jahanara.[219] She also owned a garden at Ambala[220] and another at Surat[221] and also a garden in Bachchol which had many canals and a variety of trees.[222] In 1650 A.D. she laid a lovely garden in Delhi which came to be known as Begum Ka Bagh.[223] It extended from the present National Club to the site where is now the Lajpat Rai Market. The Begum Ka Bagh had pools, water channels, fountains, canopies (chhatris) supported on 12 pillars of red sandstone (baradari) providing cool resting places and lots of flowers and fruit trees. Ali Mardan Khan's canal flowed through it providing plentiful irrigation round the year. Many festivals were also celebrated here. The concluding part of Pankhon Ka Mela meant for the ladies were celebrated here.[224] Also the Tees Hazari gardens outside Kashmere Gate later became the Jagir of Jahanara Begam.[225]

Roshanara Begam's garden tomb in Delhi, which was once her pleasure garden, is situated in the north-western suburbs of Shahjahanabad (Delhi).[226] It is called after her as the Roshanara gardens. The tomb is built of white marble, standing on a low wide platform in the centre of the upper terrace in the gardens with creeper clad walls. A raised canal bordered by flower beds and ornamented with a row of little fountains runs between this building and the entrance gate.[227]

Gardens of Zeb-Un-Nisa Begam

Zeb-un-Nisa, the artistic, poetic, learned and one of the most outstanding of all Mughal princesses and the eldest daughter of

Aurangzeb, did not lag behind the other royal Mughal ladies where constructing buildings and gardens were concerned. Out of all her gardens the Chau-Burji Bagh and the Nawan Kot Bagh were the most outstanding.

Much of the Chau-Burji (Four towered) Bagh does not remain now except the portions of walls and gates, one of them being covered all over with turquoise, amber and azure tiles.[228] Also remains three of the four tall minarets over the main archway, ornamented with tiles in patterns of cypress trees and flowers and also inscriptions in Arabic and Persian.[229] From one of these inscriptions it is known that she presented this garden to her old friend and instructress Miya Bai.[230]

Zeb-un-Nisa's garden at Nawan Kot was not far away from the Chau-Burji. She was buried here after death.[231] But some other sources say that she was buried in the Tees Hazari gardens in Delhi, which belonged to Jahanara Begam and later became the Jagir of Zeb-un-Nisa Begam.[232]

OTHER ARTS

The Mughals were men of refinement, sophistication and artistic ability and understanding. Other than undertaking construction works and laying gardens, the Mughal men and their ladies were interested and themselves engaged in a number of other forms of arts like painting, music, dance, dress designing, decoration, etc. Much is not known about the achievement of Mughal women in these fields. Even then we come across Mughal ladies like Nur Jahan Begam, whose accomplishments in these fields and more, made her one of the most outstanding personalities of that age. Some other such talented royal ladies will also be discussed here.

Music and Dance

Since ancient times music and dance have been popular forms of art and self-expression. In India too they have existed since hundreds and thousands of years. With the coming of the Mughals to our land, many new concepts were introduced into the already existing musical patterns, thus giving rise to new trends in both vocal and instrumental music. Dance too received encouragement from the Mughals.

The Mughal Emperors were very fond of music. Their Darbars were adorned with great musicians who were greatly patronised and even given high ranks like that of amirs.[233] Some of the Mughal Emperors like Shahjahan and Aurangzeb could even play some musical instruments, though Aurangzeb at a later stage in his reign forbade music and musicians from his Court.[234] Babar, Humayun, Akbar and Jehangir too loved music. In Akbar's Court there were musical geniuses like Mian Tan Sen, whose Deepak Raga set fire, and his Meghamallhar Raga brought rain and suppressed the fire.

Apart from these male court musicians, there were female court singers and dancers too during the Mughal times. They performed at marriages, festivals and feasts. There were many groups of them known by different names. The most popular among them were the Kanchanis, formerly known as Kanjaris and given the name of Kanchanis by Akbar.[235] By the time of Shahjahan they became very popular and much favoured and appeared twice at court.[236]

Famous Female Singers

During the Mughal times there were famous female singers like Meera Bai of Mewar, Mrignayani, the eighth queen of Raja Man Singh, and Roop Mati of Malwa. Since music as a form of art was so well known to the Mughal emperors, it is not unnatural that their ladies were well acquainted with this art form. They certainly attended the court festivities and had the opportunity to hear the compositions of famous musicians. Some royal Mughal ladies too sang beautifully, played musical instruments and composed songs.

Nur Jahan Begam was accomplished in music[237] and so were Mumtaz Mahal and Zeb-un-Nisa Begam.[238] Nur Jahan, herself a poetess, even composed song lyrics. Shahjahan seemed to have been very much moved by Mumtaz's sweet voice whenever she sang.[239] Nadira Begam, the beautiful daughter of Prince Parvez, a son of Jehangir, and the devoted wife of Dara Shukoh, the eldest son of Shahjahan, is believed to have been a talented singer of classical music. Her rendering of the Dhrupad was much liked by Shahjahan.[240] Shahjahan had presented her with a volume of *ragas* and *raginis* composed by Mian Tansen.[241] Hira Bai or Zainabadi, as we know her, was a slave girl much loved by Aurangzeb in his youth. Zainabadi's musical skills[242] and charm captivated the hearts of many including Aurangzeb, who never forget her even after her death.

Dancing

Dancing was not considered respectable during the Mughal times and aristocratic ladies did not usually take interest in learning this art. It was confined to some professional groups alone. The Mughal emperors entertained themselves with dance performances at their Darbar. The royal ladies watched these performances from behind veils. They were very fond of watching these and often watched dance performances in the harem too. Many Mughal paintings reveal the Mughal women's love for dance performances.[243] Nur Jahan was not in favour of cheap forms of entertainment in the harem. She encouraged classical music and dance.[244] During Aurangzeb's time dancing and singing were prohibited at court, but they were allowed in the harem.[245]

The Art of Decoration and Dress Designing

The ladies of the Mughal harem were very fond of the art of decoration and applied it in various aspects of their lives and on festivals and special occasions. Gulbadan Begam in her *Humayun Nama* speaks of several occasions when the royal ladies took upon themselves the task of looking into the decoration of their palaces, gardens and the surrounding areas. Maham Begam, wife of Babar and the mother of Humayun took such initiatives many a times.[246] On occasion of a feast given by her, she gave orders not only to illuminate the bazaars, as was usually done, but also the nobles' and soldiers' quarters and after this "illumination became general in India", says Gulbadan.[247] On this very same occasion Maham Begam had set up brocaded, gilded and heavily ornamented pavilions and large audience tents.[248]

Nur Jahan's creativity knew no bounds and it was under her that the art of decoration was at its zenith. She had a wonderful sense of colour combination and symmetry in design. The Musamman Burj at the Agra Fort, where Shahjahan spent his days of imprisonment and which was Nur Jahan's apartments and living quarters during her days, was decorated after her own designs.[249] The fine "pietra dura" inlay work of Etimad-ud-Daula's tomb at Agra were also of her own design. The Emperor's Court was redecorated tastefully.[250] Her superb art of household management curtailed the expenditures considerably. The royal chambers now had good quality furniture of new designs and other decorative pieces.[251]

Nur Jahan invented new ways of arranging feasts and entertaining guests.[252] Emperor Jehangir greatly appreciated her ability to arrange feasts perfectly. Jehangir in his memoirs speaks of several occasions when feasts were arranged by Nur Jahan Begam. On the occasion of Shab-i-Barat, Nur Jahan arranged a feast in one of her houses which was situated in the midst of large tanks.[253] Jehangir also speaks of the wonderful feast given at the Nur-Afshan garden which Jehangir attended with his other ladies.[254]

On 2nd September 1621, Nur Jahan Begam arranged the feast of Jehangir's solar weighing. Talking of it Jehangir writes:

> ...Nur Jehan Begam begged that her Vakils might make the arrangements for the entertainment.. In truth, they prepared one which increased the astonishment of beholders. From the date on which Nur Jahan Begam entered into the bond of marriage with this suppliant, although in all weighing entertainment, both solar and lunar, she had made such arrangements as were becoming to the State, and knew what were the requirements of good fortune and prosperity; yet on this occasion she had paid great attention than ever to adorn the assembly, and arrange the feast.[255]

Under the able hands of Nur Jahan Begam textile, dress and jewellery designing reached great heights. It is well-known that since her childhood days she was very much interested in embroidery in which she excelled. This childhood trait later developed into her flair for innovation in dress and textiles. There were a variety of new textiles that were introduced by Nur Jahan. Among them were *dudami*, which was a flowered muslin weighing two *dams* and used for gowns, the *panchtoliya*, a cotton cloth weighing five tolas and used for veils, the *kinari*, a type of silver-threaded lace, and *badla* or *badhah*, a kind of silver-threaded brocade.[256] She also introduced an inexpensive marriage costume of brocade called the Nur Mahal which could be got for just Rs. 25, and was easily affordable for poor people. Her *farsh-i-chandani* or sandalwood carpet became very famous all over the country and was available in different colours and designs. Some of these designs are still famous.[257] Nur Jahan's interest and innovation in carpet design can be seen in the designs of the exterior and interior surfaces of her father's tomb and also in its inlay work. A female dress known as Jammu consisting of a tight fitting *kurti* upto the knee and tight sleeves fastened upto the breasts, decorated with frills in front and worn with the Angiya (jacket), tight fitting trousers and thin cotton *dupattas* became very popular.[258]

Nur Jahan also designed a number of gold and silver ornaments. New patterns and elegant designs of gold ornaments were introduced by her.[259] Khafi Khan, who wrote a century later said that the fashions introduced by Nur Jahan still governed the society and the old ones survived only among the Afghans in backward towns.[260]

Aurangzeb's daughter Princess Zeb-un-Nisa also had great interest in the art of stitching and embroidery.[261]

Cooking

It has already been discussed how the Mughal taste for fineries extended to their royal kitchen and to their stomachs as well. The variety of dishes prepared in the Mughal kitchen is proof enough for this. And what the Mughals introduced in their menu is found even now in what is known as the Mughalai cuisine all over the world. Women all over the world are known to be the ones in-charge of the cooking in any household. The Mughals had a number of kitchen staff to look into the cooking. But it is not absurd or totally unbelievable that the Mughal ladies too supervised the kitchen work and sometimes even cooked special dishes themselves.

Nur Jahan Begam introduced a number of speciality dishes in the Mughlai cuisine which are still found in standard cookbooks and finest restaurants.[262] A finely carved jade and gem-studded fruit knife in the Salar Jung Museum in Hyderabad is said to have belonged to Nur Jahan Begam.[263] Princess Jahanara was fond of preparing certain dishes. She herself prepared vegetables, bread and other varieties of food for the Sufi saint Hazrat Miyan Meer.[264] Aurangzeb's wife Udipuri Mahal once prepared a *ragout* or stew when she had invited Aurangzeb to her apartments.[265]

Painting

Last, but not the least, the Mughals were extremely fond of painting, and some Mughal emperors like Babar and Jehangir were fine painters themselves. As in the case of poets and musicians, the Mughal Court was adorned by many famous painters, many of whom came from Persia and other Central Asian countries.

Nothing is clearly known about the specific contribution made by the Mughal ladies in the field of painting, but there are enough evidences to reveal their interest in this field. Quite a few paintings of that time are proof enough for this,[266] for example, a *nim qalam* drawing named 'Lady painter in the harem' (c. 1635-40) in the Bharat Kala Bhavan, Varanasi (No. 683) shows a Mughal lady engaged in painting,[267] but her identity is not known. In another painting, painter Hasan Ghulam is seen showing a portrait to Nur Jahan which she is examining in the Darbar.[268] There were some lady painters during Jehangir's time like Nadira Banu, Ruqaiya Banu, Sahifa Banu and Nini.[269] But no painting exists which can be attributed to any royal Mughal lady.

Nur Jahan's Influence

According to Beni Prasad, Nur Jahan could paint well.[270] But, as in the case of other royal ladies, there exists no paintings that can be attributed to her hand. Even then, Nur Jahan Begam is said to have influenced Mughal paintings in a subtle way and herself took a lot of interest in this field. A copy of Hafiz's diwan, written by Khwaja Abdus Samad Shirinqalam during Akbar's time and illustrated with miniatures under Jehangir, bears the seal of Nur Jahan and indicated that it was presented to her by Jehangir on some occasion.[271] It is said that it was due to her influence that women became more and more popular as the subject matter of painting during Jahangir's time.[272] She must have also influenced Jehangir's choice of paintings. In earlier days he was fond of paintings with religious images of the Madonna and Christ which he got from the European merchants and Portuguese missionaries. But later these subjects gave way to female images including those of Roman goddesses. The manner in which women were portrayed also changed considerably. Previously they were shown veiled and so called bad women were shown being eaten up by wild animals or getting drowned in sea. But now "women came to be shown with open necklines and midriffs, comfortable postures and pursuing pleasure in all its forms."[273]

Nothing much is known about the contribution, direct or indirect, of any other royal Mughal lady in this field. It is known that Dara Shukoh had presented his album, a wonderful collection of Mughal miniatures, to his wife, Princess Nadira.[274] It might have been not only for his love for his wife, but also for Princess Nadira's great interest in painting.

Thus, we see that the Mughal age saw substantial development in the field of architecture and other forms of art where the Mughal ladies contributed considerably. Though what they could do was much less than what their men did, but once again if we think of the existing social system in those days, then the contribution of these women cannot be taken for granted. Also, their creativity and aesthetic sense is revealed to a high degree in their achievements in the field of art and architecture.

REFERENCE

1. R.C. Mazumdar ed., *An Advanced History of India* (Madras: 1978), p. 577.
2. A.S. Beveridge in Gulbadan Begam's *Humayun Nama*, p. 219.
3. *Ibid.*, p. 218.
4. Md. Yasin, *Studies: Historical and Cultural* (Jammu [Tawi]: 1964), p. 76.
5. A.S. Beveridge in *Humayun Nama*, p. 220; Sylvia Crowe & Sheila Haywood, *The Gardens of Mughal India* (Delhi: 1973), p. 71; Percy Brown, *Indian Architecture* (*Islamic Period*) (Bombay: 1981), p. 89.
6. Crowe and Haywood, *The Gardens of Mughal India*, p. 71; Md. Yasin, *Studies: Historical and Cultural*, p. 76.
7. Md. Yasin, *Studies: Historical and Cultural*, p. 76: James Fergusson, *History of Indian and Eastern Architecture*, Vol. II (Delhi: 1967), p. 290.
8. Percy Brown, *Indian Architecture* (*Islamic Period*), p. 96.
9. E.B. Havell, *Indian ArchitectureThrough the Ages* (New Delhi: 1978), p. 160.

10. Crowe & Haywood, *The Gardens of Mughal India*, p. 71.
11. *Ibid.*, p. 71.
12. Fergusson, *History of Indian and Eastern* Architecture, Vol. II, p. 290.
13. *Ibid.*, p. 290.
14. *Ibid.*, p. 290.
15. *Ibid.*, p. 290.
16. Sir Sayyid Ahmad Khan quoted in Md. Yasin's *Studies: Historical and Cultural*, p. 76.
17. Monserrate, *The Commentary*, tr. J.S. Hoyland (Oxford: 1922), p. 96: Jagdish Narain Sarkar, *Mughal Economy* (Calcutta: 1987), p. 115; S.K. Banerji, *Humayun Badshah*, Vol. II (Lucknow: 1941), p. 317.
18. *Tuzuk-i-Jahangiri* (tr.), Vol. II, p. 64.
19. *Ibid.*, p. 64.
20. Finch in Foster ed., *Early Travels in India* (London: 1921), p. 148.
21. Ellison Banks Findly, *Noorjahan Empress of Mughal India* (New York: 1993), p. 230; E.B. Havell, *A Handbook to Agra and the Taj* (London: 1904), p. 87.
22. Fergusson, *History of Indian and Eastern Architecture*, Vol. II, p. 305.
23. Fergusson, *History of Indian and Eastern Architecture*, Vol. II, p. 305; Findly, *Noorjahan...*, p. 231.
24. Findly, *Noorjahan...*, p. 231.
25. A.L. Srivastava, *Medieval Indian Culture* (Agra: 1964), p. 207.
26. A.L. Srivastava, *Medieval Indian Culture*, p. 207; E.B. Havell, *A Handbook to Agra and the Taj*, p. 86.
27. Findly, *Noorjahan...*, p. 231.
28. *Ibid.*, p. 239.
29. Findly, *Noorjahan...*, p. 231-32; Fergusson, *History of Indian and Eastern Architecture*, Vol. II, p. 305.
30. Findly, *Noorjahan..*, p. 232; Bamber Gascoigne, *The Great Moghuls* (London: 1976), p. 159.
31. De Laet, *The Empire of Great Mogol*, tr. J.S. Hoyland (New Delhi: 1974), p. 41.
32. Pelsaert, *The Remonstrantie...*, tr. W.H. Moreland and P. Geyl, p. 5.
33. Findly, *Noorjahan...*, p. 230.
34. Findly, *Noorjahan...*, p. 233; Md. Yasin, *Studies: Historical and Cultural*, p. 81; Havell, *A Handbook to Agra and the Taj*, p. 87; George Michell, ed. *Architecture of the Islamic World* (London: 1978), p. 266.
35. Findly, *Noorjahan...*, p. 233; Md. Yasin, *Studies: Historical and Cultural*, p. 81; Crowe & Haywood, *The Gardens of Mughal India*, p. 123.
36. Crowe & Haywood, *The Gardens of Mughal India*, p. 123.
37. Percy Brown quoted in *The Cambridge History of India*, Vol. IV (*The Mughal Period*), ed. Richard Burn (Cambridge: 1937), pp. 552-53.
38. Findly, *Noorjahan...*, p. 229.
39. *Ibid.*, p. 229.
40. *Ibid.*, p. 229.
41. Findly, *Noorjahan...*, p. 229.
42. *Tuzuk-i-Jahangiri* (tr.), Vol. II, p. 192.
43. *Ibid.*, p. 338.
44. Findly, *Noorjahan...*, p. 229.

45. R.C. Temple in *The Travels of Peter Mundy in Europe and Asia*, Vol. II (London: 1914), p. 78 n.
46. Peter Mundy, Vol. II, pp. 78-79.
47. *Ibid.*, pp. 78-79.
48. *Ibid.*, pp. 78-79.
49. R.C. Temple in *The Travels of Peter Mundy ...*, Vol. II, pp. 78 n to 79 n.
50. Findly, *Noorjahan...*, p. 238; Pant, *Economic History of India Under the Mughals* (Delhi: 1990), p. 119.
51. Findly, *Noorjahan...*, p. 239.
52. Pant, *Economic History of India Under the Mughals*, p. 119.
53. Fergusson, *History of Indian and Eastern Architecture*, Vol. II, p. 304; Havell, *A Handbook to Agra and the Taj*, p. 28; Crowe & Haywood, *The Gardens of Mughal India*, p. 131; S.M. Jaffar, *Some Cultural Aspects of Muslim Rule in India* (Delhi: 1972), p. 107.
54. Crowe & Haywood, *The Gardens of Mughal India*, p. 131.
55. Crowe & Haywood, *The Gardens of Mughal India*, p. 131; C.M.V. Stuart, *Gardens of the Great Mughals* (London: 1913), p. 131.
56. C.M.V. Stuart, *Gardens of the Great Mughals*, p. 131; A.L. Srivastava, *Medieval Indian Culture*, p. 208.
57. Crowe & Haywood, *The Gardens of Mughal India*, p. 131.
58. Fergusson, *History of Indian and* Eastern Architecture, Vol. II, p. 305.
59. *Ibid.*, p. 305.
60. *Ibid.*, p. 305.
61. Richard Burn (ed.), *The Cambridge History of India*, Vol. IV, p. 151.
62. C.M.V. Stuart, *Gardens of the Great Mughals*, p. 131; Crowe & Haywood, *The Gardens of Mughal India*, p. 131.
63. Crowe & Haywood, *The Gardens of Mughal India*, p. 131.
64. Findly, *Noorjahan...*, p. 241.
65. Findly, *Noorjahan...*, pp. 241-42.
66. *Ibid.*, p. 242.
67. *Ibid.*, p. 242.
68. Nur Jahan's epitaph translated by poet John Bowen in Crowe & Haywood, *The Gardens of Mughal India*, p. 131.
69. Maheshwar Dayal, *Rediscovering Delhi, The Story of Shahjahanabad* (New Delhi: 1982), p. 71.
70. Inayat Khan, *The Shah Jahan Nama*, tr. & ed. Begley and Desai, p. 458.
71. *Ibid.*, p. 458.
72. *Ibid.*, p. 458.
73. Khafi Khan, *Muntakhab-ul-Lubab*, Vol. I, p. 706.
74. Abdul Hamid Lahori, *Badshah Nama*, Vol. I, Pt. II, p. 252.
75. Lahori, Vol. I, Pt. II, p. 252; Qazwini, *Padshah Nama*, fol. 406; Fergusson, *History of Indian and Eastern Architecture*, Vol. II, pp. 318-20; S.M. Latif, *Agra, Historical and Descriptive* (Calcutta: 1896), pp. 184-88.
76. Lahori, Vol. II, Pt. II, p. 469.
77. Manucci, *Storia do Magor*, tr. William Irvine (London: 1907), Vol. I, p. 221; Bernier, *Travels in the Mogul Empire*, pp. 280-81; Jean De Thevenot, *Accounts of Surat*, ed. H.G. Rawlinson (Bombay: 1927), pp. 60, 280-81; Tavernier, *Travels in India*, tr. & ed. V. Ball (London: 1889), Vol. I, p. 49.

78. Bernier, pp. 280-81.
79. Bernier, p. 281; Manucci, *Storia...*, Vol. I, p. 221.
80. Bernier, p. 281 n.
81. Muhammad Saleh Kambu, *Amal-i-Saleh*, Vol. III, p. 47.
82. The "Son et Lumiere" show conducted at the Red Fort, Delhi.
83. C.M.V. Stuart, *Gardens of the Great Mughals*, pp. 109-10.
84. *Ibid.*, p. 110.
85. Jadunath Sarkar tr., Mustaid Khan's *Maasir-i-Alamgiri* (Calcutta: 1947), p. 90.
86. Jadunath Sarkar, *History of Aurangzib*, Vol. I (Calcutta: 1912), p. 63.
87. Magan Lal tr.,*The Diwan of Zeb-un-Nissa* (London: 1913), pp. 19-20.
88. Jadunath Sarkar, *History of Aurangzib*, Vol. I, p. 69.
89. *Ibid.*
90. Rekha Misra, *Women in Mughal India*, p. 112.
91. Muni Lal, *Aurangzeb* (New Delhi: 1988), p. 63.
92. Jadunath Sarkar, *History of Aurangzib*, Vol. I, p. 70.
93. *Ibid.*, p. 70.
94. *Ibid.*, p. 70.
95. S.C. Welch, *India, Art and Culture* (New York: 1985), p. 173.
96. Lahori, Vol. I, Pt. II, p. 403.
97. Khafi Khan, Vol. I, p. 596.
98. Lahori, Vol. II, Pt. II, p. 322.
99. A.L.Srivastava, *Medieval Indian Culture*, p. 225.
100. *Ibid.*, p. 252.
101. *Ibid.*, p. 252.
102. C.M.V. Stuart, *Gardens of the Great Mughals*, p. 4.
103. A.L. Srivastava, *Medieval Indian Culture*, pp. 252-53.
104. C.M.V. Stuart, *Gardens of the Great Mughals*, p. 246.
105. *Ibid.*, p. 246.
106. S.M. Jaffar, *Some Cultural Aspects of Muslim Rule in India*, p. 115.
107. *Ibid.*, p. 115.
108. *Ibid.*, p. 116.
109. *Ibid.*, p. 120.
110. *Ibid.*, p. 116.
111. Edward Terry in *Early Travels in India*, p. 283.
112. C.M.V. Stuart, *Gardens of the Great Mughals*, p. 279.
113. *Tuzuk-i-Jahangiri* (tr.), Vol. II, p. 143.
114. *Tuzuk-i-Jahangiri* p. 199.
115. *Tuzuk-i-Jahangiri* (tr.), Vol. II, p. 192.
116. C.M.V. Stuart, *Gardens of the Great Mughals*, p. 105.
117. A.S. Beveridge in *Humayun Nama* , p. 216.
118. *Tuzuk-i-Jahangiri* (tr.), Vol. I, p. 107n.
119. Gulbadan Begam, *Humayun Nama* (tr.), p. 179.
120. *Tuzuk-i-Jahangiri* (tr.), Vol. I, pp. 106-107.
121. Crowe & Haywood, *The Gardens of Mughal India*, p. 60.
122. Crowe & Haywood, *The Gardens of Mughal India*, p. 63; S.M. Latif, *Agra, Historical and Descriptive*, p. 190.

123. Crowe & Haywood, *The Gardens of Mughal India*, p. 63.
124. *Ibid.*, p. 71.
125. *Ibid.*, p. 73.
126. *Ibid.*, p. 73.
127. *Tuzuk-i-Jahangiri* (tr.), Vol. II, p. 64.
128. *Ibid.*, p. 64.
129. *Ibid.*, p. 64 n.
130. William Finch in *Early Travels in India*, p. 148.
131. C.M.V. Stuart, *Gardens of the Great Mughals*, p. 126.
132. *Ibid.*, pp. 42-43.
133. *Tuzuk-i-Jahangiri* (tr.), Vol. II, pp. 134, 151, 178; Bernier, pp. 406-407.
134. Findly, *Noorjahan...*, p. 256; Crowe & Haywood, *The Gardens of Mughal India*, p. 98.
135. *Tuzuk-i-Jahangiri* (tr.), Vol. II, p. 151.
136. Findly, *Noorjahan...*, p. 256.
137. Findly, *Noorjahan...*, p. 256; Crowe & Haywood, *The Gardens of Mughal India*, p. 96.
138. Findly, *Noorjahan...*, p. 256.
139. Bernier, pp. 399-400.
140. Findly, *Noorjahan...*, p. 256-57.
141. Crowe & Haywood, *The Gardens of Mughal India*, p. 96.
142. Findly, *Noorjahan...*, p. 257.
143. *Ibid.*, p. 257.
144. Crowe & Haywood, p. 98.
145. *Ibid.*, p. 98.
146. *Ibid.*, p. 108.
147. C.M.V. Stuart, *Gardens of the Great Mughals*, p. 191.
148. Findly, *Noorjahan...*, p. 257.
149. Crowe & Haywood, *The Gardens of Mughal India*, p. 108.
150. Findly, *Noorjahan...*, p. 257.
151. Richard Carnac Temple ed., *The Travels of Peter Mundy in Europe & Asia*, Vol. II, p. 159.
152. Findly, *Noorjahan...*, p. 257.
153. *Tuzuk-i-Jahangiri* (tr.), Vol. II, p. 173.
154. *Ibid.*, p. 173.
155. Bernier, p. 413.
156. *Tuzuk-i-Jahangiri* (tr.), Vol. I, p. 92.
157. *Ibid.*, Vol. II, pp. 173-74.
158. Bernier, p. 414.
159. *Tuzuk-i-Jahangiri* (tr.), Vol. II, p. 174.
160. *Tuzuk-i-Jahangiri* (tr.), Vol. II, p. 150-51.
161. *Ibid.*, p. 151.
162. *Tuzuk-i-Jahangiri* (tr.), Vol. II, p. 238.
163. *Ibid.*, Vol. II, pp. 150-51.
164. Findly, *Noorjahan...*, p. 255.
165. *Ibid.*, p. 255.
166. Pant, *Economic History of India Under the Mughals*, p. 117.

167. *Ibid.*, p. 117.
168. C.M.V. Stuart, *Gardens of the Great Mughals*, p. 159.
169. Pant, *Economic History of India Under the Mughal*, p. 117.
170. Sugam Anand, *The History of Begum Nurjahan*, p. 69.
171. Findly, *Noorjahan...*, p. 255.
172. C.M.V. Stuart, *Gardens of the Great Mughals*, p. 157.
173. Findly, *Noorjahan...*, p. 255.
174. Elizabeth B. Moynihan, *Paradise as a Garden in Persia and Mughal India* (London: 1982), p. 128; Findly, *Noorjahan...*, p. 252; C.M.V. Stuart, *Gardens of the Great Mughals*, p. 130.
175. C.M.V. Stuart, *Gardens of the Great Mughals*, p. 131; Crowe & Haywood, *The Gardens of Mughal India*, p. 131.
176. Findly, *Noorjahan...*, p. 252; C.M.V. Stuart, *Gardens of the Great Mughals*, p. 130; Crowe & Haywood, *The Gardens of Mughal India*, p. 131.
177. Crowe & Haywood, *The Gardens of Mughal India*, p. 131.
178. Fergusson, *History of Indian and Eastern Architecture*, Vol. II, p. 304.
179. Crowe & Haywood, *The Gardens of Mughal India*, p. 131.
180. C.M.V. Stuart, *Gardens of the Great Mughals*, p. 131.
181. E.B. Moynihan, *Paradise as a Garden...*, p. 128.
182. *Ibid.*, p. 128.
183. *Ibid.*, p. 129.
184. *Tuzuk-i-Jahangiri* (tr.), Vol. II, p. 192.
185. C.M.V. Stuart, *Gardens of the Great Mughals*, p. 52.
186. Findly, *Noorjahan...*, p. 251.
187. Findly, *Noorjahan...*, p. 251; Crowe & Haywood, *The Gardens of Mughal India*, p. 123.
188. Peter Mundy, Vol. II, p. 214.
189. Pelsaert, p. 5.
190. Peter Mundy, Vol. II, p. 78-79.
191. R.C. Temple in Peter Mundy, Vol. II, p. 79 n.
192. Findly, *Noorjahan...*, p. 248.
193. Findly, *Noorjahan...*, p. 248; C.M.V. Stuart, *Gardens of the Great Mughals*, p. 42; *Tuzuk-i-Jahangiri*, (tr.), Vol. II, p. 199; E.B. Moynihan, *Paradise as a Garden...*, P. 102.
194. Moynihan, *Paradise as a Garden...*, p. 102.
195. Findly, *Noorjahan...*, p. 249.
196. *Tuzuk-i-Jahangiri* (tr.), Vol. I, p. 5.
197. *Tuzuk-i-Jahangiri* (tr.), Vol. II, p. 199.
198. *Ibid.*, p. 199 n.
199. H. Beveridge in *Tuzuk-i-Jahangiri*, Vol. II, p. 76 n.
200. *Tuzuk-i-Jahangiri* (tr.), Vol. I, pp. 232, 252.
201. Findly, *Noorjahan...*, p. 249.
202. *Ibid.*, p. 249.
203. Findly, *Noorjahan...*, p. 249.
204. *Tuzuk-i-Jahangiri* (tr.), Vol. II, p. 98.
205. E.B. Moynihan, *Paradise as a Garden...*, p. 131.
206. *Ibid.*, p. 132.

207. Crowe & Haywood, *The Gardens of Mughal India,* p. 146; C.M.V. Stuart, *Gardens of the Great Mughals*, p. 103.
208. Inayat Khan, *The Shah Jahan Nama* (tr.), p. 451.
209. C.M.V. Stuart, *Gardens of the Great Mughals*, p. 103.
210. *The Shah Jahan Nama* (tr.), p. 451.
211. Muhammad Saleh Kambu quoted in C.M.V. Stuart, *Gardens of the Great Mughals*, p. 105.
212. *The Shah Jahan Nama* (tr.), p. 451.
213. Crowe & Haywood, *The Gardens of Mughal India,* p. 148.
214. Bernier quoted in Crowe & Haywood, p. 148.
215. Qazwini, *Padshah Nama*, fol. 279a; Lahori, *Badshah Nama,* Vol. II, Pt. I, p. 99.
216. Lahori, *Badshah Nama*, Vol. I, Pt. I, p. 195; Qazwini, fol. 279 a.
217. Qazwini, fol. 279 a; Lahori, Vol. I, Pt. II, p. 27.
218. Md. Saleh Kambu, *Amal-i-Saleh;* Vol. II, p. 36.
219. Lahori, Vol. II, Pt. I, p. 99.
220. Lahori, Vol. I, Pt. II, p. 7 and Vol. II, Pt. I, p. 115; Qazwini, ff. 279a and 584.
221. S.N. Sen ed., *The Indian Travels of Thevenot and Careri* (New Delhi : 1949), p. 25; Stavorinus, *Voyage too the East Indies.*, tr., S.H. Wilcocke, Vol. II, p. 468, and Vol. III, p. 177.
222. Lahori, Vol. II, Pt. II, p. 428.
223. Maheshwar Dayal, *Rediscovering Delhi, The Story of Shahjahanabad*, p. 29.
224. *Ibid.*, pp. 29-31.
225. *Rediscovering Delhi...*, p. 60; *Maasir-i-Alamgiri*, tr. J. Sarkar, p. 275.
226. Crowe & Haywood, *The Gardens of Mughal India,* p. 184.
227. C.M.V. Stuart, *Gardens of the Great Mughals*, p. 110.
228. *Ibid.*, p. 134.
229. C.M.V. Stuart, p. 135; Magan Lal tr., *Diwan of Zeb-un-Nissa,* p. 20 (Introduction).
230. Magan Lal tr., *Diwan of Zeb-un-Nissa,* p. 20.
231. C.M.V. Stuart, *Gardens of the Great Mughals*, p. 135.
232. *Maasir-i-Alamgiri,* tr. J. Sarkar, p. 275.
233. M.A. Ansari, *Social Life of the Mughal Emperors* (New Delhi : 1974), p. 175.
234. *Ibid.*, p. 176.
235. *Ibid.*, p. 176.
236. *Ibid.*, p. 176.
237. Beni Prasad, *History of Jehangir,* p. 172; John J. Pool, *Famous Women of India* (Calcutta: 1954), pp. 91-92.
238. Rekha Misra, *Women in Mughal India*, p. 95.
239. Maharani Sunity Devee, *The Beautiful Mogul Princesses,* pp. 17-18.
240. Muni Lal, *Shah Jahan* (Ghaziabad : 1986), p. 209.
241. *Ibid.*, p. 209.
242. Jadunath Sarkar, *History of Aurangzib*, Vol. I, p. 65.
243. Percy Brown, *Indian Painting Under the Mughals* (New York : 1975), Plate lvii, Fig. 1; Ivan Vasilevich Shchukin, *La Pienture Indienne; al' epoque des grands Moghols* (Paris: 1929), Plate lvii.
244. Sugam Anand, *History of Begum Nurjahan,* p. 73.
245. Manucci, *Storia...*, Vol. II, p. 335.

246. Gulbadan Begam, *Humayun Nama* (tr.), pp. 113-14.
247. *Humayun Nama* (tr.), p. 113.
248. *Ibid.*, p. 113.
249. E.B. Havell, *A Handbook to Agra and the Taj*, p. 27.
250. Sugam Anand, *History of Begum Nurjahan*, p. 71.
251. *Ibid.*, p. 72.
252. Khafi Khan, Vol. I, p. 269.
253. *Tuzuk-i-Jahangiri* (tr.), Vol. I, p. 385.
254. *Ibid.*, Vol. II, p. 199.
255. *Tuzuk-i-Jahangiri* (tr.), Vol. II, p. 214.
256. Findly, *Noorjahan...*, p. 222; Beni Prasad, *History of Jehangir*, pp. 184-85.
257. Beni Prasad, *History of Jehangir*, p. 185.
258. Sugam Anand, *History of Nurjahan*, p. 71.
259. Beni Prasad, *History of Jehangir*, p. 185.
260. Khafi Khan, Vol. I, p. 269.
261. Zinat Kausar, *Muslim Women in Medieval India* (New Delhi: 1992), p. 181.
262. Findly, *Noorjahan...*, p. 221.
263. *Ibid.*, p. 221.
264. Rekha Misra, *Women in Mughal India*, p. 93.
265. Manucci, *Storia...*, Vol. III, pp. 258-59.
266. George Michell, et. al., *In the Image of Man* (New Delhi: 1982), p. 136, no. 141; Vijay Krishna, Chiteri-Lady Artist and her Model', *Journal of the Indian Society of Oriental Art*, Vol. XI (Calcutta : 1970), pp. 60-63.
267. Asok Kumar Das in A. Jan Qaisar & S.P. Verma (eds.), *Art and Culture* (Jaipur: 1993), p. 44.
268. Stchoukine, plate vii.
269. Asok Kumar Das in *Art and Culture*, p. 44.
270. Beni Prasad, *History of Jehangir*, p. 172.
271. A.K. Das, *Dawn of Mughal Painting* (Bombay: 1982), p. 83.
272. P. Pal, *Court Paintings of India* (New York & New Delhi: 1983), p. 44.
273. Findly, *Noorjahan...*, pp. 224-26.
274. C.M.V. Stuart, *Gardens of the Great Mughals*, p. 135.

Seven

Contributions of Royal Mughal Ladies in Economic Life

The royal life in the Mughal harem and cultural heritage bears testimony to the economic affluence and prosperity of the Mughal age which was one of the most glorious periods of Indian history. The Mughal empire witnessed developments in all spheres of economy which included agriculture, internal and external trade, commerce and industries, banking and currency. Much has been discussed and written by eminent scholars on various aspects of economic condition of the Mughal age. The present chapter deals with contribution of the royal Mughal ladies in economic prosperity of the Mughal empire which occupies a unique place in the annals of India.

Sea Trade

The Mughal emperors took a lot of personal interest in trade and commerce especially in sea-trade. Side by side with merchant vessels, there were ships owned by the Mughal emperors that were used for sea-trade. Akbar was greatly interested in this field. Jehangir too had his own ships and participated in sea-trade. When Shahjahan as Prince Khurram was the governor of Gujarat he carried on a highly profitable trade in broad cloth, textiles, gumlac, indigo and tobacco and carried on this even when he became emperor.[1] This profitable Red Sea trade became an area of conflict between Prince Khurram and the English East India Company.[2]

With such a flourishing atmosphere of trade and commerce prevailing during the Mughal period, it is not very unnatural that side by side with the Mughal emperors, the Mughal ladies, their close relatives and the nobles also took a lot of interest in this field and participated actively in the economic scenario of the Mughal Age. Though too many royal ladies of the Mughal harem did not actively participate in the economic field, yet there were distinguished ladies of that time like Jehangir's mother Maryam-uz-Zamani, Nur Jahan Begam and Shahjahan's daughter Princess Jahanara, who are known to have taken an active participation in the trade and commerce of that time. There were also some others who contributed indirectly to trade and commerce.

Participation of Mughal Ladies

The royal Mughal ladies built market places where there were a lot of buying and selling, built Caravansarais for the travellers and merchants, and also owned ships which carried on sea-trade on their behalf. These ships usually operated between Surat and the ports on the Red Sea. They were of different types, like the pilgrim ships of 400 to 1500 tons, and the junks, built on Chinese model and roughly of 30 to 400 tons.[3] The Mughal ladies also owned large jagirs, the revenues of which went to them. Since owning these jagirs meant a lot of income for them, it can be said without doubt that they must have tried their best to improve the economic condition of these jagirs.

Even in an indirect manner the Mughal ladies contributed to the flourishing economy of the Mughal age. The needs and requirements of the Mughal harem gave an impetus to many industries, including both the imperial *karkhanas* and also those which flourished in other parts of the country. To fulfil certain requirements of their goods were also brought from foreign lands. Starting with textiles, it is already known to us that the harem ladies dressed in the costliest clothes made from the finest material whether of cotton, silk or wool. The muslins used for their clothes were of three types — Ab-e-Rawan (running water), Baft Hawa (woven air) and Shabnam (evening dew).[4] Muslins called Shabnam were famous as Dhaka Malmal and came from Dhaka. The great love of Mughal ladies for silk especially in making their dresses resulted in a lot of silk being imported from foreign countries like China and Persia, and also brought from many parts of the country like Banaras, Bengal and Orissa. Some of the other well-known fabrics used by the Mughal ladies were Satin, Kimkhab, Kattan, Tasser, Tafta, Ambari, Atlas, etc. Both plain and brocaded velvet called Makhmal was brought from Europe, Sashan, Yazd, Mashad, Herat and some other places.[5] From these materials beautiful and gorgeous dresses were made by expert dressmakers for these royal ladies. These dresses were also exquisitely embroidered by experts.

Apart from fine fabrics and beautiful dresses, the Mughal ladies were also interested in jewellery, items of decoration needed in their palaces, furniture items, looking glasses, laces, carpets, shoes and slippers, cutlery, vases, quilts, bedsheets, pillow-covers, shawls and many other things. Many of these were manufactured in the imperial *karkhanas* by skilled artisans, but some of them were brought from foreign countries. For example, equisite carpets were made in Kashmir, Fatehpur and Jaunpur, but the most wonderful ones were brought from Iran and Central Asia. Since many goods came from other places including foreign lands, this certainly helped in trade and commerce to some extent, both internal and external.

However, too many Mughal ladies were not interested in the economic field. In fact, till Akbar's time we practically do not come across any royal lady who contributed in some way towards this field, except one of Humayun's wives named Haji Begam, who happened to built a sarai called Arban Sarai near Delhi in 1560 A.D., which had an accommodation of 300.[6] This same Haji Begam had built the Humayun's Tomb in Delhi. Haji Begam's motive behind building this sarai was certainly a charitable one owing to her charitable nature, but, building of sarais during the Mughal times, as in times before and after, certainly helped as means to boost up trade and commerce by providing shelter and security to pilgrims and also traders and travellers, who went from one place to another. Because such safe provisions were made, traders could freely and fearlessly move with their goods to other places for selling and buying of goods. In the Mughal period, the emperors and other members of the royal family and also the nobles and other rich and prominent men, all undertook the construction of sarais as works of public utility.

Participation of Jodha Bai in Sea Trade

Akbar's wife and Jehangir's mother Jodha Bai, who had the title of Maryam-uz-Zamani, was greatly interested in trade and commerce of her time and was the first royal Mughal lady who participated directly in it. She had her own ships and carried on brisk trade from the Surat port to various ports on the Red Sea. One of her ships was the famous Rahimi of Surat.[7] It carried about 1500 passengers and pilgrims to Mocha or Jedda port of Mecca. John Jourdian calls it Beheme.[8] Sometimes the foreigners called it Remee.[9]

Many foreigners who were in India during Jehangir's time make mention of the ships of Queen Mother Maryam-uz-Zamani and the brisk trade that was carried on by them between India and Arabia, in their accounts. William Finch wrote that, "the Emperor's mother, or others acting under her protection, carried on extensive trading operations, and at this time a vessel belonging too her was being laden for a voyage to Mocha."[10] The position of the English ambassador Hawkins, seems to have suffered at the Mughal court as a result of the dealings that Finch had with the Queen Mother's agents who were sent to Bayana to buy indigo.[11]

The foreign merchant powers had an eye for the Queen Mother's ships including Rahimi. The English wanted to capture them to make the Mughal Emperor (Jehangir) aware of the impatience of the English merchants and their grievances.[12] In 1613 A.D. the Portuguese came into direct conflict with the Mughals for capturing one of Queen Mother's ships "which was to be laden for Mocha."[13] This ship had valuable cargo and passengers and also had a Portuguese pass guaranteeing her against molestation.[14] The Mughals were greatly angered by this high-handed behaviour of the Portuguese. When the Portuguese showed no signs of restoring the ship, Mukarrab Khan was sent to Surat "with orders to stop all traffic and to lay seige to the Portuguese town of Daman by way of reprisals. At the same time the Jesuit Church at Agra was closed, and the Fathers were deprived of the allowances they had hitherto received."[15]

Sir Thomas Roe also mentioned Maryam-uz-Zamani's ships in his accounts.[16] From his accounts we know that,

> "On 7 June 1615 A.D. by the mediation of the Jesuit Javier, Mukarrab Khan and Gonzalo Pinto da Fonseca, had signed

> a preliminary treaty of peace, which it was agreed should be submitted to the great Mogul and the Viceroy respectively for ratification within fifty days. Amongst other things, it provided that the English should be expelled from Surat, ... the Portuguese effects which had been confiscated were to be restored after deducting 70,000 xerafins as compensation for the merchandise seized by the Portuguese, and the latter were to present a ship to the Queen-Mother in lieu of the one they had burnt at Gogo, ..."[17]

The accounts of these contemporary writers give enough proof of the trading activities of Jehangir's mother Jodha Bai. It can also be seen that the trading activities of these important royal ladies of the Mughal harem were given due importance by the Mughal emperors and all possible arrangements were made to provide them with the best trading facilities and also to protect their goods and vessels.

One of Jehangir's Hindu wives Jagat Gosain who was the daughter of Raja Udai Singh of Jodhpur and who was the mother of Prince Khurram, later Shahjahan, did not contribute directly towards the economic field, but she is said to have founded a village called Sohagpura where ruins of her palace and tomb are still found. This village was a famous manufacturing centre for fine bangles of glass which were quite popular and considered auspicious by unmarried and married ladies.[18]

Commercial Activities of Nur Jahan Begam

Other than Jehangir's mother and in a scale much larger than her, it was Jehangir's last wife, the illustrious Nur Jahan Begam who took a very active part in trade and commerce of her time. As in other fields like art, architecture, education, literature and even politics, Nur Jahan's participation in the economic field too was quite substantial and much more than any other Mughal lady of the royal household, except perhaps Princess Jahanara, the eldest daughter of Shahjahan.

Unlike her mother-in-law Jodha Bai, Nur Jahan Begam's commercial activities were not confined to sea-trade alone. She is famed to have built market places and sarais, had ships of her own that carried on brisk sea-trade and even coins were struck in her name. No other Muslim women enjoyed this privilege of having coins struck in their name. Nur Jahan's coins were made of gold and bore the twelve signs of the zodiac, one sign on each coin.[19] It is not clearly known how much of an economic transaction was carried on by these coins. Manucci calls them "current money"[20] whereas Pelsaert said that they were not so.[21]

Nur Jahan had unlimited wealth around her. She was the pivot of the Mughal administration of Jehangir's time and the whole administrative set up revolved around her. Apart from the wealth lavished on her by her Emperor husband, she received a lot of *nazrs* or offerings from many people who wished to please her in order to gain her favours. Nur Jahan owned vast *jagirs,* one of her *jagirs* being that of Ramsar, which was about 20 miles south-east of Ajmer.[22] The *pargana* of Toda, 80 km. south east of Ajmer on the trade route from Surat to Ajmer, and with an annual revenue of 2 lakhs of rupees, were given to her by Jehangir as a part of the celebrations of Shahjahan's victory in the Deccan.[23] According to Beni Prasad, "If she (Nur Jahan) could have been admitted to the order of *mansabdars,* her *jagirs* would have entitled her too the rank of 30,000."[24] But Nur Jahan was never known to waste this money that she had. With it she did a lot of charitable works and built many a great monuments. It can be undoubtedly said that she invested a large amount from her personal accounts in carrying out a profitable trade.

Building of Sarais

Nur Jahan Begam built *sarais* too, the most famous of her *sarais* being the Nur Mahal Sarai in Jalandhar. This sarai was built around 1620 A.D. and Nur Jahan bore the entire expenses of its construction.[25] This *sarai* is situated 16 miles south of Jalandhar, 25 miles east south-east of Sultanpur and 13 miles west of Phalor. This *sarai* was a very famous one and could accommodate a large number of people. Jehangir speaks of this *sarai* in his memoirs.[26] Nur Jahan Begam built another *sarai,* again by the name of Nur Mahal Sarai near Agra. Peter Mundy mentioned this *sarai* in his accounts and said that it could accommodate two to three thousand people and 500 horses.[27]

Crafts and Designing

We have already discussed about Nur Jahan Begam's interests, talents and contributions in the fields of dress, textiles, carpet and jewellery designing. All her new innovations in these fields must have encouraged craftsmen a lot, especially the craftsmen engaged in such types of works. During her times and because of her encouragement in Agra there seems to have existed a whole market called the Kinari Bazar where the craftsmen were engaged in the manufacture of the famous *Kimkhab* textile. The dress making, carpet making and jewellery making industries also got a boost under her encouragement and innovations. More and more skilled craftsmen also got employment in these industrial units.

Nur Jahan Begam carried on sea-trade with foreign lands with a lot of enthusiastic vigour. She owned a number of ships. Her chief agent in her activities concerning foreign trade was her brother Asaf Khan.[28] Her ships too operated between Surat and the Arabian coasts. Nur Jahan was a very intelligent woman. She realised that the rivalry and tensions that existed between the Mughals and the Portuguese would prevent her ships from taking her goods to foreign lands. So she tried to favour the English so that she could send her goods out on English ships.[29] According to Sir Thomas Roe and John Fryer:

> The one and twentieth at this instant, came unto me from Asaph Chan, a servant, in the name of Normahal, that she had moved the Prince for another firman, and that shee had obtained it, and was readie to send down her servant with that, to see and take order for our good establishment, that shee would see that wee should not bee wronged."[30]
> Indigo and embroidered cloth were the main articles of foreign trade undertaken by Nur Jahan.[31]

Nur Jahan Begam also took an active interest in internal trade. Through the river Jamuna in Agra, a number of articles manufactured in Agra were sent to other parts of the country and similarly many articles of trade and commerce entered Agra through this route. Pelsaert, while describing the city of Agra in his accounts, wrote that Nur Jahan Begam had offices there which "collect duties on all these goods before they can be shipped across the river: and also on innumerable kinds of grain, butter and other provisions, which are produced in the Eastern provinces, and imported thence."[32] De Laet too in his description of Sikandra mentioned, "Hither are brought all kinds of merchandise from Purob, Bengala, Purbet and Bouten (Bhutan); these pay dues to the queen before they are taken across the river."[33]

Commercial Activities of Jahanara Begam

During the reign of Shahjahan, his eldest daughter Jahanar Begam was the only royal Mughal lady who took an active interest and participated wholeheartedly in the prosperous trade and commerce of that time. Jahanara's mother and Shahjahan's favourite wife Mumtaz Mahal, though an influential lady of the royal court and seraglio, did not take part in trade and commerce. After her name stands the name of a flourishing and prosperous area, Mumtazabad, which Shahjahan built to immortalise her name after her untimely death. This city of Mumtazabad was built in twelve years, 1631-1642 A.D. at a cost of 50 lakhs of rupees, and apart from many buildings, had many markets and inns.[34] Private merchants too built inns and buildings here. But other than the name, Mumtaz Mahal did not contribute anything in it. In course of time the city of Mumtazabad merged with the older city of Agra, but the most famous of its buildings the mausoleum of Mumtaz Mahal known as the Taj Mahal, still stands there. A secondary wife of Shahjahan, Akbarabadi Mahal seems to have built a *sarai*.[35] But, it was only Jahanara Begam who participated actively and contributed largely towards economy in those days.

Revenue through Sarais, Jagirs and Ports

Princess Jahanara built the famous caravansarai known as the caravanasarai of Begam Saheb or the Begam Sarai. It was built in Delhi and foreigners like Manucci, Bernier, Tavernier and Thevenot speak of it in their accounts. In it provision was made for adequate safety of the travellers and merchants, the gates being closed at night. This carvansarai was said to have been meant for the rich Persian, Usbek and other foreign merchants.[36] The Begam Sarai was destroyed after the Sepoy Mutiny.[37] No doubt this *sarai* with its special facilities encouraged merchants to carry on trade and commerce between different places through Delhi.

Princess Jahanara, like Nur Jahan Begam, built Caravansarais and market places, engaged in sea-trade and on the whole, took an active interest in trade and commerce. Again, like Nur Jahan Begam, she owned many *jagirs*, the revenues of which came to her, apart from the annual allowances given to her by her doting father and the gifts that she received from other sources. Some of her *jagirs* were Panipat,[38] Achchol,[39] Bachchol,[40] Safipur,[41] Dohraha,[42] and Farjahara.[43] The revenue of the flourishing Surat port was given to the Princess for her expenditure of betel which she provided for her entire household, and the revenue of the Sarkar of Dohraha was given to her for the maintenance of her gardens.[44] The pargana of Panipat yielded an annual revenue of one crore dams.[45] Since Princess Jahanara had great influence in her father's administration, many people, even foreigners tried to please her through valuable gifts and presents in order to gain her favours. The Dutch sought her intervention to solve their problems.[46] The English too tried to please her with gifts like broad cloth, embroidered cloth, mirrors, perfumed oil, cabinets, etc.[47] Tavernier speaks of presenting the Princess with gifts.[48]

Foreign Trade

Jahanara Begam invested her wealth in conducting brisk foreign trade and also got back in return huge profits. She owned a large number of ships and established friendly commercial relations with the Dutch and the English. Their co-operation helped her to carry on extensive trade and make huge profits.[49] Manucci estimates her income to 30 lakhs of rupees a year apart from the precious stones and jewels owned by her.[50] The most famous and largest of Jahanara Begam's ships was called Sahebi after Begam Saheb, the popular title of Jahanara Begam. It was constructed by the Begam at Surat, from where it operated. Usually the captain, crew and other officials of the ship such as the Darogha and Munshrif were appointed by the Emperor himself. But Princess Jahanara once left the selection of the captain and the crew of her ship to her officials. But in the next year she made the appointment of the Darogha of her ship herself and Muhammed Rafi was given the post.[51] This ship Sahebi was used by the Princess for profits as well as to assist Haj pilgrims.[52]

On her first voyage on 29th November, 1643 A.D., The Sahebi was reserved for pilgrims to Mecca and Medina. Jahanara Begam also gave orders that every year 50 Koni of rice was to be sent by the ship for distribution among the destitutes and needy people of Mecca. No fare was charged from the pilgrims. But they were warned against carrying the goods of other merchants in their names.[53] Merchants with cargo were also allowed to travel in it, though the naul (freight) collected from them was given away in alms. The cargo of the Princess carried on this vessel was worth 10 to 15 thousands of rupees. The goods usually went to Jedda. The treasurer of the ship was in charge of keeping in his custody the amount received from fright and also the money got from the sale of the Princess's cargo. The captain of the ship was under instructions to bring as many horses as he was able to procure at Jedda. The Sahebi, is known to have operated till 1663 A.D.[54] Another ship by the name of Gunjawar, which originally belonged to Shahjahan was given by him to Princess Jahanara in December 1629 A.D., along with the instruments, valuables, drugs and material. It also operated from Surat.[55]

Building of Market Places

Jahanara Begam is credited with the work of building two famous market places, one at Lahore and the other at Delhi. These market places became the most important commercial centres of those cities where merchants even from foreign lands came with their goods. In Lahore, Jahanara Begam planned and supervised the building of the Chowk Sarai Bazaar.[56] The famous Chandni Chowk built around 1650 A.D. in Delhi was also a contribution of Princess Jahanara.[57] It is situated opposite to the Lahore Gate of the Red Fort Delhi. There was a pool in the centre of the Chandni Chowk, fed by the water of Ali Mardan Khan's canal flowing nearby. On moonlit nights the whole complex and the pool shimmering in silvery moonlight acquired the name of Chandni Chowk.[58] At each end of the Chandni Chowk there was a beautiful ornamented gate. During the time of the Mughals, Chandi chowk was a famous and flourishing trade centre where traders came from all parts of Hindustan and also from abroad. Each shop specialised in a particular commodity. There were jewellery shops selling exquisite ornaments and rare gems and pearls. There were fruit shops selling choicest fruits from Afghanistan and Kashgar. Some shops sold fine wine some sold ornamented hookahs and decoration materials. There were shops selling even different kinds of birds and pet animals. Many of the articles sold here were rare and very costly. The rich people and the nobles often visited the Chandni Chowk for shopping.[59] The Chandi Chowk even today continues to be one of the busiest commercial centres of the capital, Delhi.

Economic Contribution of Royal Ladies During Aurangzeb's Time

Building of Sarais

During the times of Emperor Aurangzeb there seems to have been no royal lady who actively participated in commercial activities. Aurangzeb's second daughter, the charitable Zinat-un-Nisa Begam built fourteen Caravansarais for poor travellers and merchants.[60] Then there was Aurangzeb's wife Nawab Bai who is said to have built a *sarai* at Fardapur.[61] Other than these two ladies it is difficult to say whether any other royal Mughal lady contributed in any way towards the economic field.

This short survey of the commercial interests, activities and contribution of Mughal ladies from the times of Babar to Aurangzeb reveal that even in the intricate field of economy, the royal ladies of that age, if at all they came forward and participated, they did it actively and with a lot of interest. They invested large amounts in trade and commerce and got back many times more as returns in the form of profits. Also, their building market places and sarais and having their own ships carrying on external trade, certainly helped in the existing process of trade and commerce. May be, very few ladies came forward to take part in commercial activities, even then, the few that came forward left their deep mark in this field.

REFERENCES

1. Jagdish Narain Sarkar, *Mughal Economy* (Calcutta: 1987), p. 228.
2. *Ibid.*, p. 228.
3. Jagdish Narain Sarkar, *Mughal Economy*, p. 193.

4. K.S. Lal, *The Mughal Harem* (New Delhi: 1988), p. 122.
5. K.S. Lal, *The Mughal Harem*, p. 123.
6. S.K. Benerji, *Humayun Badshah* (Calcutta: 1983), Vol. II, p. 317; Antonio Monserrate, *Commentaries*, tr. J.S. Hoyland (London, Calcutta, etc. : 1922), p. 96; Jagdish Narain Sarkar, *Mughal Economy*, p. 115.
7. Jagdish Narain Sarkar, *Studies in Economic Life in Mughal India* (Delhi: 1975), p. 274.
8. *Journal of John Jourdain*, ed. William Foster (Cambridge: 1905), pp. 186, 191 and 209.
9. Nicholas Downton as quoted in J.N. Sarkar's *Studies in Economic Life in Mughal India*, p. 275.
10. William Finch in Foster ed. *Early Travels in India*, p. 123.
11. *Ibid.*, p. 123.
12. Jagdish Narain Sarkar, *Studies in Economic Life in Mughal India*, p. 274.
13. Finch in Foster ed. *Early Travels in India*, p. 129.
14. Nicholas Withington in Foster ed. *Early Travels in India*, p. 191.
15. *Ibid.*, p. 192.
16. William Foster ed., *The Embassy of Sir Thomas Roe to India* (London : 1926), pp. 74 (n), 387-88.
17. *Ibid.*, p. 74 (n).
18. Kabir Kausar and Inamul Kabir, *Biographical Dictionary of Prominent Muslim Ladies* (New Delhi: 1982), p. 151.
19. Pelsaert, *The Remonstrantie...*, tr. Moreland & Geyl, p. 29.
20. Manucci, *Storia do Magor*, tr. W. Irvine, Vol. I, p. 157.
21. Pelsaert, p. 29.
22. *Tuzuk-i-Jahangiri* (tr.), Vol. I, p. 342 and n.
23. *Ibid.*, Vol. I, p. 380.
24. Beni Prasad, *History of Jahangir*, p. 194.
25. E.B. Findly, *Noor Jahan, Empress of Mughal India* (New York: 1993), p. 229.
26. *Tuzuk-i-Jahangiri* (tr.), Vol. II, pp. 192, 338.
27. Peter Mundy, *Travels (in Asia)*, ed. R.C. Temple (Cambridge: 1907-36), Vol. III, pp. 78-79.
28. D. Pant, *The Commercial Policy of the Mughals* (Bombay: 1930), p. 166.
29. *Ibid.*, p. 165.
30. Thomas Roe, John Fryer, *Travels in India in the Seventeenth Century* (London: 1873), p. 144.
31. D. Pant, *The Commercial Policy of the Mughals*, p. 165.
32. Pelsaert, p. 4.
33. De Laet, *The Empire of the Great Mogol*, tr. J.S. Hoyland (New Delhi: 1974 reprint), p. 41.
34. K.S. Lal, *The Mughal Harem*, p. 85.
35. Maheshwar Dayal, *Rediscovering Delhi, The Story of Shahjahanabad* (New Delhi: 1982), p. 71.
36. Bernier, pp. 280-81; Manucci, *Storia...*, Vol. I, p. 221.
37. Bernier, p. 281 (n).
38. Inayat Khan, *The Shahjahan Nama*, tr. & ed. Begley and Desai (Delhi: 1990), p. 447; Md. Saleh Kambu, *Amal-i-Saleh*, Vol. III, p. 109.

39. Lahori, *Badshah Nama*, Vol. I, Pt. II, p. 51 and Vol. II, Pt. I, p. 209; Qazwini, *Padshah Nama*, f. 626.
40. Lahori, Vol. I, Pt. II, p. 51 & Vol. II, Pt. I, p. 209; Qazwini, f. 626.
41. Lahori, Vol. II, Pt. II, p. 426.
42. *Ibid.*, Vol. I, Pt. II, p. 51; Vol. II, Pt. I, p. 207.
43. *Ibid.*, Vol. II, Pt. II, p. 582.
44. Manucci, *Storia...*, Vol. I, pp. 67, 216.
45. *Ibid.*, p. 216.
46. *English Factory Records* (1651-1654), pp. 11-12, 50 (1646-1650), pp. 219-20.
47. *Ibid.* (1646-1650), p. 304.
48. Travernier, *Travels in India*, tr. & ed. V. Ball (London: 1873), Vol, I, p. 141.
49. *English Factory Records*, 1642-1645, p. 148; 1646-1650, pp. 219-20; 1651-1654, pp. 11-12, 50.
50. Manucci, *Storia...*, Vol. I, p. 216.
51. Shireen Moosvi, 'Mughal Shipping at Surat in the First Half of 17th Century', *Proceedings of the Indian Historical Congress*, 51st Session (Calcutta : 1990), pp. 309, 313.
52. *Ibid.*, p. 312.
53. Shireen Moosvi, 'Mughal Shipping at Surat in the First Half of 17th Century', p. 312.
54. *Ibid.*, pp. 312-13.
55. *Ibid.*, p. 311.
56. *Amal-i-Saleh*, Vol. III, p. 47.
57. The 'Son et Lumiere' Show conducted at the Red Fort, Delhi.
58. Maheshwar Dayal, *Rediscovering Delhi, The Story of Shahjahanabad*, p. 15.
59. *Ibid.*, pp. 15-16.
60. Rekha Misra, *Women in Mughal India*, p. 110.
61. Jadunath Sarkar, *History of Aurangzib*, Vol. I, p. 63.

Eight

Travels of the Mughal Harem

The life of Mughal ladies was not always confined within the four walls of the mahal. A lot of the time in their lives were spent in travelling to other parts, both in and outside the country, for various purposes, along with their menfolk. Sometimes the Mughal women accompanied their men in military expeditions, or during exiles or in hunting expeditions, or to look after widely scattered family holdings, or to go to cooler parts for escaping summer temperatures, or for the simple joy of sightseeing.

Encampments

Proper care was taken of the Mughal women when they went on journeys. Several guards looked after their safety during the journeys, as well as when they encamped. The ladies were always placed near the emperor's tents according to their ranks and positions in the harem, along with their servants and attendants. "Each Begam was to encamp with her own establishment and within her own enclosure (Saraparda)..."[1] Bermier reported:

> Adjoining the royal tents are those of the Begams, or Princesses, and of the great ladies and principal female attendants of the Seraglio. These tents are also enclosed on every side by rich Kanates and in the midst of them are the tents of the inferior female domestics and other women connected with the Seraglio, placed generally in much the same order, according to the offices of the respective occupants.[2]

Pilgrimages and Sight-seeing

During the course of their journeys, the Mughal women, with the permission of the emperor or the person in charge of them, could make pilgrimages to local shrines, or watch natural wonders like waterfalls, etc., or visit nearby buildings and gardens.[3] Jehangir in his memoirs mentions several such pleasure trips when his women accompanied him. He mentions the hunt in the neighbourhood of Rohtas,[4] an occasion when Nur Jahan Begam killed four tigers with six shots, feasts arranged on the bank of a tank,[5] another feast on the bank of the lake of Fathpur[6] and his visit to the Nur Afghan garden which belonged to Nur Jahan Begam.[7] Gulbadan Begam too mentions the hunting trips in Iraq when Hamida Banu accompanied Humayun[8] and also his visits to flower gardens and splendid buildings of Sultan Husain Mirza in Khurasan.[9] In those days Humayun along with Hamida Banu saw many other noteworthy places like Herat; Jam, where he saw the shrines of his own and of Hamida's ancestor Ahmad; and also visited the tomb of the founder of the Safi dynasty at Ardabil.[10]

Travelling Placement

When on a journey the women usually travelled behind the men.[11] This certainly slowed down the pace of the group.[12] Manucci however says that "although the princesses and ladies start the last, they always arrive the first, having taken some shorter route."[13] Sometimes, the women travelled as a smaller group with their ladies-in-waiting, ahead of the main group. This was done to save them a tedious journey or long wait[14] or to keep the emperor's journey a secret.[15]

Modes of Travelling

There were different modes of travelling or conveyances used by the royal ladies during the Mughal times. Whenever these ladies went out, the needs of purdah were well looked into. Several contemporary native and foreign accounts have described different kinds of conveyances used by the royal and noble women of those times.

Edward Terry wrote:

> "His (Jahangir's) wives and women... are carryed in palankas or upon elephants, or else in cradles hanging on the sides of dromedaries, covered close and attended by eunuchs."[16]

Abul Fazl speaks of the foot-servants who carried the *palkis, singhasans, chandols* and *dolis* and says that, "they walk so evenly that the man inside is not inconvenienced by any jolting."[17]

The royal Mughal ladies usually travelled in *hauda* set up on the backs of elephants. Elephants, because of their strength and massiveness have always been considered useful for carrying heavy loads, men and baggage over long distances. The *hauda* which was set up on the elephant back was a square structure, richly furnished with gold, covered with screens of gold on every side and a covering over the top for protection which was made "of cloth of silver".[18] Terry described the *haudas* as "pretty receptacles, surrounded with curtains, which stand up like low and little turrents upon their (the elephant's) backs."[19] Bernier calls the *hauda* as Mikdembar (Mekdamber) and says:

> These lovely and distinguished females, seated in Mikdembers, are thus elevated above the earth, like so many superior beings borne along with through the middle region of the air.[20]

These Mikdembers could accommodate upto eight women, four on each side.[21] They were latticed and covered with silken nets.[22] The richness of these haudas have been mentioned by Manucci too who described them as, "dome-roofed" thrones, "very brilliant, made all of enamelled gold, and highly adored."[23] Jehangir in his memoirs has estimated that these grand *haudas* used by the imperial family were each worth Rs. 30,000.[24] Proper care was taken to hide the ladies from public view[25] when they went in the hauda. Although the women were not seen, they could observe the passers by.[26]

The palanquin or *palki* was another popular kind of conveyance. It was a kind of bed, six or seven feet long and three feet wide, with a small rail around it, usually made of bamboo and roofed over with rich brocade and satin and carried on poles by men at each corner.[27] Sometimes, they were suspended between two camels or two small elephants.[28] The palanquins of the royal ladies were also covered with "different nettings of gold thread,"[29] sometimes ornamented with precious stones or pieces of looking glass.[30] About the Palanquin (palki), Ovingtom said that their carriage was "as easier and pleasant as that of our chairs in the streets of London, but far surpasseth them in point of state and quick dispatches of a Journey.[31] Even during the times of Babar, the palki with bearers was a common mode of travel for women.[32]

Sometimes, the women of those times travelled in Chaudoles which were carried on men's shoulders and similar to tact-ravans.[33] They were "gilt and painted and covered with magnificent silk nets of many colours, enriched with embroidery, fringes and beautiful tassels."[34] The women travelled comfortably in these chaudoles which had tiger skins spread below and silk adorned windows.[35]

Carriages were another kind of conveyances in the Mughal age, popular in the royal families and with 'long-distance' travellers. These carriages were usually drawn by oxen, sometimes by bullocks, but usually not by horses.[36] Della Valle found an "abundance of coaches" in India, for travel not only in cities but also in the country.[37] He also found these oxen running and galloping like horses.[38] As in any other conveyance of that time, when the royal ladies went out, these carriages were covered on all sides to maintain purdah.[39] Della Valle described these as `closed coaches'.[40] Bullock carriages were called bahals.[41] Akbar is said to have invented a carriage which could be used as a conveyance, or for carrying load and even for the purpose of grinding corn sometimes.[42] He had another special carriage which was drawn by one elephant and used as a travelling bath.[43] A very famous carriage of Jehangir's time was the English coach given to Jehangir by Sir Thomas Roe in 1616 A.D. Jehangir gave this coach as a gift to Nur Jahan, who according to Roe had it "newly covered and trimed rich."[44] Jehangir liked the coach so much that he got another one made like it which he used for himself.[45]

Women sometimes travelled on horsebacks for faster travel,[46] either riding directly on a saddle or in a horse litter.[47] Horses were useful modes of travel in hilly regions. Camel and camel litters (Kajawas) were also used.[48] Gulbadan Begam while describing Humayun's journey and hunting expeditions in Iraq mentions Hamida Banu enjoying these sights from a distance in either a camel or a horse litter.[49]

When the royal ladies had to cross rivers or seas on their journeys they went in boats or ships. Gulbadan Begam mentions an occasion when the ladies of Babar's household accompanied him to Dholpur by boat.[50] The boats were luxurious with cushions, awnings and sails.

> They were rowed by oarsmen in gallery fashion or else driven by the heart-shaped paddles as seen in Kashmir today, the boatman sitting behind the curtained 'drawing-rooms' of the ladies. There was no tiller but a helsman steered with a long oar and chanted the rhythm.[51]

Women were not allowed to cross rivers on rafts as they were very dangerous.[52] We also know from various sources about the pilgrimage made to Mecca by some royal ladies during the time of Akbar and this was done by ship.[53] The return journey was very tedious and the women suffered a lot.

Whenever the royal princesses and other ladies of rank went out, proper arrangements were made to look after their comfort and protection. Whenever these ladies went "young, well-dressed female slave, with a peacock's tail in ... hand,[54] brushed away the dust and flies and men in front sprinkled water on the roadways to lay the dust."[55]

Manucci reported:

> When Begam Sahib leaves her palace to go to court, she proceeds in great pomp, with much cavalry and infantry and many eunuchs... surrounded her closely, push on one side everyone they find in front of them, shouting out, pushing and assaulting everyone without the least respect of persons. The same is done by all the princsses of the blood-royal when they come out.[56]

Manucci, giving an account of Roshanara Begam's retinue on a journey, which he had once seen, speaks of similar sort of arrangements. He observed before the Begam's elephant "a number of bold and aggressive men on foot to drive away everybody, noble or pauper, with blows from sticks and with pushes."[57] During the journey if a princess met a nobleman who was anxious to gain her favours at the court, she usually accepted his compliments and gifts. If she was pleased with him betel in a decorated bag, and, if she was not, she ordered that he "receive a shower of blows which makes him run."[58]

A lady while on journey, however, could be approached only with great difficulty. Bermier writes—

> Woe to any unlucky cavalier, however, exalted in rank, who, meeting the procession, is found too near. Nothing can exceed the insolence of the tribes of eunuchs and footmen which he has to encounter; and they eagerly avail themselves of any such opportunity to beat a man in the most unmerciful manner.[59]

Wherever the emperor went, his ladies accompanied him. Sometimes the women were subjected to a lot of difficulties during their journeys because of lack of adequate provisions or bad weather or dangerous routes. No doubt they suffered a lot. But we hardly come across any instances when these Mughal ladies refused to accompany their men even under adverse circumstances. We can here give the example of Babar's grandmother Aisan Daulat Begam and his mother Qutlug Nigar Khanum, who accompanied Babar or went for his sake anywhere and everywhere even under extremely difficult conditions. So did Hamida Banu Begam during the days of Humayun's exile. Nur Jahan Begam, Mumtaz Mahal and Dara's wife Nadira Begam, also stood by their husbands at all times and suffered the most tedious and dangerous journeys for their husbands' sakes. Such was the loyalty and courage of these remarkable women of the Mughal Age.

REFERENCES

1. A.S. Beveridge in Gulbadan Begam's *Humayun Nama* (New Delhi : 1983), p. 95 n.
2. Bernier, *Travels In the Mogul Empire*, tr. Constable and Smith (New Delhi : 1983), p. 361.
3. *Tuzuk-i-Jahangiri*, tr. A. Rogers, ed. H. Beveridge (Delhi : 1989), Vol. I, p. 130.
4, *Ibid.*, Vol. I, p. 375.
5. *Ibid.*, Vol. II, p. 53.
6. *Ibid.*, p. 66.
7. *Ibid.*, p. 199.
8. Gulbadan Begam, *Humayun Nama* (Bev.), p. 169 n.
9. *Ibid.*, p. 169.
10. A.S. Beveridge in *Humayun Nama*, p. 169 n.
11. Foster ed. *The Embassy of Sir Thomas Roe to India* (London : 1926), Vol. II, p. 324.
12. A.S. Bev. in *Humayun Nama*, pp. 70-71; Nizamuddin Ahmad's *Tabqat-i-Akbari* tr. in Elliot & Dowson, Vol. 5, pp. 457 and 465.
13. Manucci, *A Pepys of Mogul India*, tr. W. Irvine (London : 1913), p. 109.
14. Gulbadan Begam, *Humayun Nama* (Bev.), p. 100; A.S. Bev. in *Humayun Nama*, p. 20 (Introduction); *Tuzuk-i-Jahangiri* (R&B), Vol. II, p. 123.

15. Foster ed., *The Embassy of Sir Thomas Roe to India*, Vol. II, p. 274.
16. Terry in Foster ed., *Early Travels in India* (London : 1921), p. 329.
17. Abul Fazl, *Ain-i-Akbari*, Vol. I, tr. H. Blochmann (Delhi : 1989), p. 264.
18. Roe, Vol. II, p. 321.
19. Terry in *Early Travels* .... p. 405.
20. Bermier, *Travels*....p. 372.
21. *Ibid.*, p. 372.
22. *Ibid.*, p. 372.
23. Manucci, *A Pepys of Mogul India*, p. 107.
24. *Tuzuk-i-Jahangiri* (R & B), Vol. II, p. 79.
25. Monserrate, *The Commentary*, tr. J.S. Hoyland (Oxford : 1922), p. 79.
26. Manucci, *A Pepys of Mogul India*, p. 107.
27. Travernier, *Travels in India*, tr. V. Ball (London: 1889), Vol. I, pp. 37-38.
28. Bernier, p. 372.
29. Manucci, *A Pepys of Mogul India*, p. 108.
30. Manucci, *Storia do Magor*, tr. W. Irvine (London : 1907), Vol. I, p. 212.
31. John Ovington quoted in Jagidsh Narain Sarkar's *Mughal Economy*, p. 111.
32. A.S. Beveridge in *Hamayun Nama*, p. 20.
33. Bernier, pp. 371-72.
34. *Ibid.*, pp. 371-72.
35. Waldemar Hansen, *The Peacock Throne* (Great Britain : 1973), p. 31.
36. Abul Fazl, *Ain-i-Akbari* (Bloch), Vol. I, p. 265; Terry in *Early Travels*, pp. 144-45.
37. Della Valle, *The Travels of Pietro Della Valle in India*, Ed. Edward Grey (London : 1891), Vol. I, p. 44.
38. *Ibid.*, p. 44.
39. Terry in *Early Travels*, p. 404.
40. Della Valle, Vol. I, p. 44.
41. A.L. Srivastava, *Akbar The Great*, (Agra : 1967), Vol. II, p. 97.
42. *Ibid.*, p. 97.
43. *Ibid.*, p. 97.
44. Roe, Vol. I, pp. 118-19; Vol. II, p. 324.
45. *Ibid.*
46. A.S. Bev. in *Humayun Nama*, p. 45 (Intro.).
47. *Ibid.*, p. 20; Gulbadan Begam, *Humayun Nama* (Bev.), p. 169; Della Valle, Vol. I, p. 44.
48. *Ibid.*, p. 169.
49. *Ibid.*
50. Gulbadan Begam, *Humayun Nama* (Bev.), p. 104.
51. Rumer Godden, Gulbadan (London : 1980), pp. 62-64.
52. A.S. Bev. in *Humayun Nama*, p. 20 (Introduction).
53. *Ibid.*, pp. 69-72 (Introduction); Abul Fazl, *Akbar Nama* (Bev.), Vol. III, p.
54. Bernier, p. 372.
55. Manucci, *Storia....*, Vol. I, p. 230.
56. *Ibid.*, p. 220.
57. Manucci, *A Pepys of Mogul India*, p. 107.
58. Manucci, *Storia...*, Vol. I, p. 212.
59. Bernier, p. 373.

Conclusion

While making a study of the life, activities, achievements and contributions of the royal Mughal ladies from the times of Babar to Aurangzeb, it is observed that the harems of the Mughal emperors consisted of a large number of women of various religious and cultural background. In these harems resided the wives, mothers, step-mothers, foster-mothers, aunts, grandmothers, sisters, daughters and other female relatives of the emperor. Also in it lived the emperor's concubines, dancing and singing girls, slaves and servant women and a number of women officials and guards who were appointed by the emperor for looking after the various needs of the harem. Women usually came into the harem through marriage, birth, purchase, appointment or as gifts. To the emperors the royal seraglio, more than anything else, was a status symbol and the size of the Mughal harem increased from age to age.

The life of a Mughal lady revolved round the emperor. Their position in the harem was determined by the place they had in the emperor's life. The harem women usually maintained cordial relationship amongst themselves but jealousies prevailed and the women competed among themselves in order to please the emperor better than the others around her. To give the emperor or prince his first male child was a great honour. Very important ladies of the harem enjoyed many more privileges than the others. If she was childless, she was allowed to adopt the child of some other harem lady. They had their separate living quarters or palaces. They had many servants to attend upon them and their annual allowances were huge sums added to the jagirs that they owned. They even became the recipients of lofty titles.

Marriages in the Mughal royal family were usually settled by the parents or near relatives. But there were found certain cases of love marriages too. The Mughal emperors not only had Muslim wives, but they married Hindu women too. The daughters or relatives of Indian princes and kings who were married to Mughal emperors and princes mostly as a part of diplomatic dealings or because of the defeat of the girl's family in battles against the Mughals, were generally considered as inferior wives and were known as Bais and Mahals. But some of these wives came to enjoy important places in the harem because they became the mothers of emperor's or prince's first son.

The Mughal emperor's had great respect and honour for the ladies related to them and had strong sense of family ties. The mothers enjoyed the foremost position in the harem. The step-mothers, foster mothers, grand mothers, aunts and sisters were also held in esteem. The Mughal emperors loved their daughters even though the birth of a girl was usually not welcomed in those days. They got the best arrangements made for educating their daughters and for the cultivation of their talents. Thus we come across quite a few talented and highly educated Mughal princesses.

The royal Mughal ladies led lives of great material comforts and luxuries. These ladies lived in grand apartments which formed a part of the fort complex and were luxuriously furnished with exotic gardens, fountains, orchards, tanks, etc., attached to them. These residences were known as Mahals. Separate Mahals were provided for important harem ladies. The harem staff, dancing and singing girls and even the slave and servant girls were provided accommodation by the emperors inside the fort. The harem staff were paid high salaries. The harem was strictly guarded. No outsiders were allowed inside the harem. Spies were present inside the harem who kept the emperor informed about the activities of the harem inmates. Very important harem ladies had their own officials to look after their estates and properties.

The lives of the harem ladies were governed by the strict rules of purdah and seclusion. These women rarely went out of the palaces, but when they did, their faces, were well hidden behind veils. When they travelled, their palanquins, chaudoles, carriages and howdahs were well covered so that they were not seen by the outsiders. But inside the harem quarters these women could move about freely.

The Mughal emperors made adequate arrangements for the entertainment of their harem ladies. These ladies often entertained themselves by musical and dance performances inside the harem. They also attended musical performances conducted in the royal Darbar, though sitting behind curtains. There were a number of indoor games like chess, chaupar, cards, pachisi, chandal-mandal, ankh-michauli, etc., that the ladies played and outdoor games and amusements like hunting, chaugan (polo), Ishq-bazi (pigeon flying), watching animal fights, wrestling matches and combats, etc. where the women participated as spectators usually. But some Mughal ladies were experts at the use of arms and they themselves participated in hunting. Some of them, the young and active ones played chaugan too. There were a number of festivals including Hindu festivals like Dasshera, Diwali, Holi, Raksha Bandhan, Shivaratri and Janamasthami and Persian festivals like Nauroz and Ab-i-Pashan, that were celebrated by the Mughals side by side with the Muslim festivals like Id-uz-Azha, Id-i-Qurban, Shab-i-Barat, Barawafat, etc. Other festive occasions were the Emperor's birthday, marriages, coronation ceremonies, Jashns, or the times when special guests were entertained. In all these occasions the Mughal ladies also joined in the festivities. A special kind of women's fair called the Mina Bazaar was also organised from time to time and especially during the Nauroz celebrations. It was an exclusively women's affair where emperor and royal princes became the buyers and the harem women the sellers of various commodities.Whatever might have been the occasion, the Mughal ladies, though veiled and kept in seclusion, were not deprived of taking part in the festivities and merry-making.

The lavish lifestyle of the Mughal ladies, apart from their grand living apartments and dainty dishes of food, included the wearing of gorgeous dresses and exquisite ornaments. Their dresses were made of the finest silks, brocades, satins or malmals and the cloth was brought from far and wide. The Mughal ladies decorated themselves with ornaments from head to toe. There were a number of ornaments suited for the different parts of the body. A lot of cosmetics were also used by these ladies which added to their beauty. In spite of the material luxuries and comforts that the Mughal ladies enjoyed, there was a distinct void in their lives which only love and companionship could fill. In fact, love was what they wanted most and seldom got. This want for love and companionship led them into many love affairs including extra-marital affairs and relationships with eunuchs. Their frustrations also led them to get addicted to intoxicating drinks and drugs.

All the royal ladies of the Mughal harem were not simply concerned with the superficial side of life like leading a life of pleasure and luxury. They had a serious side of their lives too. Many of them had a deep interest in religion and religious matters. They went on pilgrimages to the shrines of holy men, they undertook the Haj pilgrimage to Mecca, built mosques and undertook works of great charity. Some of them had belief in Sufi philosophy and were mystics themselves. Many royal ladies engaged themselves in serious and constructive activities and there was no scarcity of talent among them.

The Mughal times witnessed many politically ambitious and powerful royal ladies. The intervention of the harem in political matters of the Mughal age was quite prominent. Right from the times of Babar, the Mughal ladies either directly or indirectly played a role in political matters. They sometimes acted as peace-makers and tried to solve differences of opinions, settled disputes, acted as instruments to conclude peace with the enemy, secured pardon for their near and dear ones, took interest in the administration of the empire and some very brave and capable ones even went out themselves to face the enemy. But too much harem intervention in political matters sometimes gave rise to chaotic situations. In spite of that, the courage, determination and strength of mind exhibited by some of the Mughal ladies is worthy of praise and will surely be a guiding light for women all over the world and for all ages that went and are to come.

Many of the royal ladies were educated, but their interest in learning did not stop with their receiving good education. Many of them composed beautiful verses and some of them have left behind works of great literary value. They spent much of their personal allowances in giving active support to the spread of education, establishing education institutions, patronising men of learning, maintaining their own libraries and collecting rare and valuable books.

The royal Mughal ladies contributed much in the field of art and architecture too. Many of them took an active interest and even spent a lot of their personal allowances in constructing beautiful monuments and exotic gardens, many of which survive even today. They constructed palaces, *sarais,* garden tombs, mosques, market places, step-wells, etc. for themselves and also for their husbands or fathers. Their beautiful gardens were laid amidst beautiful location of Kashmir, Kabul, Lahore, Agra and Delhi. These royal ladies also took a lot of interest in other forms of art like music, painting, cooking and also in the art of decoration and designing. Some extremely talented ones even went for textile, dress and jewellery designing. They also knew the art of perfumery. Their aesthetic sense and creativity is revealed to a great degree in their contributions in the field of art and architecture.

Too many royal Mughal ladies did not take interest in the flourishing arena of trade and commerce of the Mughal times. But the ones who were interested took an active part in the economic field. These royal ladies built caravansarais for travellers and merchants, set up market places and also owned ships to carry on sea-trade. These ships usually operated between Surat and the ports on the Red Sea. These economic ventures earned them huge profits. Since these royal ladies had a lot of wealth and owned vast jagirs, investing in trade was not a problem for them. The Mughal emperors too made suitable arrangements for their ladies to participate freely in all these fields.

As compared to the contributions made by the Mughal emperors in different fields, the contributions made by their ladies were quite less. But, if we take into consideration the medieval society in which they lived and the prevailing social conditions with its many aspects like purdah, seclusion, polygamy, discouragement of women's education and on the whole the low status of women, then, the contributions of these royal ladies in various fields cannot be taken for granted. Their many-sided contributions can in no way be considered a mean achievement. Through these mediums, in their own special way, the Mughal women have managed to carve a niche for themselves in the vast course of events collectively known as Mughal history.

Bibliography

Primary Sources

I. Persian and English Translation of Persian Sources

Abul Fazl Allami, *Ain-i-Akbari,* Text. ed. H. Blochmann, Calcutta: Vol. I, 1872, Vol. II, 1877; English tr. in 3 Vols., Asiatic Society of Bengal, Calcutta 1873-1949; Vol. I, tr. H. Blochmann, Vol. II and Vol. III tr. H.S. Jarrett.

———, *Akbar Nama*. MS. nos. 534 and 535 of Vol. I and Vol. II at the National Archives of India, New Delhi; English tr. in 3 vols. by H. Beveridge, pub. by Asiatic Society of Bengal, Calcutta, 1907, 1912 and 1939.

———, *Insha-i-Abul Fazl* or *Maktubat-i-Allami*. Compiled by Abd-ul-Samad bin Afzal Muhammad. MSS. Nos. 317, 322, 378 and 381, National Archives of India, New Delhi.

———, *Ruqqat-i-Shaikh Abul Fazl*. Compiled by Maulvi Nur Muhammad. MS. no. 165, Sir Jadunath Sarkar Collection, National Library, Calcutta.

Aftabchi, Jauhar, *Tazkirat-ul-Waqiat*. Also known as *Tarikh-i-Humayun or Humayunshahi* MS. no. 173, Sir Jadunath Sarkar Collection, National Library, Calcutta. Eng. tr. Major Charles Stewart, London: Oriental Translation Fund, 1832.

Agahi, *Dastur-Al-Amal-i-Agahi* MS. no. 2201, National Archives of India, New Delhi. MS no. 70, Sir Jadunath Sarkar Collection, National Library, Calcutta.

Anonymous Work, *Mina Bazaar*. Available as the 3rd part of a volume of three books bound together at the Fort William College Collection, National Archives of India, New Delhi.

Aqil Khan Razi, *Waqiat-i-Alamgiri*. Also known as *Zafar Nama-i-Alamgiri,* MS. no. 227, National Archives of India, New Delhi, MS no. 206, Sir Jadunath Sarkar Collection, National Library, Calcutta.

Aurangzeb Alamgir, *Ruqaim-i-Karaim*. MS. no. 154, Sir Jadunath Sarkar Collection, National Library, Calcutta.

———, *Ruka' at-i-Alamgiri* or *Letters of Aurangzebe*. Tr. Jamshid H. Bilimoria. Delhi : Idarah-i- Adabiyat-i Delli, 1972.

Babur, Zahir-ud-Din Muhammad, *Babar-Nama*. Eng. tr. from the Turki text by A.S. Beveridge (2 Vols.). New Delhi: Oriental Book Reprint Corporation, 1979.

Badauni, Abdul Qadir, *Muntakhab-ut-Tawarikh*. English tr. in 3 vols.

———, Vol. I tr. Ranking, Calcutta: Asiatic Society of Bengal, 1898; Patna; Academica Asiatica, 1973.

———, Vol. II tr. Lowe, Calcutta: Asiatic Society of Bengal, 1924; Delhi: Idarah-i-Adabiyat-i-Delhi, 1973.

———, Vol. III, tr. Haig, London: Royal Asiatic Society, 1912; Calcutta: Asiatic Society of Bengal, 1924; Patna: Academica Asiatica, 1973.

Bahadur Singh, *Majmua-i-Khwurrami or Shahjahan Nama*, MS. no. 371, National Archives of India, New Delhi.

Bakhtawar Khan, *Mirat-ul-Adam*. MS. no. 11, Buhar Collection, National Library, Calcutta; MS. no. 385, National Archives, New Delhi.

———, *Mirat-i-Jahan Numa*, MS. no. 13, Buhar Collection, National Library, Calcutta.

Barahman, Chandra Bhan, *Chaar Chaman*. MS. no. 67, Sir Jadunath Sarkar Collection, National Library, Calcutta.

Biyat, Bayazid, *Mukhtasar* or *Tarikh-i-Humayun Wa Akbar*. Ed. Hidayat Hussain; Calcutta; Asiatic Society of Bengal, 1941.

Burhanpuri, Bhimsen, *Tarikh-i-Dilkusha*. Also known as *Nushha-i-Dilkusha*. MS. no. 182, Sir Jadunath Sarkar Collection, National Library, Calcutta.

Dara Shukoh, *Majma 'Al-Bahrin*. MS no. 291, National Archives of India, New Delhi.

Dughlat, Mirza Md. Haider, *Tarikh-i-Rashidi*. Tr. E. Denison Ross. London: Sampson, Low, Marston, 1895.

Ferishta, *Tarikh-i-Ferishta*. Tr. Alexander Dow under the title of *The History of Hindostan* (3 vols.). New Delhi: Today and Tomorrow's Printers and Publishers, 1973.

Gilani, Abul Fath, *Ruqqat-i-Abul Fath Gilani*, MS. no. 158, Sir Jadunath Sarkar Collection, National Library, Calcutta.

Gulbadan Begam, *Humayun Nama*, Tr. A.S. Beveridge, New Delhi: Oriental Books Reprint Corporation, 1983.

Haqiri, Shaikh Rifat, *Aurangnama*, MS. no. 59, Sir Jadunath Sarkar Collection, National Library, Calcutta.

Inayat Khan, Muhammad Tahir, *Shah Jahan Nama*. MS. no. 70, Buhar Collection, National Library, Calcutta. Tr. and Ed. W.E. Begley and Z.A. Desai: Oxford University Press, 1990.

Jehangir, Nur-ud-Din Muhammad, *Tuzuk-i-Jahangiri*. Tr. Alexander Rogers, Ed. Henry Beveridge (2 Vols.). Delhi: Low Price Publications, 1989.

Jehangir Nama, MS. no. 67, Buhar Collection, National Library, Calcutta. Tr. under the title of *Memoirs of the Emperor Jahangueir* by David Price. New Delhi: Mittal Publications, 1995.

Kambu, Mohammad Salih, *Amal-i-Salih*. Ed. G. Yazdini (3 Vols.) Calcutta: Bibliotheca Indica, 1923-46. MS no. 55, Sir Jadunath Sarkar Collection, National Library, Calcutta.

Kamwar Khan, Md. Hadi, *Tadkirat-us-Salatin Chagata* (2 Vols.). MS no. 77 (Vol. I) and no. 78 (Vol. 2), Buhar Collection, National Library, Calcutta.

Khafi Khan, Muhammad Hashim, *Muntakhab-ul-Lubab*. Ed. Kabir-al-Din Ahmad and Woolseley Haig. Calcutta: Bibliotheca Indica, 1869.

Khawand Amir, *Humayun Nama* or *Qanun-i-Humayuni*. Ed. Hidayat Husain Tr. Beni Prasad. Calcutta: Bibliotheca Indica. 1940.

Lahori, Abdul Hamid, *Badshahnama* (2 Vols.). Ed. Kabiruddin and Abdur Rahim. Calcutta: Bibliotheca Indica, 1867 and 1868. MS no. 2526 (Vol. I). National Archives, New Delhi, MS no. 74 (Vol. I), Buhar Collection, National Library, Calcutta.

Malikzada, Munshi. *Nigar Nama-i-Munshi*. MS. no. 374, National Archives, New Delhi.

Musta'idd Khan, Mohammad Saqi, *Maasir-i-Alamgiri*. MS. no. 2400, National Archives, New Delhi. Ed. Ahmed Ali. Calcutta: Bibliotheca Indica, 1870-73. Tr. Sir Jadunath Sarkar, National Library, Calcutta.

Mutamid Khan, Muhammad Sharif, *Iqbal Nama-i-Jahangiri*. Text Pub. by College Press, Calcutta, 1865. MS. no. 66 (Vol. II), Buhar Collection, National Library, Calcutta, MS. no. 472 (Vol. III), National Archives, New Delhi.

Nagar, Ishwardas, *Futuhat-i-Alamgiri*. MS. no. 83, Sir Jadunath Sarkar Collection, National Library, Calcutta. Tr. and Ed. Tasneem Ahmad. Delhi: Idarah-i Adabiyat-i Delli, 1978.

Nizamuddin Ahmed *Tabqat-i-Akbari*. Tr. B. De (3 Vols.). Calcutta: Royal Asiatic Society of Bengal, 1927, 1963, 1939.

Qabil Khan, Abul Fath, *Adab-i-Alamgiri*. MS. no. 2019, National Archives, New Delhi.

Qazwini, Muhammad Amin bin Abul Husays, *Padshahnama*. MS. no. 69. Buhar Collection, National Library, Calcutta.

Sarhindi, Illahadad Faizi, *Tarikh-i-Humayun Shahi*. MS. no. 108, Oriental Public Library, Patna.

Shah Nawaz Khan, *et. al. Maathir-ul-Ummara*. Tr. H. Beveridge, Calcutta: Bibliotheca Indica, 1911-14.

Sujan Rai Khatri, *Khulasat-ut-Tawarikh*. Ed. Zafar Hassan. Delhi: G.S. Sons, 1918, MS. no. 387, National Archives, New Delhi. MS. no. 114, Sir Jadunath Sarkar Collection, National Library, Calcutta.

Waris, Muhammad, *Padshah Nama*, MSS. no. 147 (3rd Daftar) and no. 148 (4th Daftar), Sir Jadunath Sarkar Collection, National Library, Calcutta.

Zeb-un-Nisa Begam, *Diwan-i-Makhfi*. Tr. Magan Lal and Jessie Duncan Westbook under the title of The Diwan of Zeb-un-Nissa. London: John Murray, 1913.

II. European Travellers and Factors

Bernier, Francois, *Travels in the Mogul Empire* (1656-1668). Tr. on basis of Irving Brocks' version. Annt. Archibald Constable, 2nd ed. revised by V.A. Smith. New Delhi: Oriental Books Reprint Corporation, 1983.

Best, Thomas, *The Voyage of Thomas Best to the East Indies* (1612-1614). Ed. William Foster. London: The Hakluyt Society, 1934.

De Laet, *The Empire of the Great Mogol*. Tr. J.S. Hoyland, annt. S.N. Banerjee. New Delhi: Oriental Books Reprint Corporation, 1974.

Della Valle, Pietro, *The Travels of Pietro Della Valle in India* (2 Vols.). Ed. Edward Grey. London: The Hakluyt Society, 1891.

Downton, Nicholas, *The Voyages of Nicholas Downton to the East India* (1614-1615). Ed. William Foster. London: The Haklyut Society, 1905.

Du Jarric, Pierre, *Akbar and the Jesuits*: An Account of the Jesuit Missions to the Court of Akbar. Tr. C.H. Payne. London: George Routledge & Sons. Ltd., 1926.

Floris, Peter, *Peter Floris: His Voyage to the East Indies in the Globe* (1611-1615). The Contemporary Translation of His Journal. Ed. W.H. Moreland, *et. al.* London: The Hakluyt Society, 1934.

Foster, William ed., *Early Travels in India* (1583-1619). Personal travel accounts of Ralph Fitch (1583-1591), John Mildenhall (1599-1606), William Hawkins (1608-1613), William Finch (1608-1611), Nicholas Withington (1612-1616), Thomas Croyat (1612-1617), and Edward Terry (1616-1619). London: Humphrey Milford, Oxford University Press, 1921.

——— ed., *The English Factories in India* (1618-1621). *The English Factories in India* (1622-1623). A Calendar of Documents in the Indian Office; British Museum and Public Record Office. Oxford: The Clarendon Press, 1906, 1908.

Frayer, John, *A New Account of East Indies and Persia,* Being Nine Year's Travel (1672-1681) (3 vols.) Ed. W. Crooke. London: The Hakluyt Society, 1909-1915.

Grose, John Henry, *A Voyage to the East Indies.* London: S. Hooper, 1772.

Hamilton, Alexander, *A New Account of the East Indies,* Ed. William Foster. London: The Argonaut Press 1930.

Hawkins, William, *The Hawkins* (William, Sir John, Sir Richard) Voyages during the reign of Henry VIII, Queen Elizabeth, and James I. Ed. C.R. Markham. London: The Hakluyt Society, 1878.

Hedges, William, *The Diary of William Hedges* (3 Vols.). Ed. H. Yule. London: The Haklyut Society, 1887-1889.

Herbert, Thomas, *Travels,* London: Printed by R. Everingham, 1677.

Jourdain, John, *The Journal of John Jourdain* (1608-1617), describing his experiences in Arabia, India and the Malay Archipelago. Ed. William Foster. Cambridge: Printed for the Hakluyt Society, 1905.

Maclagan, Edward Doughlas, *The Jesuits and the Great Mogul.* London: Burns Oates & Washbourne, 1932.

Mandelslo, Johann Albrecht Von, *Mandelslo's Travels in Western India,* ed. M.S. Commissariat. London: Humphrey Milford, Oxford University Press, 1931.

Manrique, Fray Sebastian, *Travels of Fray Sebastian Manrique* (2 Vols.) Tr. and Ed. C. Eckford Luard and H. Hosten. Oxford: The Hakluyt Society, 1927.

Manucci, Niccolao, *A Pepys of Mogul India* (1653-1708), being an abridged edition of the "Storia Do Mogor". Tr. William Irvine, London: John Murray 1913.

———, *Memoirs of the Mughal Court.* Ed. Michael Edwardes. London: Folio Society, 1963.

———, *Storia Do Mogor* (4 Vols.). Tr. William Irvine. London: John Murray, 1907.

Marshall, John, *John Marshall in India;* Notes and Observations in Bengal (1668-1672). Ed. Shafaat Ahmad Khan. London: Humphrey Milford, Oxford University Press, 1927.

Monserrate, Antonio, *Mongolica Legationis Commentarius,* or, The Commentary of Father Monserrae on his journey to the Court of Akbar. Tr. J.S. Hoyland, annt. S.N. Banerjee. London, Calcutta (etc.): Humphrey Milford, Oxford University Press, 1922.

Mundy, Peter, *The Travels of Peter Mundy in Europe and Asia* (3 Vols.), Vol. 3, Travels in Asia. Ed. Richard Carnac Temple, Cambridge: Hakluyt Society, 1907-36.

Oaten, E.F., *European Travellers in India During the 15th, 16th and 17th Centuries.* London: Kegan Paul Trench, Trubner & Co., 1909.

Ovington, John, *A Voyage to Surat in the Year 1689.* Ed. H.G. Ranelingson. London: Oxford University Press, Humphrey Milford, 1929.

Pelsaert, Francisco, *Jahangir's India,* The Remonstrantie of Francisco Pelsaert. Tr. W.H. Moreland and P. Geyl. Delhi: Idarah-i-Adabiyat-i-Delli, 1972.

Purchas, Samuel, *Early Travels in India.* Glasgow: James Maclehose, 1864.

———, *His Pilgrims,* containing a history of the world in sea voyages and land travels by Englishmen and others. Glasgow: James Maclehose & Sons, 1905-1907.

Pyrard, Francois, *The Voyage of Francois Pyrard.* (2 Vols.). Tr. Albert Gray London : The Hakluyt Society, 1887-1890.

Roe, Thomas, *The Embassy of Sir Thomas Roe to the Court of the Great Mogul,* 1615-1619. Ed. William Foster. London : The Hakluyt Society, 1899.

———, *The Embassy of Sir Thomas Roe to India, 1615-1619,* as narrated in his journal and correspondence. Ed. William Foster. London: Himphrey Milford, Oxford University Press, 1926.

Roe, Thomas and John Fryer, *Travels in India in the Seventeenth Century*. London : Frubner & Co.; 1873.

Stavorinus, John Splinter, *Voyages to the East Indies.* Tr. S.H. Wilcocke. London: G.G. and J. Robinson, 1798.

Tavernier, Jean Baptiste, *Travels in India* (1640-1667), (2 Vols.) Ed. and tr. V. Ball, London, New York: Macmillan & Co., 1889. 2nd ed. William Crooke, London: Oxford University Press, 1925.

Thevenot, Jean De, *Accounts of Surat*. Ed. H.G. Rawlinson. Bombay: British India Press, 1927.

Thevenot and Careri, *India in the Seventeenth Century* (Vol. II). The Voyages of Thevenot and Careri. Ed. J.P. Guha. New Delhi: Associated Publishing House, 1976.

Secondary Sources

Books

Agarwal, Ashvini, *Studies in Mughal History,* Delhi (etc.): Motilal Banarsidas, 1983.

Agarwal, C.M., *Studies in Medieval Indian History.* Jalandhar : ABS Publications, 1988.

Ahmad, Aziz, *Studies in Islamic Culture in the Indian Environment.* Oxford : Clarendon Press, 1964.

Altekar, A.S., *The Position of Women in Hindu Civilization; from Prehistoric Times to the Present Day*. Varanasi : Banaras Hindu University, Cultural Publication House, 1938.

Anand, Sugam, *History of Begum Nur Jahan,* New Delhi : Radha Publications, 1992.

Ansari, M.A., *Social Life of the Mughal Emperors.* New Delhi : Gitanjali Publishing House, 1983.

Arora, R.C., *The City of the Taj,* Aligarh : Published by the author, 1937.

Avasthy, R.S., *The Mughal Emperor Humayun*, Allahabad: History Department, University of Allahabad, 1967.

Aziz, Abdul, *Arms and Jewellery of the Indian Mughals.* Lahore: Published by the author, 1947.

———, *The Imperial Library of the Mughals.* Delhi: Idarah-i-Adabiyat-i-Delli, 1974.

———, *The Imperial Treasury of the Indian Mughals.* Delhi: Idarah-i-Adabiyat-i-Delli, 1972.

Banerjee, S.K., *Humayun Badsahah.* Calcutta: Oxford University Press, 1983.

Begley, W.E. and Z.A. Desai, compiled and tr., *Taj Mahal-The Illumined Tomb,* An anthology of 17th Century Mughal and European Documentary Sources. Cambridge, Massachusetts : The Aga Khan Program for Islamic Architecture, Harvard University Art Museums, 1989.

Beni Prasad, *History of Jehangir,* Madras: Humphrey Milford, Oxford University Press, 1922.

Bilgrami, Rafat Mashood, *Religious and Quasi-Religious Departments of the Mughal Period* (1556-1707). Delhi: Munshiram Manoharlal, 1984.

Binyon, Lawrence, *Akbar:* London: Peter Davies Ltd. 1932.

Brown, Percy, *Indian Architecture (Islamic Period).* Bombay : D.B. Taraporevala Sons & Co. Pvt. Ltd., 1981.

———, *Indian Paintings Under the Mughals* (A.D. 1550 to A.D. 1750). New York : Hacker Art Books, 1975.

———, *List of Painters of the Mughal School Together with their Principal Works.* Oxford: Clarendon Press, 1924.

Burn, Richard ed., *Cambridge History of India* (Vol. 4), *The Mughal Period.* Cambridge: University Press, 1937.

Butenschon, Andrea, *The Life of A Mogul Princess, Jahanara Begam.* London: George Routledge & Sons Ltd., 1931.

Caldecott, R.M., *The Life of Babur: The Emperor of Hindustan.* London: James Darling: Edinburgh: John Chisholm, 1844.

Caunter, Robert, M. Elphinstone & S. Lanepoole, *Nur Jahan and Jehangir.* Calcutta: Susil Gupta (India) Ltd., 1950.

Chatterjee, Anjali (Basu), *Bengal in the Reign of Aurangzeb* (1658-1707), Calcutta : Progressive, 1967.

Chauhan, D.S., *Trends of Urbanization in Agra.* New Delhi: Allied Publishers, 1966.

Chitnis, K.N., *Glimpses of Medieval Indian Ideas and Institutions.* Poona: D.S. Joshi, 1974.

Chopra, P.N., *Life and Letters under the Mughals.* New Delhi: Ashajanak Publications, 1976.

———, *Some Aspects of Society and Culture During the Mughal Age* (1526-1707), Agra: Shiva Lal Agarwala & Co. Ltd., Educational Publishers, 1955.

Coomaraswamy, A.K., *History of Indian and Indonesian Art.* New York : Dover, 1965.

———, *The Arts & Crafts of India and Ceylon,* New Delhi: Today and Tomorrow Printers and Publishers, 1971.

Crowe, Sylvia and Sheila Haywood, *The Gardens of Mughal India.* Delhi: Vikas Publishing House Pvt. Ltd., 1973.

Dar, S.N., *Costumes of India and Pakistan, a Historical and Cultural Study.* Bombay: D.B. Taraporevala Sons & Co. Pvt. Ltd., 1969.

Das, Asok Kumar, *Dawn of Mughal Painting.* Bombay: Vakils, Feffer & Simons, 1982.

Dass, Diwan Jarmani and Rakesh Bhan Dass, *Maharani — Love Adventures of Indian Maharanis and Princesses.* New Delhi: S. Chand & Co. (Pvt.) Ltd., 1972.

Dayal, Maheshwar, *Rediscovering Delhi, The Story of Shahjahanabad.* New Delhi: S. Chand & Co. Ltd., 1982.

Deva, B. Chaitanya, *Musical Instruments of India.* New Delhi: Munshiram Manoharlal Publishers Pvt. Ltd., 1987.

Devee, Maharani Sunity, *The Beautiful Mogul Princesses.* London: W. Thacker & Co., 1918.

Edwardes, S.M., *Babur, Diarist and Despot,* New Delhi: Heritage Publishers, 1977.

———, *Mughal Rule in India.* London: Oxford University Press, 1930. New Delhi: Asian Publication Services, 1979.

Erskine, William, *History of India. Under the Two First Sovereigns of the House of Tamur, Baber and Humayun* (2 Vols.). London: Longman, Brown, Green and Longmans, 1854.

Fabri, Charles, *Indian Dress, A Brief History.* New Delhi: Orient Longman Ltd., 1977.

Fanshawe, Herbert Charles, *Delhi, Past and Present.* London: John Murray, 1902.

Farooqi, Naimur Rahman, *Mughal Ottoman Relations.* Delhi: Idarah-i-Adabiyat-i-Delli, 1989.

Faruqi, Abul Khair Md., *Roads and Communications in Mughal India.* Delhi: Idarah-i-Adabiyat-i-Delli, 1977.

Fergusson, James, *History of Indian and Eastern Architecture* (Vol. 2). New Delhi: Munshiram Manoharlal Oriental Publishers, 1967.

Festing, Gabrielle, *When Kings Rode to Delhi.* Edinburgh & London: William Blackwood and Sons, 1912.

Findly, Ellison Banks, *Noorjahan, Empress of Mughal India.* New York: Oxford University Press, 1993.

Fox, Ralph Winston, *Genghis Khan.* Essex: Diamon Press Ltd., 1962.

Gascoigne, Bamber, *The Great Moghuls.* London: Jonathan Cape, 1976.

Ghauri, Iftikar Ahmad, *War of Succession Between the Sons of Shahjahan.* Lahore: Publishers United Ltd., 1964.

Ghurye, Govind Sadashiv, *Indian Costume.* Bombay: Popular Prakashan, 1966.

Godden, Rumer, *Gulbadan.* London: Macmillan London Ltd., 1980.

Gorham, A., *Indian Masons' Marks of the Moghul Dynasty.* London: Published for the "Societas Rosicruciana in Anglia" by John M. Watkins, 1911.

Grenard, Fernand, *Baber, First of the Moguls.* London: Thornton Butterworth, 1931.

Habib, Irfan, *The Agrarian System of Mughal India* (1556-1770). Bombay: Asia Publishing House, 1963.

Hambly, Gavin, *Cities of Mughal India; Delhi, Agra and Fatehpur Sikri.* Delhi: UBS Publishers, 1968.

Hansen, Waldemar, *The Peacock Throne.* Great Britain: Weidenfeld and Nicolson, 1973.

Hasan, Hadi, *A Golden Treasury of Persian Poetry.* Ed. M.S. Israeli. New Delhi: Published by Indian Council for Cultural Relations, 1992.

———, *Mughal Poetry.* Aligarh: 1952.

Hasan, Ibn, *The Central Structure of the Mughal Empire, and Its Practical Working upto the Year 1657.* New Delhi: Munshiram Manoharlal, 1970.

Hasrat, Bikramjit, *Dara Shukoh, Life and Works.* Shantiniketan: Visva-Bharati University Publications, 1953.

Havell, E.B., *A Handbook to Agra and the Taj, Sikandra, Fatehpur Sikri and the Neighbourhood.* London, New York and Bombay : Longmans, Green & Co., 1904.

———, *Indian Architecture Through the Ages.* New Delhi: Asian Publication Services, 1978.

Hendley, T.H., *Indian Jewellery.* London: W. Griggs & Sons, 1909.

Herklots, G.A., tr. *Islam in India or the Qanun-i-Islam of Jafar Sharif.* London, Edinburgh (etc.): Oxford University Press, 1921.

Hodiwala, S.H., *Historical Studies in Mughal Numismatics,* Calcutta: The Numismatic Society of India, 1923.

Holden, E.S., *The Mogul Emperors of Hindustan,* New York: Scribner's, 1895.

Munter, W.W. ed., *The Imperial Gazetter of India* (2nd edition). London: Trubner & Co., 1885-1887.

Husain, Md. Ashraf, *A Guide to Fatehpur Sikri.* Delhi: Manager of Publications, 1937.

———, *A Historical Guide to the Agra Fort.* Delhi: Manager of Publications, 1937.

Husain, Yusuf, *Glimpses of Medieval Indian Culture.* Bombay: Asia Publishing House, 1962.

Imperial Gazetter of India, Reprinted from the 3rd ed. of the Imperial Gazetter of India (1907-1909). Oxford: The Clarendon Press, 1924.

Ishwari Prasad, *A Short History of Muslim Rule in India (from the Conquest of Islam to the Death of Aurangzeb).* Allahabad: Indian Press, 1931.

———, *History of Medieval India* 3rd ed. Allahabad: Indian Press, 1940.

———, *The Life and Times of Humayun.* Bombay: Orient Longman, 1955.

Jaffar, S.M., *Some Cultural Aspects of Muslim Rule in India.* Delhi: Idarah-i-Adabiyat-i-Delli, 1972.

Jain, Devaki ed., *Indian Women.* New Delhi: Publications Division, Ministry of Information and Broadcasting, Govt. of India, 1976.

Kausar, Kabir and Innamul Kabir, *Biographical Dictionary of Prominent Muslim Ladies.* New Delhi: Light and Life Publishers, 1982.

Kausar, Zinat, *Muslim Women in Medieval India.* Patna, New Delhi: Janaki Prakashan, 1992.

Keay, F.E., *Indian Education in Ancient and Later Times.* London: Humphrey Milford, Oxford University Press, 1938.

Khan, Mazhar ul Haq, *Purdah and Polygamy*. Delhi: Amar Prakashan, 1982.

Kulshrestha, S.S., *Development of Trade and Industry Under the Mughals* (1526-1707 A.D.). Allahabad: Kitab Mahal Pvt. Ltd., 1964.

Lal, K.S., *The Legacy of Muslim Rule in India*, New Delhi: Aditya Prakashan, 1992.

———, *The Mughal Harem*. New Delhi: Aditya Prakashan, 1988.

———, *Studies in Medieval Indian History*. Delhi: Ranjit Printers and Publishers, 1966.

Lane-Poole, Stanley, *Aurangzeb*. London: Clarendon Press, 1893.

———, *Babar*, Delhi: S. Chand & Co., 1964.

———, *Medieval India Under Mohammedan Rule*. Delhi: Low Price Publications, 1992.

Latif, S.M., *Agra, Historical and Descriptive*. Calcutta: Central Press Company Ltd., 1896.

Law, N.N., *Promotion of Learning in India During Mohammadan Rule*. Delhi: Idarah-i-Adabiyat-i-Delli, 1973 (reprint).

Macnicol, Margaret ed., *Poems by Indian Women*, Calcutta: Association Press (Y.M.C.A.). London: Oxford University Press, 1923.

Malleson, G.B., *Rulers of India - Akbar and the Rise of the Mughal Empire*. Delhi: Low Price Publications, 1990.

Mathur, N.L., *Red Fort and Mughal Life*. New Delhi: National Museum, 1964.

Maududi, S.A.A., *Purdah and the Status of Women in Islam*. Delhi: Markazi Maktaba Islami, 1974.

Mazumdar, K.C., *Imperial Agra of the Moguls*. Agra: Gaya Prasad and Sons, 1946.

Mazumdar, R.C. (ed.), *The History and Culture of the Indian People*, Vol. III — The Mughal Empire. Bombay: Bharatiya Vidya Bhavan, 1974.

Michell, George (ed.), *Architecture of the Islamic World*. London: Themes and Hudson Ltd., 1978.

Ministry of Information and Broadcasting, Govt. of India, *India-Government and Economic Life in Ancient and Medieval Periods*. New Delhi : Publications Divisions, Ministry of Information and Broadcasting, Govt. of India, 1979.

Misra, Rekha, *Women in Mughal India* (1526-1748 A.D.), Delhi; Munshiram Manoharlal Oriental Publishers and Booksellers, 1967.

Moreland, W.H., *From Akbar to Aurangzeb,* London : Macmillan, 1923.

———, *India at the Death of Akbar.* New Delhi : Munshiram Manoharlal Publishers Pvt. Ltd., 1983.

Moreland, W.H. and A.C. Chatterji, *A Short History of India.* London (etc.): Longmans, 1936.

Moosvi, Shireen, *The Economy of the Mughal Empire.* Delhi: Oxford University Press, 1987.

Moynihan, E.B., *Paradise as a Garden in Persia and Mughal India.* London: Scolar Press, 1982.

Muin-ud-Din, Mohummad, *The History of the Taj and the Buildings in its Vicinity,* Agra: The Moon Press, 1905.

Mukharji, Ila, *Social Status of North Indian Women* (1526-1707 A.D.). Agra: Shiva Lal Agarwala & Co. Educational Publishers, 1972.

Nath, R., *Agra and Its Monumental Glory.* Bombay: D.B. Taraporevala Sons & Co. Pvt. Ltd., 1977.

———, *Some Aspects of Mughal Architecture.* New Delhi: Abhinav Publications, 1976.

———, *The Immortal Taj Mahal,* The Evolution of the Tomb in Mughal Architecture. Bombay: D.B. Taraporevala, 1972.

Nizami, K.A., *Studies in Medieval Indian History and Culture.* Allahabad: Kitab Mahal, 1966.

Ojha, P.N., *Some Aspects of North Indian Social Life* (1556-1707 A.D.). Patna: Nagari Prakashan Pvt. Ltd., 1961.

Pal, Pratapaditya, *Court Paintings of India, 16th-17th Centuries.* Published by Navin Kumar, New York for Kumar Gallery. New Delhi, India, 1993.

Pandey, A.B., *Later Medieval India : A History of the Mughals.* Allahabad: Central Book Depot, 1963.

Pant, *Economic History of India Under the Mughals.* Delhi: Kanishka Publishing House, 1990.

Pant, D., *The Commercial Policy of the Mughals.* Bombay: D.B. Taraporevala Sons & Co., 1930.

Parihar, Subhash, *Mughal Monuments in Punjab and Haryana.* New Delhi: Inter-India Publications, 1985.

Pool, J.J., *Famous Women of India.* Calcutta: Susil Gupta (India) Ltd., 1954.

Qaisar, A.J. and S.P. Verma (ed.) *Art & Culture* - Felicitation Volume in Honour of Prof. S. Nurul Hasan. Jaipur: Publication Scheme, 1993.

Qanungo, K.R., *Dara Shukoh.* Calcutta: S.C. Sarkar & Sons, 1935.

———, *Historical Essays.* Agra: Shiva Lal Agarwala & Co. (Pvt.) Ltd., 1960.

———, *Islam and Its Impacts on India.* Calcutta: General Printers and Publishers Pvt. Ltd., 1968.

Radhey Shyam, *Babar.* Patna: Janaki Prakashan, 1978.

Ramachandran C.E. and K.V. Raman (eds.), *Aspects of Indian History and Culture.* New Delhi: Books and Books Publishers and Distributors, 1984.

Ray, Aniruddha, *Some Aspects of Mughal Administration.* New Delhi: Kalyani Publishers, 1984.

Ray Chaudhary, S.C., *Social, Cultural and Economic History of Indian (Medieval Age).* Surjeet Publications, 1985.

Ray Chaudhary, Tapan Kumar, *Bengal Under Akbar and Jehangir.* Calcutta: A. Mukherjee & Co. Ltd., 1953.

Ray Chaudhary, T.K. and Irfan Habib, *The Cambridge Economic History of India* (Vol. I) Hyderabad: Orient Longman in Association with Cambridge University Press, 1984.

Rothfeld, Otto, *Women of India.* Bombay: D.B. Taraporevala Sons & Co., 1928.

Roy, D.N., *The Spirit of Indian Civilization.* Calcutta: University of Calcutta Publications, 1938.

Roy, D.S., *Warring Women of Ind.* Bombay: Colour Publications Pvt. Ltd., 1973.

Rizvi, S.A.A., *A History of Sufism in India* (2 Vols.) Delhi: Munshiram Manoharlal, 1983.

———, *Religious and Intellectual History of the Muslims in Akbar's Reign, with special reference to Abul Fazl (1556-1605).* New Delhi: Munshiram Manoharlal, 1975.

Rizvi, S.A.A., V.J.A. Flynn and Saksena, B.P., *Fatehpur Sikri.* Bombay: D.B. Taraporevala, 1975.

———, *History of Shahjahan of Dihli.* Allahabad: The Indian Press Ltd., 1932.

Sanders, J.H. tr., *Tamerlane or Timur the Great Amir—from the Arabic Life by Ahmed Ibn Arabshah.* London: Luzac & Co., 1936.

Sanderson, G., *A Guide to the Buildings and Gardens: Delhi Fort.* Delhi: Manager of Publications, 1937.

Sardesai, G.S., *New History of the Marathas.* Bombay: Phoenix Publications, 1946.

Sarkar, Jadunath, *Anecdotes of Aurangzib.* Calcutta: M.C. Sarkar & Sons, 1912.

———, *History of Aurangzib* (mainly based on Persian sources) (Vol. I). Calcutta: M.C. Sarkar & Sons, 1912.

———, *History of Aurangzib* (Vols. I & II). Calcutta: Orient Longman Ltd., 1973.

———, *India Through the Ages.* Calcutta: M.C. Sarkar & Sons, 1928.

———, *Studies in Aurangzib's Reign*. Calcutta: M.C. Sarkar & Sons Ltd., 1933.

———, *Studies in Mughal India.* Calcutta: M.C. Sarkar & Sons. Cambridge: W. Heffer & Sons, 1919.

———, *The India of Aurangzib* (with extracts from the Khulsatu-t-Tawarikh and the Chahar Gulshan translated). Calcutta: Bose Brothers, 1901.

Sarkar, Jagdish Narain, *India and Iran in the Medieval Period.* Calcutta: Iran Society, 1974.

———, *Mughal Economy.* Calcutta: Naya Prokash, 1987.

———, *Mughal Polity.* Delhi: Idarah-i-Adabiyat-i-Delli, 1984.

———, *Private Trade in Seventeenth Century India.* Calcutta: Scientific Book Agency, 1969.

———, *Studies in Economic Life in Mughal India.* Delhi: Oriental Publishers and Distributors, 1975.

Satish Chandra, *Mughal Religious Policies, the Rajputs and the Deccan.* New Delhi : Vikas Publishing House Pvt. Ltd., 1993.

———, *The Parties and Politics at the Mughal Court* (1707-1740). Aligarh: Deptt. of History, A.M.U., 1959.

Sengupta, Padmini, *The Story of Women in India*. New Delhi: Indian Book Company, 1974.

Sharma, Sri Ram, *The Religious Policy of the Mughal Emperors.* Calcutta: Humphrey Milford, 1940.

Sharma, Tripat, *Women in Ancient India* (from 320 A.D. to C. 1200 A.D.) New Delhi: Ess Ess Publications, 1987.

Shchukin, I.V., *La Peinture Indienne; a l'epoque des grands Moghols.* Paris: Ernest Leroux, 1929.

Shelat, J.M., *Akbar.* Bombay: Bharatiya Vidya Bhavan, 1959.

Shustery, A.M.A., *Outlines of Islamic Culture* (2 Vols.). Mysore: Published by the author, 1938.

Siddiqui, I.H., *Mughal Relations with Indian Ruling Elite.* New Delhi: Munshiram Manoharlal Publishers, 1983.

Smith, Edmund W., *Moghul Colour Decoration of Agra.* Allahabad: Supdt. Government Press, 1901.

Smith, V.A., *A History of Fine Art in India and Ceylon.* Oxford: Clarendon Press, 1911.

———, *Akbar, The Great Mogul.* Oxford: Clarendon Press, 1917. Delhi: Vinod Publications, 1988.

———, *Oxford History of India.* Oxford: Clarendon Press, 1920-34.

Spear, T.G. Percival, *A History of India.* Harmondsworth, Middlesex: Penguin, 1965.

———, *A History of India* (Vol. 2). Baltimore: Penguin Books, 1965.

———, *Delhi, A Historical Sketch.* London: Humphrey Milford, Oxford University Press, 1937.

———, *Delhi, Its Monuments and History.* London: Geoffrey Cumberlage, 1945.

Srivastava, A.L., *Akbar the Great* (3 Vols.). Agra: Shiva Lal Agarwala & Co., 1962 (Vol. I), 1967 (Vol. II), 1972 (Vol. III).

———, *Medieval Indian Culture.* Agra: Shiva Lal Agarwala & Co. (P) Ltd., 1964.

———, *The Mughal Empire.* Agra: Shiva Lal Agarwala & Co., 1979.

Srivastava, D.B., *The Province of Agra, Its History and Administration.* New Delhi: Concept Publishers, 1979.

Srivastava, K.P. (ed.), *Mughal Farmans* (1540-1706 A.D.) (Vol. I). Lucknow: Published by Uttar Pradesh State Archives, 1974.

Stuart, C.M. Villiers, *Gardens of the Great Mughals.* London: Adam and Charles Black, 1913.

Sullivan, Edward, *Mughal Empire in India.* Delhi: Royal Publications, 1990.

Tara Chand, *A Short History of the Indian People;* from the earliest time to the present day. Calcutta (etc.): Macmillan & Co. Ltd. 1950.

———, *Influence of Islam on Indian Culture.* Allahabad: The Indian Press Ltd., 1936.

Thapar, Romila, *A History of India* (Vol. I). Baltimore: Penguin Books, 1966.

The Indian Heritage—Court Life and Arts Under the Mughals. London: Victoria and Albert Museum, 1982.

Thomas, P., *Indian Women Through the Ages.* Bombay: Asia Publishing House, 1964.

Tod, James, *Annals and Antiquities of Rajasthan or the Central and Western Rajpoot States of India.* Ed. William Crooke (3 Vols.). London (etc.): Humphrey Milford, Oxford University Press, 1920.

Tripathi, R.P., *Rise and Fall of the Mughal Empire.* Allahabad: Central Book Depot., 1960.

Varma, H.N. and Amrit Varma, *Eminent Indian Women.* New Delhi: Great Indian Publishers, 1978.

Vashistha, B.K. (ed.), *Encyclopaedia of Women in India.* New Delhi: Praveen Encyclopaedia Publications, 1976.

Walia, J.M., *Mughal Empire in India.* New Delhi: Enkay Publishers, 1988.

Welch, S.C., *India, Art and Culture* (1300-1900 A.D.). New York: Published by the Metropolitan Museum of Art and Holt, Rinehart and Winston.

Wheeler, James Talboys, *The History of India Under Mussulman Rule.* London: Trubner & Co., 1876.

Wheeler, J.T. and M. Macmillan, *European Travellers in India.* Calcutta: Susil Gupta (India) Ltd., 1956.

Williams, L.F. Rushbrook, *An Empire Builder of the Sixteenth Century.* London: Longmans Green & Co., 1918.

Yasin, Mohammad, *A Social History of Islamic India.* Lucknow: The Upper India Publishing House Ltd., 1958.

———, *Studies: Historical and Cultural* Jammu (Tawi): Published by the author, 1964.

II. Selected Articles from Journals

Ahmad, N.L., "Some Aspects of Life and Culture in Mughal India during the Shah Jahan Period". *Jammu and Kashmir University Review* 6 (1962): 35-62.

Ali, Syed Ameer, "Islamic Culture Under the Moguls". *Islamic Culture,* (October 1927): 499-521.

Ansari, Azher, "Social Condition at the Court of Akbar and its Influence on Society". *Islamic Culture,* 33 (1959): 124-38.

Ansari, M.A., "Akbar's Contribution to Social Life at the Court". *University of Allahabad Studies,* History Section (1958): 1-18.

———, "Amusements and Games under the Great Mughals". *Islamic Culture,* 35 (Jan. 1961): 21-31.

———, "Court Ceremonies of the Great Mughals". *Islamic Culture,* 35 (July 1961): 183-97.

———, "Some Aspects of the Social Life at the Court of the Great Mughals". *Islamic Culture,* 36 (July 1962): 182-195.

———, "The Harem of the Great Mughals". *Islamic Culture,* 34 (Jan. 1960): 1-13; (April 1960): 107-24.

Beni Prasad, "The Accession of Shah Jahan". *Journal of Indian History,* Vol. 2 (November 1922): 1-19.

Chakraborthy, P.N., "Nurjahan's Commercial Relations with the English". *Indian History Congress Proceedings,* 34th session, Chandigarh, 1973.

Chowdhari, J.N., "Mumtaz Mahal (1593-1631)". *Islamic Culture* (July 1937): 373-81.

Findly, E.B., "The Capture of Maryam-uz-Zamani's Ship: Mughal Women and European Traders". *Journal of American Oriental Society,* 108.2 (1988): 227-38.

Gopal, S., "Gujarati Shipping in the 17th Century". *Indian Economic and Social History Review,* 8 (1971): 31-39.

Halim, A., "Music and Musicians at the Court of Shah Jahan". *Islamic Culture,* 19 (1945): 354-60.

Hasan, S. Nurul, "The Theory of the Nur Jahan Junta". *Indian History Congress Proceedings,* Trivandrum Session (1958): 324-35.

Khan, Md. Afzal, "Position of Itimad-ud-Daula's Family During the Reign of Shah Jahan". *Indian History Congress Proceedings,* 39th Session, Osmania University, Hyderabad (1978).

Lal, K.S., "The Mughal Harem". *Journal of Indian History,* Vol. LIII (April 1975).

Moosvi, Shireen, "Mughal Shipping at Surat in the First Half of 17th Century". *Indian History Congress Proceedings,* 51st Session, Calcutta University.

Nadvi, S.A. Zafar, "Libraries During the Muslim Rule in India". *Islamic Culture* (January 1946): 18.

Pawar, Kiran, "Role of Some of the Royal Women in the Career of Babur". *Indian History Congress Proceedings,* 52nd Session, New Delhi (1991-92): 349.

Qaiser, A.J., "Shipbuilding in Mughal Empire During the 17th Century". *Indian Economic and Social History Review,* 5 (June 1968): 149-70.

Qanungo, K.R., "Some Side-Lights on the Character and Court-Life of Shah Jahan". *Journal of Indian History,* 9 (1929): 45-52.

Shafi, Muhammad, "The Shalimar Gardens of Lahore". *Islamic Culture* (January 1929): 58-66.

Solomon, W.E. Gladstone, "Impressions of the Taj Mahal". *Islamic Culture* (April 1927): 231-37.

———, "In the Garden of the Taj Mahal". *Islamic Culture* (January 1923): 147-59.

———, "Masterpieces of Moghul Painting". *Islamic Culture* (January 1930): 144-50.

Srivastava, A.L., "Akbar and National Integration". *Journal of Indian History,* 40 (1962): 1-8.

Standish, J.F., "Persian Influence in Mughal India". *Islamic Quarterly,* 3 (July/September, 1968): 160-73.

Tripathi, R.P., "Maham Anagah and Akbar". *Journal of Indian History,* 1 (1921-22): 327-44.

Umar, M., "Life of Mughal Royalty in India During 18th Century". *Medieval Indian Quarterly,* 5 (1963): 88-112.

III. Encyclopaedia and Dictionary

Dictionary of Islam, Ed. T.P. Huges, London: 1899; New Delhi: 1976.

Encyclopaedia of Islam, Vol. A, B. Leiden, London: 1960.

Encyclopedia of Asian History, Vol. 3, New York: Macmillan Publishing Company, 1988.

Encyclopedia of Social Sciences, Vol. 14, 1919.

Persian English Dictionary, P. Steingass, Ist Indian Edition, New Delhi: 1973.

IV. Gazetteers, Journals and Reports

District Gazetteers of Delhi.

The Imperial Gazetters of India, Oxford, 1908.

Epigraphica Indica.
Epigraphica Indica (Arabic and Persian Supplement).
Epigraphica Indo-Moselemia.
Indian Antiquary, Bombay.
Indian Culture, Calcutta.
Indian Economic and Social History Review.
Indian Historical Review.
Islamic Culture, Hyderabad.
Jammu and Kashmir University Review.
Journal of Aligarh Historical Research Institute.
Journal of American Oriental Society.
Journal of Indian History, Trivandrum.
Journal of Indian Society of Oriental Art.
Journal of Pakistan Historical Society.
Journal of Royal Asiatic Society, London.
Journal of Royal Asiatic Society of Bengal, Calcutta.
Medieval India A Miscellany, Aligarh.
Medieval Indian Quarterly, Aligarh.
Proceedings of Indian History Congress.
The Indian Historical Quarterly, Calcutta.
The Islamic Review.
University of Allahabad Studies.

Index

A

Abbas, Shah, 142
Ab-e-Rawan, 84
Achabal Kashmir, 212
Aghacha, Gulnar, 24
Aghacha Nargul, 24
Ain-i-Akbari, 74
Ajmer, 31
Akbar, 15
Akbarabadi, 24
Akbar-Anagas, 19
Amber, 22
Ambha, Bibi, 10
amirs, 35
Amritsar, 10
Amuli, Taliba, 70
Anaga, Ji Ji, 19
Anaga, Maham, 109
Anarkali, 51
Ardheli, Mulla Safi-ud-Din, 73
Arthashastra, 44
Ashraf, A. D. Saiyed, 39
Atum Mana, 70
Azam, Muhammad, 106
Aurangzeb, 15, 24, 33, 70
Azam, Sultan, 106

B

Babar, 15
Babar Nama, 19
Badan, Nazuk, 24
Bagh-i-Bahar Ara, 214
Bai, Jodha, 20, 22
Bai, Man, 23, 51
Bai, Nawab. 71
Bandis, 38
Banu, Hamida, 19, 37
Banu, Hira Bibi, 37
Banu, Manik, 37
Banu, Niyaz Bibi, 37
Begam, Arjumand Banu, 23, 52, 104
Begam, Asmat Banu, 75
Begam, Ayisha Sultan, 22
Begam, Dildar, 18, 109
Begam, Gulbadan, 11, 20
Begam, Gul-Chihra, 21
Beg, Ghiyas, 50
Begam, Hamida Banu, 11
Begam, Jahanara, 27
Begam, Jani, 33
Begam, Ladli, 52
Begam, Maham, 22, 34
Begam, Nadira, 53
Begam, Nur Jahan, 18
Begam, Ruqqaiah Sultan, 18, 22
Begam, Shukr-un-Nisa, 21, 33
Begam, Zainab Sultan, 22
Bhim, Rawal, 23
Bichhwah, 80
Bibi, Hafiza Mariam, 70
Bijapuri Mahal, 33
Bimar Khanah, 18
Bostan, 97
Bundela, Ramchandra, 23

C

Chadar, 45
Chandni Chowk, 201
Chikan Kari, 10

Coryat, Thomas, 49

D

Dain, Sukh, 24
Dal Lake, 207
Das, Raja Bhagwan, 23
Dhaka Malmal, 84
Din Panah, 43
Diwali, 41
Diwani-i-Makhfi, 182
Dussehra, 41

E

Etimad-ud-Daula, 47, 133, 195, 197

F

farsh-i-Chandani, 85
Fatehpuri, 24
Fatehpuri Mosque, 201
Fatehpuri Sikri, 27
Fatehpur Sikri palace, 69
Fatima, Bibi, 38
Fazl, Abul, 17, 19, 27, 93
Finch, William, 29, 48
Firoz, Ruknuddin, 9

G

Gol Conda, 151
Gossain, Jagat, 128
Gulstan, 17, 97
Guvarati, Itimad khan, 164

H

Hamam, Hakin, 19, 39
Harkha, 22
Hassan, Khwaja, 23
Havan Kund, 40
Hawkins, A. D. William, 33, 135
howdaks, 16
Humayun Nama, 11, 15, 21, 26, 70–71, 168
Humayun's Tomb, 194
Hussain, Muzaffar, 23

I

Id-ul-Fitr, 41
Istalju, Ali Quli, 133

J

Jahanara's Tomb, 202
Jahan, Nur, 18, 132
Jahagir, 15
Jahangir's Tomb, 199
Jagirs, 31
Jagulfi, 83
Jama Masjid, 163
Jami Masjid, 44, 201
Jamuna river, 28
Jodha Bai Mahal, 193

K

Karamsi, Raj Kumari, 23, 129
Karim, Mir Abdul, 205
Kashi, Hakim, 39
Kanchanis, 25
Karnphul, 78
Kausar, Zinat, 11
Kautilya, 44
Khalifa, Bachaka, 26
Khalji, Jalaluddin, 9
Khan, Bakhtawar, 70
Khan, Didar, 55
Khan, Inayat, 49, 85
Khan, Jafar, 57
Khan, Qasin, 23
Khan, Sir Sayyed Ahmad, 195
Khana, Akbar, 17
Khatura, Shams, 10
Khanum, Qutlug-Nigar, 26, 114
Khudavandzada, 9
Khusrau, 26
Koka, Haji, 37
Koka, Qutub-ud-din, 20
Koka, Saadat Yar, 19

Koka, Zain Khan, 19
Khwaja Muin-ud-din Chisti, 42
Khwaja Saras, 39
Kuntila, 78
Kusum, 74

L

Lal, K.S. 11, 55
Lodi, Bahlal, 10

M

Madrasas, 69
Mahabharata, 44
Main Mir, 43
Maktabs, 69
Malika-i-Jahan, 9, 20
Malika-i-Zaman, 147
Mal, Raja Bihari, 22, 127
Mansabs, 39
Mariam's Kothi, 193
Matbakh, 17
Mati, Roop, 221
Mazumdar, R. C., 193
Mecca, 24
Meena Bazar, 82
Mehr-un-Nisa, 71, 133
Mirza, Jehangir, 115
Moti Mahal, 27
Mughal, Abdullah Khan, 22
Mughal Days, 211
Mughal Harem, education of, 69
  learning of, 69
Mughal Harem Ladies, 15
  life style of, 16
  diet of, 17
  recreation of, 17
  status/position of, 18
  foster mothers, 19
  elder women, 20
  girl child status, 21
  emperor wives, 22
  Babar's queens, 22
  Akbar's queens, 22
  Jahangir's wives, 23
  Shahjahan's wives, 23
  concubines, 24
  slave/servant girls, 25
  wealth sources of, 30
  administration set-up, 36
  security of, 38
  religious life, 40
  purdah system, 44
Mughal Harem, travels of, 249
  pilgrimages/sight-seeing, 249
  travelling modes, 250
Mughal ladies, politics of 113
  Babar time, 114
  Aisan Daulat Begam, 114
  Qutlug-Nigar Khanun, 116
  Humayun's time, 119
  Hamida Begam, 119
  Khanzada Begam, 121
  Akbar's time, 122
  Mahan Anaga, 122
  Mahchu Chak Begam, 126
  Bakhtunnisa Begam, 126
  Akbar time, 127
  Hindu/Rajput wives, 127
Mughal women, dress of, 81
  bodice, 82
  jacket, 82
  breaches, 82
Muharram, 41
Mulla Shah, 43
Mumtaz Mahal, 18, 26, 147
Munis-ul-Arwah, 72
Muslim Women in Medieval India, 11

N

Nakmachi, 78
Narayana, 74
Nawab Ulya, 27
Nawan Kot Bagh, 207

Nawis, Waqia, 37
Nur Afza Garden, 213
Nur Jahan's Tomb, 200
Nur Mahal Sarai, 197

P

Pachisi, 94
Pathar Masjid, 43, 199
Phul katara, 35
Pietra Dalla Valle, 47
Pratap, Maharana, 131
Pravarasena II, 211
Prince Daulat Afza, 32
Prince Khusrau, 136–37
Prince Salim, 52, 133
Prince Jahanara, 31
Purdah, 9

Q

Qadiriya Sufi, 43
Quran, 40
Qazurini, 31
Qandhar, 142

R

Rai, Rawal Hari, 22, 128
Rang Mahal, 27, 193
Ramayana, 44
Rathor, Keshav Das, 23
Raksha Bandhan, 41
Royal Mughal ladies, outdoor amusements of, 98
  hunting, 98
  ishq-bauzi, 100
  animal fight, 100
Risala-i-Sahibiya, 43
Roe, Sir Thomas, 33, 252
Roshanara Begam Tomb, 203
Royal Mughal ladies, ornaments of, 76
  head ornaments, 77
  ear ornaments, 78
  nose ornaments, 78
  necklaces, 79
Royal Mughal ladies, amusements of, 93
  indoor amusements, 93
  chess, 93
  chaupar, 94
  pachisi, 94
  cards, 95
  Chandal Mandal, 95
  gambling, 95
  ankh michauli, 96
  dancing, 96
  intoxicants use of, 97

S

Safawi Mirza Rustam, 106
Sahibat-uz-Zamani, 27
Salim, 22
Sarkar, Sir Jadunath, 53, 203
Shabb-i-Barat, 41
Shabistan-i-Iqbal, 27
Shad, Bibi Daulat. 22
Shahjahan, 21
Shah Jahan Nama, 85
Shah, Abdullah Qutb, 150
Shah, Miran Mubarak, 22
Shah, Muhammad Muazzam Bahadur, 37
Shaikh Nizamuddin Aulia, 42
Shivaji, 156
Shalamar Bagh, 210
Shukh, Dara, 53, 105
Singh, Rana Amar, 131
Singh, Raja Man, 23, 204
Shirazi, Shaikh Sadi, 17, 97
Smith, Vincent, 58
Sonahla Makan, 27
Sultan, Ilbari, 9
Sultan, Razia, 9
Sultan, Ruqaiya, 28